The Letters to the Seven Churches of Asia

By W. M. Ramsay,

Edited by Anthony Uyl

Devoted Publishing

Woodstock, Ontario, 2017

The Letters to the Seven Churches of Asia
And their place in the plan of the Apocalypse
By W. M. Ramsay,
D.C.L., Litt.D., LL.D. Professor of Humanity in the University of Aberdeen 1904
Edited by Anthony Uyl

What kind of philosophies do you have?
Let us know!

Contact us at: devotedpub@hotmail.com
Visit our shop on Facebook: @DevotedPublishing
Published in Woodstock, Ontario, Canada 2017.

For bulk educational rates, please contact us at the above email address.

ISBN: 978-1-77356-003-8

Table of Contents

Preface

In the contact of East and West originates the movement of history. The historical position of Christianity cannot be rightly understood except in its relation to this immemorial meeting and conflict. The present book is based on the view that Christianity is the religion which associates East and West in a higher range of thought than either can reach alone, and tends to substitute a peaceful union for the war into which the essential difference of Asiatic and European character too often leads the two continents. So profound is the difference, that in their meeting either war must result, or each of them must modify itself. There is no power except religion strong enough to modify both sufficiently to make a peaceful union possible; and there is no religion but Christianity which is wholly penetrated both with the European and with the Asiatic spirit--so penetrated that many are sensitive only to one or the other.

Only a divine origin is competent to explain the perfect union of Eastern and Western thought in this religion. It adapted itself in the earliest stages of its growth to the great Graeco-Asiatic cities with their mixed population and social system, to Rome, not as the Latin city, but as the capital of the Greek-speaking world, and to Corinth as the halting-place between Greek Asia and its capital. Several chapters of the present book are devoted to an account of the motley peoples and manners of those cities. The adaptation of Christianity to the double nationality can be best seen in the Apocalypse, because there the two elements which unite in Christianity are less perfectly reconciled than in any other book of the New Testament. The Judaic element in the Apocalypse has been hitherto studied to the entire neglect of the Greek element in it. Hence it has been the most misunderstood book in the New Testament.

The collision of East and West throughout history has been a subject of special interest to the present writer from early youth; and he has watched for more than twenty-five years the recent revival of the Asiatic spirit, often from a very close point of view. In 1897, in a book entitled Impressions of Turkey, he tried to analyse and describe, as he had seen it, "the great historic movement" through which "Mohammedanism and Orientalism have gathered fresh strength to defy the feeling of Europe." It is now becoming plain to all that the relation of Asia to Europe is in process of being profoundly changed; and very soon this will be a matter of general discussion. The long-unquestioned domination of European over Asiatic is now being put to the test, and is probably coming to an end. What is to be the issue? That depends entirely on the influence of Christianity, and on the degree to which it has affected the aims both of Christian and of non-Christian nations: there are cases in which it has affected the latter almost more than the former. The ignorant European fancies that progress for the East lies in Europeanising it. The ordinary traveller in the East can tell that it is as impossible to Europeanise the Asiatic as it is to make an Asiatic out of a European; but he has not learned that there is a higher plane on which Asia and Europe may "mix and meet." That plane was once in an imperfect degree reached in the Graeco-Asiatic cities, whose creative influence in the formation of Roman and modern society is beginning to be recognised by some of the latest historical students, and the new stage towards which Christianity is moving, and in which it will be better understood than it has been by purely European thought, will be a synthesis of European and Asiatic nature and ideas.

This book is a very imperfect essay towards the understanding of that synthesis, which now lies before us as a possibility of the immediate future. How imperfect it is has become clearer to the writer as in the writing of it he came to comprehend better the nature of the Apocalypse.

The illustrations are intended to be steps in the argument. The Apocalypse reads the history and the fate of the Churches in the natural features, the relations of earth and sea, winds and mountains, which affected the cities; this study distinguishes some of those influences; and the Plates furnish the evidence that the natural features are not misapprehended in the study.

The Figures in the text are intended as examples of the symbolism that was in ordinary use in the Greek world; the Apocalypse is penetrated with this way of expressing thought to the eye; and its symbolic language is not to be explained from Jewish models only (as is frequently done). It was written to be understood by the Graeco-Asiatic public; and the Figures prove that it was natural and easy for those readers to understand the symbolism. Most of the subjects are taken from coins of the Imperial period; and hearty thanks are due to Mr. Head of the British Museum for casts from originals under his care. If the style of the coins were the subject of study, photographic reproductions would be required. But what we are here interested in is the method of expressing ideas by visible forms; and a line drawing, which brings out the essential facts, is more useful for our purpose. Examples are very numerous, and this small selection gives rather the first that came to hand than the best that might be chosen.

...

In several cases it is pointed out that the spirit which is revealed in the natural features of the city was recognised in ancient times, being expressed by orators in counselling or flattering the citizens, and becoming a commonplace in popular talk. It is right to point out that in every case the impressions, gained first of all immediately from scenery, were afterwards detected in the ancient writers (who usually express them in obscure and elaborately rhetorical style).

The writing of a series of geographical articles in Dr. Hastings' Dictionary of the Bible greatly facilitated the preparation of the present book, though the writer has learned much since, often as a result of writing those articles.

It has not been part of the writer's purpose to describe the Seven Cities as they are at the present day. That was done in a series of articles by Mrs. Ramsay in the British Monthly, November, 1901, to May, 1902, better than he could do it. He has in several places used ideas and illustrations expressed in the articles, and some of the photographs which were used in them are here reproduced afresh.

W. M RAMSAY

Chapter 1: Writing, Travel, and Letters Among the Early Christians

Many writers on many occasions have perceived and described the important part which intercommunication between the widely separated congregations of early Christians, whether by travel or by letter, played in determining the organisation and cementing the unity of the Universal Church. Yet perhaps all has not been said that ought to be said on the subject. The marvellous skill and mastery, with which all the resources of the existing civilisation were turned to their own purposes by St. Paul and by the Christians generally, may well detain our attention for a brief space.

Travelling and correspondence by letter are mutually dependent. Letters are unnecessary until travelling begins: much of the usefulness and profit of travelling depends on the possibility of communication between those who are separated from one another. Except in the simplest forms, commerce and negotiation between different nations, which are among the chief incentives to travelling in early times, cannot be carried out without some method of registering thoughts and information, so as to be understood by persons at a distance.

Hence communication by letter has been commonly practised from an extremely remote antiquity. The knowledge of and readiness in writing leads to correspondence between friends who are not within speaking distance of one another, as inevitably as the possession of articulate speech produces conversation and discussion. In order to fix the period when epistolary correspondence first began, it would be necessary to discover at what period the art of writing became common. Now the progress of discovery in recent years has revolutionised opinion on this subject. The old views, which we all used to assume as self-evident, that writing was invented at a comparatively late period in human history, that it was long known only to a few persons, and that it was practised even by them only slowly and with difficulty on some special occasions and for some peculiarly important purposes, are found to be utterly erroneous. No one who possesses any knowledge of early history would now venture to make any positive assertion as to the date when writing was invented, or when it began to be widely used in the Mediterranean lands. The progress of discovery reveals the existence of various systems of writing at a remote period, and shows that they were familiarly used for the ordinary purposes of life and administration, and were not reserved, as scholars used to believe, for certain sacred purposes of religion and ritual.

The discovery that writing was familiarly used in early time has an important bearing on the early literature of the Mediterranean peoples. For example, no scholar would now employ the argument that the composition of the Iliad and the Odyssey must belong to a comparatively late day, because such great continuous poems could not come into existence without the ready use of writing--an argument which formerly seemed to tell strongly against the early date assigned by tradition for their origin. The scholars who championed the traditional date of those great works used to answer that argument by attempting to prove that they were composed and preserved by memory alone without the aid of writing. The attempt could not be successful. The scholar in his study, accustomed to deal with words and not with realities, might persuade himself that by this ingenious verbal reasoning he had got rid of the difficulty; but those who could not blind themselves to the facts of the world felt that the improbability still remained, and acquiesced in this reasoning only as the least among a choice of evils. The progress of discovery has placed the problem in an entirely new light. The difficulty originated in our ignorance. The art of writing was indeed required as an element in the complex social platform on which the Homeric poems were built up; but no doubt can now be entertained that writing was known and familiarly practised in the East Mediterranean lands long before the date to which Greek tradition assigned the composition of the two great poems.

A similar argument was formerly used by older scholars to prove that the Hebrew literature belonged to a later period than the Hebrew tradition allowed; but the more recent scholars who advocate the late date of that literature would no longer allow such reasoning, and frankly admit that their views must be supported on other grounds; though it may be doubted whether they have abandoned as thoroughly as they profess the old prejudice in favour of a late date for any long literary composition, or have fully realised how readily and familiarly writing was used in extremely remote time, together with all that is implied by that familiar use. The prejudice still exists, and it affects the study of both Hebrew and Christian literature.

In the first place, there is a general feeling that it is more prudent to bring down the composition of any ancient work to the latest date that evidence permits. But this feeling rests ultimately on the fixed idea that people have gradually become more familiar with the art of writing as the world grows older, and that the composition of a work of literature should not, without distinct and conclusive proof, be attributed to an early period.

In the second place, there is also a very strong body of opinion that the earliest Christians wrote little or nothing. It is supposed that partly they were either unable to write, or at least unused to the familiar employment of writing for the purposes of ordinary life; partly they were so entirely taken up with the idea of the immediate coming of the Lord that they never thought it necessary to record for future generations the circumstances of the life and death of Jesus, until lapse of long years on the one hand had shown that the Lord's coming was not to be expected immediately, and that for the use of the already large Church some record was required of those events round which its faith and hope centred, while on the other hand it had obscured the memory and disturbed the true tradition of those important facts. This opinion also rests on and derives all its influence from the same inveterate prejudice that, at the period in question, writing was still something great and solemn, and that it was used, not in the ordinary course of human everyday life and experience, but only for some grave purpose of legislation, government, or religion, intentionally registering certain weighty principles or important events for the benefit of future generations. Put aside that prejudice, and the whole body of opinion which maintains that the Christians at first did not set anything down in writing about the life and death of Christ--strong and widely accepted as it is, dominating as a fundamental premise much of the discussion of this whole subject in recent times--is devoid of any support.

But most discussions with regard to the origin, force, and spirit of the New Testament are founded on certain postulates and certain initial presumptions, which already contain implicit the whole train of reasoning that follows, and which in fact beg the whole question at starting. If those postulates are true, or if they are granted by the reader, then the whole series of conclusions follows with unerring and impressive logical sequence. All the more necessary, then, is it to examine very carefully the character of such postulates, and to test whether they are really true about that distant period, or are only modern fallacies springing from the mistaken views about ancient history that were widely accepted in the eighteenth and most part of the nineteenth century.

One of those initial presumptions, plausible in appearance and almost universally assumed and conceded, is that there was no early registration of the great events in the beginning of Christian history. This presumption we must set aside as a mere prejudice, contrary to the whole character and spirit of that age, and entirely improbable; though, of course, decisive disproof of it is no longer possible, for the only definite and complete disproof would be the production of the original documents in which the facts were recorded at the moment by contemporaries. But so much may be said at once, summing up in a sentence the result which arises from what is stated in the following pages. So far as antecedent probability goes, founded on the general character of preceding and contemporary Greek or Graeco-Asiatic society, the first Christian account of the circumstances connected with the death of Jesus must be presumed to have been written in the year when Jesus died.

But the objection will doubtless be made at once--If that be so, how can you account for such facts as that Mark says that the Crucifixion was completed by the third hour of the day (9 a.m., according to our modern reckoning of time), while John says that the sentence upon Jesus was only pronounced about the sixth hour, i.e. at noon. The reply is obvious and unhesitating. The difference dates from the event itself. Had evidence been collected that night or next morning, the two diverse opinions would have been observed and recorded, already hopelessly discrepant and contradictory.

One was the opinion of the ordinary people of that period, unaccustomed to note the lapse of time or to define it accurately in thought or speech: such persons loosely indicated the temporal sequence of three great events, the Crucifixion, the beginning and the end of the darkness, by assigning them to the three great successive divisions of the day--the only divisions which they were in the habit of noticing or mentioning--the third, sixth, and ninth hours. Ordinary witnesses in that age would have been nonplused, if they had been closely questioned whether full three hours had elapsed between the Crucifixion and the beginning of the darkness, and would have regarded such minuteness as unnecessary pedantry, for they had never been trained by the circumstances of life to accuracy of thought or language in regard to the lapse of time. Witnesses of that class are the authority for the account which is preserved in the three Synoptic Gospels. We observe that throughout the Gospels of Mark and Luke only the three great divisions of the day--the third, sixth and ninth hours--are mentioned. Matthew once mentions the eleventh hour (20:9); but there his expression does not show superior accuracy in observation, for he is merely using a proverbial expression to indicate that the allotted season had almost elapsed. A very precise record of time is contained in the Bezan Text of Acts 19:9; "from the fifth to the tenth hour"; but this is found only in two MSS, and is out of keeping with Luke's ordinary looseness in respect of time and chronology; and it must therefore be regarded as an addition made by a second century editor, who either had access to a correct source of information, or explained the text in accordance with the regular customs of Graeco-Roman society.

The other statement, which is contained in the Fourth Gospel, records the memory of an exceptional man, who through a certain idiosyncrasy was observant and careful in regard to the lapse of time, who in other cases noted and recorded accurate divisions of time like the seventh hour and the tenth hour (John 1:39, 4:16, 4:52). This man, present at the trial of Jesus, had observed the passage of time, which was unnoticed by others. The others would have been astonished if any one had pointed out that noon had almost come before the trial was finished. He alone marked the sun and estimated the time, with the same accuracy as made him see and remember that the two disciples came to the house of Jesus about the tenth hour, that Jesus sat on the well about the sixth hour, that the fever was said to have left the child about the seventh hour. All those little details, entirely unimportant in themselves, were remembered by a man naturally observant of time, and recorded for not other reason than that he had been present and had seen or heard.

It is a common error to leave too much out of count the change that has been produced on popular thought and accuracy of conception and expression by the habitual observation of the lapse of time according to hours and minutes. The ancients had no means of observing precisely the progress of time. They could as a rule only make a rough guess as to the hour. There was not even a name for any shorter division of time than the hour. There were no watches, and only in the rarest and most exceptional cases were there any public and generally accessible instruments for noting and making visible the lapse of time during the day. The sun-dial was necessarily an inconvenient recorder, not easy to observe. Consequently looseness in regard to the passage of time is deep-seated in ancient thought and literature, especially Greek. The Romans, with their superior endowment for practical facts and ordinary statistics, were more careful, and the effect can be traced in their literature. The lapse of time hour by hour was often noted publicly in great Roman households by the sound of a trumpet or some other device, though the public still regarded this as a rather overstrained refinement--for why should one be anxious to know how fast one's life was ebbing away? Such was the usual point of view, as is evident in Petronius. Occasionally individuals in the Greek-speaking provinces of the East were more accurate in the observation of time, either owing to their natural temperament, or because they were more receptive of the Roman habit of accuracy. On the other hand, the progress of invention has made almost every one in modern times as careful and accurate about time as even the exceptionally accurate in ancient times, because we are all trained from infancy to note the time by minutes, and we suffer loss or inconvenience occasionally from an error in observation. The use of the trumpeter after the Roman fashion to proclaim the lapse of time is said to have been kept up until recently in the old imperial city of Goslar, where, in accordance with the more minute accuracy characteristic of modern thought and custom, he sounded every quarter of an hour.

But it does not follow that, because the ancients were not accustomed to note the progress of the hours, therefore they were less habituated to use the art of writing. It is a mere popular fallacy, entirely unworthy of scholars, to suppose that people became gradually more familiar with writing and more accustomed to use it habitually in ordinary life as time progressed and history continued. The contrary is the case; at a certain period, and to a certain degree, the ancients were accustomed to use the art familiarly and readily; but at a later time writing passed out of ordinary use and became restricted to a few who used it only as a lofty possession for great purposes.

It is worth while to mention one striking example to give emphasis to the fact that, as the Roman Empire decayed, familiarity with the use of writing disappeared from society, until it became the almost exclusive possession of a few persons, who were for the most part connected with religion. About the beginning of the sixth century before Christ, a body of mercenary soldiers, Greeks, Carians, etc., marched far away up the Nile towards Ethiopia and the Sudan in the service of an Egyptian king. Those hired soldiers of fortune were likely, for the most part, to belong to the least educated section of Greek society; and, even where they had learned in childhood to write, the circumstances of their life were not of a kind likely to make writing a familiar and ordinary matter to them, or to render its exercise a natural method of whiling away an idle hour. Yet on the stones and the colossal statues at Abu Simbel many of them wrote, not merely their name and legal designation, but also accounts of the expedition on which they were engaged, with its objects and its progress.

Such was the state of education in a rather humble stratum of Greek society six centuries before Christ. Let us come down eleven centuries after Christ, to the time when great armies of Crusaders were marching across Asia Minor on their way to Palestine. Those armies were led by the noblest of their peoples, by statesmen, warriors, and great ecclesiastics. They contained among them persons of all classes, burning with zeal for a great idea, pilgrims at once and soldiers, with numerous priests and monks. Yet, so far as I am aware, not one single written memorial of all those crusading hosts has been found in the whole country. On a rock beside the lofty castle of Butrentum, commanding the approach to the great pass of the Cilician Gates--that narrow gorge which they called the Gate of Judas, because it was the enemy of their faith and the betrayer of their cause--there are engraved many memorials of their presence; but none are written; all are mere marks in the form of crosses.

In that small body of mercenaries who passed by Abu Simbel 600 years before Christ, there were probably more persons accustomed to use familiarly the art of writing than in all the hosts of the Crusaders; for, even to those Crusaders who had learned to write, the art was far from being familiar, and they were not wont to use it in their ordinary everyday life, though they might on great occasions. In those 1700 years the Mediterranean world had passed from light to darkness, from civilisation to barbarism, so far as writing was concerned. Only recently are we beginning to realise how civilised in some respects was mankind in that earlier time, and to free ourselves from many unfounded prejudices and prepossessions about the character of ancient life and society.

The cumbrousness of the materials on which ancient writing was inscribed may seem unfavourable to its easy or general use. But it must be remembered that, except in Egypt, no material that was not of the most durable character has been or could have been preserved. All writing-materials more ephemeral than stone, bronze, or terra-cotta, have inevitably been destroyed by natural causes. Only in Egypt the extreme dryness of climate and soil has enabled paper to survive. Now the question must suggest itself whether there is any reason to think that more ephemeral materials for writing were never used by the ancient Mediterranean peoples generally. Was Egypt the only country in which writers used such perishable materials? The question can be answered only in one way. There can be no doubt that the custom, which obtained in the Greek lands in the period best known to us, had come down from remote antiquity: that custom was to make a distinction between the material on which documents of national interest and public character were written and that on which mere private documents of personal or literary interest were written. The former, such as laws, decrees and other State documents, which were intended to be made as widely known as possible, were engraved in one or two copies on tablets of the most imperishable character and preserved or exposed in some public place: this was the ancient way of attaining the publicity which in modern time is got by printing large numbers of copies on ephemeral material. But those public copies were not the only ones made; there is no doubt that such documents were first of all written on some perishable material, usually on paper. In the case of private documents, as a rule, no copies were made except on perishable materials.

Wills of private persons, indeed, are often found engraved on marble or other lasting material; these were exposed in the most public manner over the graves that lined the great highways leading out from the cities; but wills were quasi-public documents in the classical period, and had been entirely public documents at an earlier time, according to their original character as records of a public act affecting the community and acquiesced in by the whole body.

Similarly, it can hardly be doubted that, in a more ancient period of Greek society, documents which were only of a private character and of personal or literary interest were likely to be recorded on more perishable substances than graver State documents. This view, of course, can never be definitely and absolutely proved, for the only complete proof would be the discovery of some of those old private documents, which in the nature of the case have decayed and disappeared. But the known facts leave no practical room for doubt.

Paper was in full use in Egypt, as a finished and perfect product, in the fourth millennium before Christ. In Greece it is incidentally referred to by Herodotus as in ordinary use during the fifth century B.C. At what date it began to be used there no evidence exists; but there is every probability that it had been imported from Egypt for a long time; and Herodotus says that, before paper came into use on the Ionian coast, skins of animals were used for writing. On these and other perishable materials the letters and other commonplace documents of private persons were written. Mr. Arthur J. Evans has found at Cnossos in Crete "ink-written inscriptions on vases," as early as 1800 or 2000 years B.C.; and he has inferred from this "the existence of writings on papyrus or other perishable materials" in that period, since ink would not be made merely for writing on terra-cotta vases (though the custom of writing in ink on pottery, especially on ostraka or fragments of broken vases, as being cheap, persisted throughout the whole period of ancient civilisation).

Accordingly, though few private letters older than the imperial time have been preserved, it need not and should not be supposed that there were only a few written. Those that were written have been lost because the material on which they were written could not last. If we except the correspondence of Cicero, the great importance of which caused it to be preserved, hardly any ancient letters not intended for publication by their writers have come down to us except in Egypt, where the original paper has in a number of cases survived. But the voluminous correspondence of Cicero cannot be regarded as a unique fact of Roman life. He and his correspondents wrote so frequently to one another, because letter-writing was then common in Roman society. Cicero says that, when he was separated from his friend Atticus, they exchanged their thought as freely by letter as they did by conversation when they were in the same place. Such a sentiment was not peculiar to one individual: it expressed a custom of contemporary society. The truth is that, just as in human nature thought and speech are linked together in such a way that (to use the expression of Plato) word is spoken thought and thought is unspoken word, so also human beings seek by the law of their nature to express their ideas permanently in writing as well as momentarily in speech; and ignorance of writing in any race points rather to a degraded and degenerate than to a truly primitive condition.

Chapter 2: Transmission of Letters in the First Century

While writing springs from a natural feeling of the human mind and must have originated at a very remote period, and while letters must be almost as old as travelling, the proper development of epistolary correspondence depends on improvement in the method and the certainty of transmission. The desire to write a letter grows weaker, when it is uncertain whether the letter will reach its destination and whether others may open and read it. In the first century this condition was fulfilled better than ever before. It was then easier and safer to send letters than it had been in earlier time. The civilised world, i.e. the Roman world, was traversed constantly by messengers of government or by the letter-carriers of the great financial and trading companies. Commercial undertakings on such a vast scale as the Roman needed frequent and regular communication between the central offices in Rome and the agents in the various provinces. There was no general postal service; but each trading company had its own staff of letter-carriers. Private persons who had not letter-carriers of their own were often able to send letters along with those business communications.

In the early Roman Empire travelling, though not rapid, was performed with an ease and certainty which were quite remarkable. The provision for travelling by sea and by land was made on a great scale. Travellers were going about in great numbers, chiefly during the summer months, occasionally even during the winter season. Their purposes were varied, not merely commerce or government business, but also education, curiosity, search for employment in many departments of life. It is true that to judge from some expressions used in Roman literature by men of letters and moralists, travelling might seem not to have been popular. Those writers occasionally speak as if travelling, especially by sea, were confined to traders who risked their life to make money, and as if the dangers were so great that none but the reckless and greedy would incur them; and the opinion is often expressed, especially by poets, that to adventure oneself on the sea is an impious and unnatural act. The well-known words of Horace's third Ode are typical:--

> Oak and brass of triple fold
> Encompassed sure that heart, which first made bold
> To the raging sea to trust
> A fragile bark, nor feared the Afric gust;
> Heaven's high providence in vain
> Has severed countries with the estranging main,
> If our vessels ne'ertheless
> With reckless plunge that sacred bar transgress

But that point of view was traditional among the poets; it had been handed down from the time when travelling was much more dangerous and difficult, when ships were small in size and fewer in numbers, when seamanship and method were inferior, when few roads had been built, and travel even by land was uncertain. Moreover, seafaring and land travel were hostile to the contentment, discipline, and quiet orderly spirit which Greek poetry and philosophy, as a rule, loved to dwell on and to recommend: they tended to encourage the spirit of self-confidence, self-assertiveness, daring and rebellion against authority, which was called by Euripides "the sailors' lawlessness" (Hecuba, 602). In Roman literature the Greek models and the Greek sentiments were looked up to as sacred and final; and those words of the Roman writers were a proof of their bondage to their Greek masters in thought.

When we look deeper, we find that very different views were expressed by the writers who came more in contact with the real facts of the Imperial world. They are full of admiration of the Imperial peace and its fruits: the sea was covered with ships interchanging the products of different regions of the earth, wealth was vastly increased, comfort and well-being improved, hill and valley covered with the dwellings of a growing population: wars and pirates and robbers had been put an end to, travel was free and safe, all men could journey where they wished, the most remote and lonely countries were opened up by roads and bridges. It is the simple truth that travelling, whether for business or for pleasure, was contemplated and performed under the Empire with an indifference, confidence, and, above all, certainty, which were unknown in after centuries until the introduction of steamers and the consequent increase in ease and sureness of communication.

This ease and frequency of communication under the Roman Empire was merely the culmination of a process that had long been going on. Here, as in many other departments of life, the Romans took up and improved the heritage of Greece. Migration and intermixture of peoples had been the natural law of the Greek world from time immemorial; and the process was immensely stimulated in the fourth century B.C. by the conquests of Alexander the Great, which opened up the East and gave free scope to adventure and trade. In the following centuries there was abundant opportunity for travelling during the fine season of the year. The powerful Monarchies and States of the Greek world keep the sea safe; and during the third century B.C., as has been said by Canon Hicks, a scholar who has studied that period with special care, "there must have been daily communication between Cos (on the west of Asia Minor) and Alexandria" (in Egypt).

When the weakness of the Senatorial administration at Rome allowed the pirates to increase and navigation too become unsafe between 79 and 67 B.C., the life of the civilised world was paralysed; and the success of Pompey in re-opening the sea was felt as the restoration of vitality and civilisation, for civilised life was impossible so long as the sea was an untraversable barrier between the countries instead of a pathway to unite them.

Thus the deep-seated bent of human nature towards letter-writing had been stimulated and cultivated by many centuries of increasing opportunity, until it became a settled habit and in some cases, as we see it in Cicero, almost a passion.

The impression given by the early Christian writings is in perfect agreement with the language of those writers who spoke from actual contact with the life of the time, and did not merely imitate older methods and utter afresh old sentiments. Probably the feature in those Christian writings, which causes most surprise at first to the traveller familiar with those countries in modern time, is the easy confidence with which extensive plans of travel were formed and announced and executed by the early Christians.

In Acts 16:1ff a journey by land and sea through parts of Syria, Cilicia, a corner of Cappadocia, Lycaonia, Phrygia, Mysia, the Troad, Thrace, Macedonia, and Greece is described, and no suggestion is made that this long journey was anything unusual, except that the heightened tone of the narrative in 16:7-9 corresponds to the perplexingly rapid changes of scene and successive frustrations of St. Paul's intentions. But those who are most intimately acquainted with those countries know best how serious an undertaking it would be at the present time to repeat that journey, how many accidents might occur in it, and how much care and thought would be advisable before one entered on so extensive a programme.

Again, in 18:21 St. Paul touched at Ephesus in the ordinary course of the pilgrim-ship which was conveying him and many other Jews to Jerusalem for the Passover. When he was asked to remain, he excused himself, but promised to return as he came back from Jerusalem by a long land-journey through Syria, Cilicia, Lycaonia, and Phrygia. That extensive journey seems to be regarded by speaker and hearers as quite an ordinary excursions. "I must by all means keep this feast that cometh in Jerusalem; but I will again return unto you, if God will." The last condition is added, not as indicating uncertainty, but in the usual spirit of Eastern religion, which forbids a resolve about the future, however simple and easy, to be declared without the express recognition of Divine approval--like the Mohammedan "inshallah," which never fails when the most ordinary resolution about the morrow is stated.

In Romans 15:24, when writing from Corinth, St. Paul sketches out a comprehensive plan. He is eager to see Rome: first he must go to Jerusalem, but thereafter he is bent on visiting Spain, and his course will naturally lead him through Rome, so that he will, without intruding himself on them, have the opportunity of seeing the Romans and affecting their Church on his way.

Throughout medieval times nothing like this off-hand way of sketching out extensive plans was natural or intelligible; there were then, indeed, many great travellers, but those travellers knew how uncertain their journeys were; they were aware that any plans would be frequently liable to interruption, and that nothing could be calculated on as reasonably certain; they entered on long journeys, but regarded them as open to modification or even frustration; in indicating their plans they knew that they would be regarded by others as attempting something great and strange. But St. Paul's method and language seem to show clearly that such journeys as he contemplated were looked on as quite natural and usual by those to whom he spoke or wrote. He could go off from Greece or Macedonia to Palestine, and reckoned with practical certainty on being in Jerusalem in time for a feast day not far distant.

It is the same with others: Aquila and Priscilla, Apollos, Silas, Epaphroditus, Timothy, etc., move back and forward, and are now found in one city, now in another far distant. Unobservant of this characteristic, some writers have argued that Romans 16:3 could not have been addressed to correspondents who lived in Rome, because Aquila and Priscilla, who were in Ephesus not long before the Epistle was written, are there spoken of as living among those correspondents. Such an argument could not be used by people who had fully understood that independence of mere local trammels and connections, and quite a marvellous freedom in locomotion, are a strongly marked feature of the early Church. That argument is one of the smallest errors into which this false prepossession has led may scholars.

Communication by letter supplemented mere travelling. Such communication is the greatest factor in the developing of the Church; it kept alive the interest of the Christian congregations in one another, and strengthened their mutual affection by giving frequent opportunity of expressing it; it prevented the strenuous activity of the widely scattered local Churches from being concentrated on purely local matters and so degenerating into absorption in their own immediate surroundings. Thus it bound together all the Provincial Churches in the one Universal Church. The Christian letters contained the saving power of the Church; and in its epistolary correspondence flowed its life-blood. The present writer has elsewhere attempted to show that the early Bishops derived their importance in great degree from their position as representatives of the several congregations in their relations with one another, charged with the duty of hospitality to travellers and the maintenance of correspondence, since through this position they became the guardians of the unity of the Universal Church and the channels through which its life-blood flowed.

The one condition which was needed to develop epistolary correspondence to a very much greater extent in the Roman Empire was a regular postal service. It seems a remarkable fact that the Roman Imperial government, keenly desirous as it was of encouraging and strengthening the common feeling and bond of unity between different parts of the Empire, never seems to have thought of establishing a general postal service within its dominions. Augustus established an Imperial service, which was maintained throughout subsequent Roman times; but it was strictly confined to Imperial and official business, and was little more than a system of special Emperor's messengers on a great scale. The consequence of this defect was that every great organisation or trading company had to create a special postal service for itself; and private correspondents, if not wealthy enough to send their own slaves as letter-carriers, had to trust to accidental opportunities for transmitting their letters.

The failure of the Imperial government to recognise how much its own aims and schemes would have been aided by facilitating communication through the Empire was connected with one of the greatest defects of the Imperial administration. It never learned that the strength and permanence of a nation and of its government are dependent on the education and character of the people: it never attempted to educate the people, but only to feed and amuse them. The Christian Church, which gradually established itself as a rival organisation, did by its own efforts what the Imperial government aimed at doing for the nation, and succeeded better, because it taught people to think for themselves, to govern themselves, and to maintain their own union by their own exertions. It seized those two great facts of the Roman world, travelling and letter-writing, and turned them to its own purposes. The former, on its purely material side, it could only accept: the latter it developed to new forms as an ideal and spiritual instrument.

Chapter 3: The Christian Letters and Their Transmission

In the preceding chapter we have described the circumstances amid which the Christian letter-writing was developed; and it was pointed out in conclusion that in the pressure of those circumstances, or rather in the energetic use of the opportunities which the circumstances of the Roman Empire offered, there came into existence a kind of letter, hitherto unknown in the world. The Christians developed the older class of letter into new forms, applied it to new purposes, and placed it on a much higher plane than it had ever before stood upon. In their hands communication by letter became one of the most important, if not the most important, of the agencies for consolidating and maintaining the sense of unity among the scattered members of the one universal Church. By means of letters the congregations expressed their mutual affection and sympathy and sense of brotherhood, asked counsel of one another, gave advice with loving freedom and plain speaking to one another, imparted mutual comfort and encouragement, and generally expressed their sense of their common life. Thus arose a new category of epistles.

Dr. Deissmann in Bible Studies, p. 1ff, following older scholars, has rightly and clearly distinguished two previously existing categories, the true letter-written by friend to friend or to friends, springing from the momentary occasion, intended only for the eye of the person or persons to whom it is addressed--and the literary epistle--written with an eye to the public, and studied with literary art. The literary epistle is obviously later in origin than the true letter. It implies the previous existence of the true letter as a well-recognised type of composition, and the deliberate choice of this type for imitation. Soon after the death of Aristotle in 322 B.C. a fictitious collection of letters purporting to have been written by him was published. Such forged letters are composed for a literary purpose with an eye to the opinion of the world. The forger deliberately writes them after a certain type and with certain characteristics, which may cause them to be taken for something which they are not really. A fabrication like this proves at least that the letter was already an established form of composition; and the forger believed that he could calculate on rousing public interest by falsely assuming this guise.

But it is impossible to follow Dr. Deissmann, it seems to me, when he goes on to reduce all the letters of the New Testament to one or other of those categories. He shows, it is true, some consciousness that the two older categories are insufficient, but the fact is that in the new conditions a new category had been developed--the general letter addressed to a whole congregation or to the entire Church of Christ.

These are true letters, in the sense that they spring from the heart of the writer and speak direct to the heart of the readers; that they were often written in answer to a question, or called forth by some special crisis in the history of the persons addressed, so that they rise out of the actual situation in which the writer conceives the readers to be placed; that they express the writer's keen and living sympathy with and participation in the fortunes of the whole class addressed; that they are not affected by any thought of a wider public than the persons whom he directly addresses; in short, he empties out his heart in them. On the other hand, the letters of this class express general principles of life and conduct, religion and ethics, applicable to a wider range of circumstances than those which have called forth the special letter; and they appeal as emphatically and intimately to all Christians in all time as they did to those addressed in the first instance.

It was not long before this wider appeal was perceived. It is evident that when St. Paul bade the Colossians send his letter to be read in the Laodicean Church, and read themselves the Laodicean letter, he saw that each was applicable to a wider circle than it directly addressed. But it is equally evident that the Colossian letter was composed not with an eye to that wider circle, but directly to suit the critical situation in Colossae. The wider application arises out of the essential similarity of human nature in both congregations and in all mankind. The crisis that has occurred in one congregation is likely at some period to occur in other similar bodies; and the letter which speaks direct to the heart of one man or one body of men will speak direct to the heart of all men in virtue of their common human nature. Here lies the essential character of this new category of letters. In the individual case they discover the universal principle, and state it in such a way as to reach the heart of every man similarly situated; and yet they state this, not in the way of formal exposition, but in the way of direct personal converse, written in place of spoken.

Some of those Christian letters are more diverse from the true letter than others; and Dr. Deissmann tries to force them into his too narrow classification by calling some of them true letters and others literary epistles. But none of the letters in the New Testament can be restricted within the narrow range of his definition of the true letter: even the letter to Philemon, intimate and personal as it is, rebels in some parts against this strictness, and rises into a far higher and broader region of thought: it is addressed not only to Philemon and Apphia and Archippus, but also "to the Church in thy house."

Such letters show a certain analogy to the Imperial rescripts. The rescript was strictly a mere reply to a request for guidance in some special case, addressed by an official to the Emperor; yet it came to be regarded as one of the chief means of improving and developing Roman public law. A rescript arose out of special circumstances and stated the Emperor's opinion on them in much the same way as if the official had consulted him face to face; the rescript was written for the eye of one official, without any thought of others; but it set forth the general principle of policy which applied to the special case. The rescripts show how inadequate Dr. Deissmann's classification is. It would be a singularly incomplete account of them to class them either as true letters or as literary epistles. They have many of the characteristics of the true letter; in them the whole mind and spirit of the Imperial writer was expressed for the benefit of one single reader; but they lack entirely the spontaneity and freshness of the true letter. As expressing general truths and universal principles, they must have been the result of long experience and careful thought, though the final expression was often hasty and roused by some special occasion. This more studied character differentiates them from the mere unstudied expression of personal affection and interest.

Similarly, those general letters of the Christians express and embody the growth in the law of the Church and in its common life and constitution. They originated in the circumstances of the Church. The letter of the Council at Jerusalem (Acts 15:23ff) arose out of a special occasion, and was the reply to a question addressed from Syria to the central Church and its leaders; the reply was addressed to the Churches of the province of Syria and Cilicia, and specially the Church of the capital of that province; but it was forthwith treated as applicable equally to other Christians, and was communicated as authoritative by Paul and Silas to the Churches of Galatia (Acts 16:4).

The peculiar relation of fatherhood and authority in which Paul stood to his own Churches developed still further this category of letters. Mr. V. Bartlet has some good remarks on it in Dr. Hastings' Dictionary of the Bible, i., p. 730, from which we may be allowed to quote two sentences. "Of a temper too ardent for the more studied forms of writing, St. Paul could yet by letter, and so on the spur of occasion, concentrate all his wealth of thought, feeling and maturing experience upon some particular religious situation, and sweep away the difficulty or danger . . . The true cause of" all his letters "lay deep in the same spirit as breathes in First Thessalonians, the essentially pastoral' instinct."

A still further development towards general philosophico-legal statement of religious dogma is apparent on the one hand in Romans, addressed to a Church which he had not founded, and on the other hand in the Pastoral Epistles. The latter have a double character, being addressed by Paul to friends and pupils of his own, partly in their capacity of personal friends--such portions of the letters being of the most intimate, incidental, and unstudied character--but far more in their official capacity as heads and overseers of a group of Churches--such parts of the letters being really intended more for the guidance of the congregations than of the nominal addressees, and being, undoubtedly, to a considerable extent merely confirmatory of the teaching already given to the congregations by Timothy and Titus. The double character of these Epistles is a strong proof of their authenticity. Such a mixture of character could only spring from the intimate friend and leader, whose interest in the work which his two subordinates were doing was at times lost in the personal relation.

The Catholic Epistles represent a further stage of this development. First Peter is addressed to a very wide yet carefully defined body of Churches in view of a serious trial to which they are about to be exposed. Second Peter, James, and First John are quite indefinite in their address to all Christians. But all of them are separated by a broad and deep division from the literary epistle written for the public eye. They are informed and inspired with the intense personal affection which the writers felt for every individual of the thousands whom they addressed. They are entirely devoid of the artificiality which is inseparable from the literary epistle; they come straight from the heart and speak straight to the heart; whereas the literary epistle is always and necessarily written with a view to its effect on the public, and the style is affected and to a certain degree forced and even unnatural. It was left for the Christian letter to prove that the heart of man is wide enough and deep enough to entertain the same love for thousands as for one. The Catholic Epistles are therefore quite as far removed from the class of "literary epistles" as the typical letters of Paul are from the class of "true letters," as those classes have been defined; and the resemblance in essentials between the Catholic and the typical Pauline Epistles is sufficient to overpower the points of difference, and to justify us in regarding them as forming a class by themselves.

This remarkable development, in which law, statesmanship, ethics, and religion meet in and transform the simple letter, was the work of St. Paul more than of any other. But it was not due to him alone, nor initiated by him. It began before him and continued after him. It sprang from the nature of the Church and the circumstances of the time. The Church was Imperial, the visible Kingdom of God. Its leaders felt that their letters expressed the will of God; and they issued their truly Imperial rescripts. "It seemed good to the Holy Spirit and to us" is the bold and regal exordium of the first Christian letter.

Christian letters in the next two or three centuries were often inspired by something of the same spirit. Congregation spoke boldly and authoritatively to congregation, as each was moved by the Spirit to write: the letter partook of the nature of an Imperial rescript, yet it was merely the expression of the intense interest taken by equal in equal, and brother in brother. The whole series of such letters is indicative of the strong interest of all individuals in the government of the entire body; and they form one of the loftiest and noblest embodiments of a high tone of feeling common to a very large number of ordinary, commonplace, undistinguished human beings.

Such a development of the letter was possible in that widely scattered body of the Church only through the greatly increased facilities for travel and intercourse. The Church showed its marvellous intuition and governing capacity by seizing this opportunity. In this, as in many other ways, it was the creature of its time, suiting itself to the needs of the time, which was ripe for it, and using the conditions and opportunities of the time with true creative statesmanship.

As has been said, correspondence is impossible without some safe means of conveyance. A confidential letter, the real outpouring of one's feelings, is impossible unless the writer feels reasonably sure that the letter will reach the proper hands, and still more that it will not fall into the wrong hands. Further, it has been pointed out that there was no public post, and that any individual or any trading company which maintained a large correspondence was forced to maintain an adequate number of private letter-carriers. The great financial associations of publicani in the last century B.C. had bodies of slave messengers, called tabellarii, to carry their letters between the central administration in Rome and the agents scattered over every province where they conducted business. Wealthy private persons employed some of their own slaves as tabellarii. But if such messengers were to be useful, they must be experienced, and they must be familiar with roads and methods of travel: in short, any great company which maintained a large correspondence must necessarily organise a postal service of its own. The best routes and halts were marked out, the tabellarii travelled along fixed roads, and the administration could say approximately where any messenger was likely to be at any moment, when a letter would arrive and the orders which it contained be put in execution, when each messenger would return and be available for a new mission. All this lies at the basis of good organisation and successful conduct of business. As to the details we know nothing; no account of such things has been preserved. But the existence of such a system must be presupposed as a condition, before great business operations like the Roman could be carried on. A large correspondence implies a special postal system.

Now we must apply this to the Christian letters. Many such letters were sent: those which have been preserved must be immensely multiplied to give any idea of the number really despatched. The importance of this correspondence for the welfare and growth of the Church was, as has been shown, very great. Some provision for the safe transmission of that large body of letters, official and private, was obviously necessary. Here is a great subject, as to which no information has been preserved.

It must be supposed as was stated above, that the bishops had the control of this department of Church work. In the first place the bishop wrote in the name of the congregation of which he was an official: this is known from the case of the Roman Clement, whose letter to the Corinthians is expressed in the name of the Roman Church. The reference to him in the Shepherd of Hermas, Vision, ii., 4, 3, as entrusted with the duty of communicating with other Churches, confirms the obvious inference from his letter, and the form of the reference shows that the case was not an exceptional, but a regular and typical one. This one case, therefore, proves sufficiently what was the practice in the Church.

In the second place the bishop was charged with the duty of hospitality, i.e. of receiving and providing for the comfort of the envoys and messengers from other Churches: this is distinctly stated in 1 Timothy 3:1ff and Titus 1:5ff. To understand what is implied in this duty, it is necessary to conceive clearly the situation. As has been already pointed out, the Christian letter-writers had to find their own messengers. It cannot be doubted that, as an almost invariable rule, those messengers were Christians. Especially, all official letters from one congregation to another must be assumed to have been borne by Christian envoys. Epaphroditus, Tychicus, Silas and others, who occur as bearers of letters in the New Testament, must be taken as examples of a large class. St. Paul himself carried and delivered the first known Christian letter. That class of travelling Christians could not be suffered to lodge in pagan inns, which were commonly places of the worst character in respect of morality and comfort and cleanliness. They were entertained by their Christian brethren; that was a duty incumbent on the congregation; and the bishops had to superintend and be responsible for the proper discharge of this duty. It must therefore be understood that such envoys would address themselves first to the bishop, when they came to any city where there was an organised body of Christians resident, and that all Christian travellers would in like manner look to the bishop for guidance to suitable quarters. Considering that the number of Christian travellers must have been large, it is entirely impossible to interpret the duty of hospitality, with which the bishop was charged, as implying that he ought to entertain them in his own house.

In the third place, it seems to follow as a necessary corollary from the two preceding duties, that the letters addressed to any congregation were received by the bishop in its name and as its representative.

From the fact that the letter-carriers were usually Christian, we must infer that they were not likely as a rule to be, like the tabellarii of the great Roman companies, slaves trained to the duty and doing nothing else. In many cases, certainly, the letters were carried by persons who had other reasons for travelling. But in a great province like Asia, it was necessary to have more regular messengers within the province, and not to depend entirely on accidental opportunities. Undoubtedly, messengers had often to be sent with letters round the congregations of the province. In the earlier stages of Church development, probably, those messengers were volunteers, discharging a duty which among the pagans was almost entirely performed by slaves: just as Luke and Aristarchus, when they travelled with St. Paul to Rome, must have voluntarily passed as his servants, i.e. as slaves, in order to be admitted to the convoy. In such cases, it is apparent how much this sense of duty ennobled labour and raised the social standing of the labourer, who was not a volunteer, making himself like a slave in the service of the Church. In this there is already involved the germ of a general emancipation of slaves and the substitution of free for slave labour.

As time passed, and the work grew heavier, the organisation must have become more complex, and professional carriers of letters were probably required. But as to the details we know nothing, though the general outlines of the system were dictated by the circumstances of the period, and can be restored accordingly. Thus, as soon as we begin to work out the idea of the preparations and equipment required in practice for this great system, we find ourselves obliged to admit the existence of a large organisation. The Church stands before those who rightly conceive its practical character, as a real antagonist in the fullest sense to the Imperial government, creating and managing its own rival administration. We thus understand better the hatred which the Imperial government could not but feel for it, a hatred which is altogether misapprehended by those who regard it as springing from religious ground. We understand too how Constantine at last recognised in the Church the one bond which could hold together the disintegrating Empire. Whether or not he was a Christian, he at least possessed a statesman's insight. And his statesmanlike insight in estimating the practical strength of rival religions stands out as all the more wonderful, if he were not a Christian at heart; for (though many years of his youth and earlier manhood had been spent in irksome detention in the East, where Christianity was the popular and widely accepted religion), yet his choice was made in the West, the country of his birth and of his hopes, where Mithraism was the popular and most influential religion: it was made amid the soldiery, which was almost entirely devoted to the religion of Mithras.

Chapter 4: The Letters to the Seven Churches

One of the most remarkable parts of that strange and difficult book, the Revelation of St. John, is the passage 2:1 to 3:22, containing the Seven Letters. The Apocalypse as a whole belongs to a large and well-known class of later Jewish literature, and has many features in common with previous Apocalypses of Jewish origin. St. John was using an established literary form, which he adapted in a certain degree to his purposes, but which seriously fettered and impeded him by its fanciful and unreal character. As a general rule he obeys the recognised laws of apocalyptic composition, and imitates the current forms so closely that his Apocalypse has been wrongly taken by some scholars, chiefly German, as a work of originally pure and unmixed Jewish character, which was modified subsequently to a Christian type.

In this work, Jewish in origin and general plan, and to a great extent Jewish in range of topics, there is inserted this episode of the Seven Letters, which appears to be almost entirely non-Jewish in character and certainly non-Jewish in origin and model. There must have been therefore some reason which seemed to the author to demand imperatively the insertion of such an episode in a work of diverse character. The reason was that the form of letters had already established itself as the most characteristic expression of the Christian mind, and as almost obligatory on a Christian writer. Though many other forms have been tried in Christian literature, e.g. the dialogue, the formal treatise, etc., yet the fact remains that--apart from the fundamental four Gospels--the highest and most stimulating and creative products of Christian thought have been expressed in the epistolary form. This was already vaguely present in the mind of St. John while he was composing the Apocalypse. Under this compelling influence he abandons the apocalyptic form for a brief interval, and expresses his thought in the form of letters. In them he makes some attempt to keep up the symbolism which was prescribed by the traditional principles of apocalyptic composition; but such imagery is too awkward and cumbrous for the epistolary form, and has exerted little influence on the Seven Letters. The traditional apocalyptic form breaks in his hands, and he throws away the shattered fragments.

In the subsequent development of St. John's thought it is plain that he had recognised the inadequacy and insufficiency of the fashionable Jewish literary forms. It seems highly probable that the perception of that fact came to him during the composition of the Revelation, and that the Seven Letters, though placed near the beginning and fitted carefully into that position, were the last part of the work to be conceived.

It must also be noticed that the book of the Revelation, as a whole, except the first three verses, is cast in the form of a letter. After the brief introduction, the fourth verse is expressed in the regular epistolary form:--

John, to the Seven Asian Churches:
Grace to you and peace, from him which is and which was and which is to come; and from the
Seven Spirits, etc.

Such a beginning is out of keeping with the ordinary apocalyptic form; but the pastoral instinct was strong in the writer, and he could never lose the sense of responsibility for the Churches that were under his charge. Just as the Roman Consul read in the sky the signs of the will of heaven on behalf of the State, so St. John saw in the heavens the vision of trial and triumph on behalf of the Churches entrusted to his care. All that he saw and heard was for them rather than for himself; and this is distinctly intimated to him, 1:11, What thou seest, write in a book, and send to the Seven Churches.

The expression just quoted from 1:11, write in a book, and send, obviously refers to the vision as a whole. It is not an introduction to the Seven Letters: it is the order to write out and send the entire Apocalypse. This the writer does, and sends it with the covering letter, which begins in 1:4. Hence 1:11 explains the origin of 1:4. The idea of the letter as the inevitable Christian form was firmly in the writer's mind. He must write an Apocalypse with the record of his vision; but he must enclose it in a letter to the Churches.

The Apocalypse would be quite complete without the Seven Letters: chapter 4 follows chapter 1 naturally. The Seven Letters spring from the sense of reality, the living vigorous instinct, from which the Christian spirit can never free itself. An Apocalypse could not content St. John: it did not bring him in close enough relation to his Churches. And so, as a second thought, he addressed the Seven representative Churches one by one; and, as the letters could not be placed last, he placed them near the beginning; but the one link of connection between them and the Apocalypse lies in the words with which each is finished: he that hath an ear, let him hear what the spirit saith to the Churches, i.e. not merely the words of the Letter, but the Apocalypse which follows.

It is also not improbable that St. John had received a greater share of the regular Jewish education than most of his fellow-Apostles, and that, through his higher education, the accepted Jewish forms of composition had a greater hold on his mind, and were more difficult for him to throw off, than for Peter, who had never been so deeply imbued with them. However that may be, it is at least evident in his later career that a new stage began for him at this point, that he discarded Hebrew literary models and adopted more distinctly Greek forms, and that his literary style and expression markedly improved at the same time. Proper consideration of these facts must surely lead to the conclusion that no very long interval of time must necessarily be supposed to have elapsed between the composition of the Revelation and of the Gospel. The change in style is indeed very marked; but it is quite in accordance with the observed facts of literary growth in other men that a critical and epoch-making step in mental development, when one frees oneself from the dominion of a too narrow early education, and strikes out in a path of originality, may be accompanied by a very marked improvement in linguistic expression and style.

The Seven Letters are farther removed from the type of the "true letter" than any other compositions in the New Testament. In their conception they are strictly "literary epistles," deliberate and intentional imitations of a literary form that was already firmly established in Christian usage. They were not intended to be sent directly to the Churches to which they were addressed. They had never any separate existence apart from one another and from the book of which they are a part. They are written on a uniform plan, which is absolutely opposed to the spontaneity and directness of the true letter. At the stage in his development, which we have supposed the author to be traversing, he passed from the domination of one literary form, the Jewish apocalyptic, to the domination of another literary form, the Christian epistolary. He had not yet attained complete literary freedom: he had not yet come to his heritage, emancipated himself from the influence of models, and launched forth on the ocean of his own wonderful genius. But he was just on the point of doing so. One step more, and he was his own master.

How near that step was is obvious, when we look more closely into the character of the Seven Letters. It is only by very close study, as in the chapters below devoted to the individual letters, that the reader can duly appreciate the special character of each. To sum up and anticipate the results of that closer study, it may here be said that the author of the Seven Letters, while composing them all on the same general lines, as mere parts of an episode in a great work of literature, imparts to them many touches, specially suitable to the individual Churches, and showing his intimate knowledge of them all. In each case, as he wrote the letter, the Church to which it was addressed stood before his imagination in its reality and its life; he was absorbed with the thought of it alone, and he almost entirely forgot that he was composing a piece of literature, and apostrophised it directly, with the same overmastering earnestness and sense of responsibility that breathe through St. Paul's letters.

As will be shown fully in chapter 14, the Seven Churches stood as representative of seven groups of congregations; but the Seven Letters are addressed to them as individual Churches, and not to the groups for which they stand. The letters were written by one who was familiar with the situation, the character, the past history, the possibilities of future development, of those Seven Cities. The Church of Sardis, for example, is addressed as the Church of that actual, single city: the facts and characteristics mentioned are proper to it alone, and not common to the other Churches of the Hermus Valley. Those others were not much in the writer's mind: he was absorbed with the thought of that one city: he saw only death before it. But the other cities which were connected with it may be warned by its fate; and he that overcometh shall be spared and honoured. Similarly, St. Paul's letter to Colossae was written specially for it alone, and with no reference to Laodicea; yet it was ordered to be communicated to Laodicea, and read publicly there also.

This singleness of vision is not equally marked on the surface of every letter. In the message to Laodicea, the thought of the other cities of the group is perhaps apparent; and possibly the obscurity of the Thyatiran Letter may be due in some degree to the outlook upon the other cities of its group, though a quite sufficient and more probable reason is our almost complete ignorance of the special character of that city.

To this singleness of vision, the clearness with which the writer sees each single city, and the directness with which he addresses himself to each, is due the remarkable variety of character in the whole series. The Seven Letters were evidently all written together, in the inspiration of one occasion and one purpose; and yet how different each is from all the rest, in spite of the similarity of purpose and plan and arrangement in them all! Each of the Seven Churches is painted with a character of its own;

and very different futures await them. The writer surveys them from the point of view of one who believes that natural scenery and geographical surroundings exercise a strong influence on the character and destiny of a people. He fixes his eye on the broad features of the landscape. In the relations of sea and land, river and mountains--relations sometimes permanent, sometimes mutable--he reads the tale of the forces that insensibly mould the minds of men. Now that is not a book which he that runs may read. It is a book with seven seals, which can be opened only by long familiarity, earnest patient thought, and the insight given by belief and love. The reader must have attuned himself to harmony with the city and the natural influences that had made it. St. John from his lofty standpoint could look forward into the future, and see what should come to each of his Churches.

He assumes always that the Church is, in a sense, the city. The local Church does not live apart from the locality and the population, amid which it has a mere temporary abode. The Church is all that is real in the city: the rest of the city has failed to reach its true self, and has been arrested in its development. Similarly, the local Church in its turn has not all attained to its own perfect development: the "angel" is the truth, the reality, the idea (in Platonic sense) of the Church. Thus in that quaint symbolism the city bears to its Church the same relation that the Church bears to its angel. But here we are led into subjects that will be more fully discussed in chapters 6 and 16. For the present we shall only review in brief the varied characters of the Seven Churches and the Seven Cities, constituting among them an epitome of the Universal Church and of the whole range of human life.

The note alike in the Church and in the history of Ephesus has been change. The Church was enthusiastic; but it has been cooling. It has fallen from its high plane of conduct and spirit. And the penalty denounced against it is that it shall be moved out of its place, unless it recreates its old spirit and enthusiasm: "I have this against thee that thou didst leave thy first love. Remember therefore from whence thou art fallen and repent and do the first works; or else I come to thee, and will move thy lamp out of its place." And, similarly, in the history of the city the same note is distinct. An extraordinary series of changes and vicissitudes had characterised it, and would continue to do so. Mutability was the law of its being. The land and the site of the city had varied from century to century. What was water became land; what was city ceased to be inhabited; what was bare hillside and cultivated lowland became a great city crowded with a teeming population; what was a harbour filled with the shipping of the whole world has become a mere inland sea of reeds, through which the wind moans with a vast volume of sound like the distant waves breaking on a long stretch of sea-coast in storm.

The distinctive note of the letter to Smyrna is faithfulness that gives life, and appearance bettered by reality. The Church "was dead and lived," like Him who addressed it: it was poor, but rich: it was about to suffer for a period, but the period is definite, and the suffering comes to an end, and the Church will prove faithful through it all and gain "the crown of life." Such also had the city been in history: it gloried in the title of the faithful friend of Rome, true to its great ally alike in danger and in prosperity. The conditions of nature amid which it was planted were firm and everlasting. Before it was an arm of the vast, unchanging, unconquerable sea, its harbour and the source of its life and strength. Behind it rose its Hill (Pagos) crowned with the fortified acropolis, as one looks at it from the front apparently only a rounded hillock of 450 feet elevation; but ascend it, and you discover it to be really a corner of the great plateau behind, supported by the immeasurable strength of the Asian continent which pushes it forward towards the sea. The letter is full of joy and life and brightness, beyond all others of the Seven; and such is the impression the city still makes on the traveller (who usually comes to it as his first experience of the towns of Asia Minor), throwing back the glittering rays of the sun with proportionate brightness, while its buildings spring sharp out of the sea and rise in tiers up the front slopes of its Pagos.

Pergamum stands before us in the letter as the city of authority, beside the throne--the throne of this world and of the power of evil, where the lord of evil dwelleth. And to its victorious Church is promised a greater authority, the power of the mighty name of God, known only to the giver and the receiver. It was the royal city of history, seat of the Attalid Kings and chief centre of the Roman Imperial administration; and the epithet "royal" is the one that rises unbidden to the traveller's lips, especially as he beholds it after seeing the other great cities of the land, with its immense acropolis on a rock rising out of the plain like a mountain, self-centred in its impregnable strength, looking out over the distant sea and over the land right away to the hills beside far off Smyrna.

Thyatira, with its low and small acropolis in its beautiful valley, stretching north and south like a long funnel between two gently swelling ridges of hill, conveys the impression of mildness, and subjection to outward influence, and inability to surmount and dominate external circumstances. The letter to Thyatira is mainly occupied with the inability of the Church to rise superior to the associations and habits of contemporary society, and its contented voluntary acquiescence in them (which was called the Nicolaitan heresy). Yet even in the humble Thyatira he that perseveres to the end and overcomes shall be rewarded with irresistible power among the nations, that smashing power which its own deity pretends to wield with his battle-axe, a power like but greater than that of mighty Rome itself. In the remnant of the Thyatiran Church, which shall have shown the will to resist temptation, weakness shall be made strong.

The letter to the Sardian Church breathes the spirit of death, of appearance without reality, promise without performance, outward show of strength betrayed by want of watchfulness and careless confidence. Thou hast a name that thou livest and thou art dead . . . I have found no works of thine fulfilled . . . I will come as a thief comes; and thou shalt not know what hour I will come upon thee. And such also was the city and its history. Looked at from a little distance to the north in the open plain, Sardis wore an imposing, commanding, impregnable aspect, as it dominated that magnificent broad valley of the Hermus from its robber stronghold on a steep spur that stands out boldly from the great mountains on the south. But, close at hand, the hill is seen to be but mud, slightly compacted, never trustworthy or lasting, crumbling under the influences of the weather, ready to yield even to a blow of the spade. Yet the Sardians always trusted to it; and their careless confidence had often been deceived, when an adventurous enemy climbed in at some unguarded point, where the weathering of the soft rock had opened a way.

Philadelphia was known to the whole world as the city of earthquakes, whose citizens for the most part lived outside, not venturing to remain in the town, and were always on the watch for the next great catastrophe. Those who knew it best were aware that its prosperity depended on the great road from the harbour of Smyrna to Phrygia and the East. Philadelphia, situated where this road is about to ascend by a difficult pass to the high central plateau of Phrygia, held the key and guarded the door. It was also of all the Seven Cities the most devoted to the name of the Emperors, and had twice taken a new title or epithet from the Imperial god, abandoning in one case its own ancient name. The Church had been a missionary Church, and Christ Himself, bearer of the key of David, had opened the door before it, which none shall shut. He Himself "will keep thee from the hour of trial," the great and imminent catastrophe that shall come upon the whole world. But for the victor there remains stability, like that of the strong column that supports the temple of God; and he shall not ever again need to go out for safety; and he shall take as his new name the name of God and of His city.

The Laodicean Church is strongly marked in the letter as the irresolute one, which had not been able to make up its mind, and halted half-heartedly, neither one thing nor another. It would fain be enriched, and clad in righteousness, and made to see the truth; but it would trust to itself; in its own gold it would find its wealth, in its own manufactures it would make its garments, in its own famous medical school it would seek its cure; it did not feel its need, but was content with what it had. It was neither truly Christian, nor frankly pagan. This letter, alone among the Seven, seems not to bring the character of the Church into close relation to the great natural features amid which the city stood; but on the other hand it shows a very intimate connection between the character attributed to the Church and the commerce by which the city had grown great.

The second half of this letter gradually passes into an epilogue to the whole Seven; and this proves that, in spite of the individual character of each letter, they form after all only parts in an elaborate and highly wrought piece of literature. It is hardly possible to say exactly where the individual letter ends and the epilogue begins; in appearance the whole bears the form after which all the letters are modelled; but there is a change from the individualisation of the letter to the general application of the epilogue.

To comprehend more fully the individuality of the Seven Letters one should compare them with the letters of Ignatius to the five Asian Churches, Ephesus, Smyrna, Magnesia, Tralleis, Philadelphia, or with the letter of Clement to the Corinthian Church. Ignatius, it is true, had probably seen only two of the five, and those only cursorily; so that the vagueness, the generality, and the lack of individual traits in all his letters were inevitable. He insists on topics which were almost equally suitable to all Christians, or on those which not unnaturally filled his own mind in view of his coming fate.

But it is a remarkable fact that the more definite and personal and individual those old Christian letters are, the more vital and full of guidance are they to all readers. The individual letters touch life most nearly; and the life of any one man or Church appeals most intimately to all men and all Churches.

The more closely we study the New Testament books and compare them with the natural conditions, the localities and the too scanty evidence from other sources about the life and society of the first century, the more full of meaning do we find them, the more strongly impressed are we with their unique character, and the more wonderful becomes the picture that is unveiled to us in them of the growth of the Christian Church. It is because they were written with the utmost fulness of vigour and life by persons who were entirely absorbed in the great practical tasks which their rapidly growing organisation imposed on them, because they stand in the closest relation to the facts of the age, that so much can be gathered from them. They rise to the loftiest heights to which man in the fulness of inspiration and perfect sympathy with the Divine will and purpose can attain, but they stand firmly planted on the facts of earth. The Asian Church was so successful in moulding and modifying the institutions around it because with unerring insight its leaders saw the deep-seated character of those Seven Cities, their strength and their weakness, as determined by their natural surroundings, their past history, and their national character.

This series of studies of the Seven Letters may perhaps be exposed to the charge of imagining fanciful connections between the natural surroundings of the Seven cities and the tone of the Letters. Those who are accustomed to the variety of character that exists in the West may refuse to acknowledge that there exists any such connection between the character of the natural surroundings and the spirit, the Angel, of the Church.

But Western analogy is misleading. We Occidentals are accustomed to struggle against Nature, and by understanding Nature's laws to subjugate her to our needs. When a waterway is needed, as at Glasgow, we transform a little stream into a navigable river. Where a harbour is necessary to supply a defect in nature, we construct with vast toil and at great cost an artificial port. We regulate the flow of dangerous rivers, utilising all that they can give us and restraining them from inflicting the harm they are capable of. Thus in numberless ways we refuse to yield to the influences that surround us, and by hard work rise superior in some degree to them.

Such analogy must not be applied without careful consideration in Asia. There man is far more under the influence of nature; and hence results a homogeneity of character in each place which is surprising to the Western traveller, and which he can hardly believe or realise without long experience. Partly that subjection may be due to the fact that nature and the powers of nature are on a vaster scale in Asia. You can climb the highest Alps, but the Himalayas present untrodden peaks, where the powers of man fail. The Eastern people have had little chance of subduing and binding to their will the mighty rivers of Asia (except the Chinese, who regulated their greatest rivers more than 2,000 years ago). The Hindus have come to recognise the jungle as unconquerable, and its wild beasts as irresistible; and they passively acquiesce in their fate. Vast Asiatic deserts are accepted as due to the will of God; and through this humble resignation other great stretches of land, which once were highly cultivated, have come to be marked on the maps as desert, because the difficulties of cultivation are no longer surmountable by a passive and uninventive population. In Asia mankind has accepted nature; and the attempts to struggle against it have been almost wholly confined to a remote past or to European settlers.

How it was that Asiatic races could do more to influence nature at a very early time than they have ever attempted in later times is a problem that deserves separate consideration. Here we only observe that they themselves attributed their early activity entirely to religion: the Mother-Goddess herself taught her children how to conquer Nature by obeying her and using her powers. In its subsequent steady degradation their religion lost that early power.

But among the experiences which specially impress the traveller who patiently explores Asia Minor step by step, village by village, and province by province, perhaps the most impressive of all is the extent to which natural circumstances mould the fate of cities and the character of men. The dominance of nature is, certainly, more complete now than it was of old; but still even in the early ages of history it was great; and it is a main factor both in molding the historical mythology, or mythical explanations of historical facts that were current among the ancient peoples, and in guiding the more reasoned and pretentious scientific explanations of history set forth by the educated and the philosophers. The writer of the Seven Letter has stated in them his view of the history of each Church in harmony with the prominent features of nature around the city.

Chapter 5: Relation of the Christian Books to Contemporary Thought and Literature

Symbolism does not take up so large a space in the Seven Letters as it does in the rest of the Apocalypse. In the letters the writer was brought more directly in contact with real life and human conduct; and the practical character of Christian teaching had a stronger hold on him when he felt himself, even in literature, face to face with a real congregation of human beings, and pictured to himself in imagination their history and their needs, their faults and excellencies. Yet even in the letters symbolism plays some part; ideas and objects are sometimes named, not in their immediate sense, but as representatives or signs of something else. Not merely is the general setting, the Seven Stars, the Lamps (candle-sticks in the Authorised and the Revised Versions), etc., symbolical: even in the letters there are many expression whose real meaning is not what lies on the surface. The "crown of life," indeed, may be treated as a mere figure of speech; but the "ten days" of suffering through which Smyrna must pass can hardly be regarded as anything more than "a time which comes to an end." Even the metaphors and other figures are not purely literary: they have had a history, and have acquired a recognised and conventional meaning. The "door," which is mentioned in 3:7, would hardly be intelligible without regard to current Christian usage.

Two points of view must be distinguished in this case. In the first place a regular, generally accepted conventional symbolism was growing up among the Christians, in which Babylon meant Rome, a door meant an opening for missionary work, and so on: this subject has not yet been properly investigated in a scientific way, apart from prejudices and prepossessions.

In the second place, the letters were written to be understood by the Asian congregations, which mainly consisted of converted pagans. The ideas expressed in the letters had to be put in a form which the readers would understand; to suit their understanding the figures and comparisons must be drawn from sources and objects familiar to them; the words must be used in the sense in which they were commonly employed in the cities addressed; illustrations, which were needed to bring home to the readers difficult ideas, must be drawn from the circle of their experience and education, chapters 11 and 13.

It has been too much the custom to regard the earliest Christian books as written in a specially Christian form of speech, standing apart and distinguishable from the common language of the eastern Roman Provinces. Had that been the case, it is not too bold to say that the new religion could not have conquered the Empire. It was because Christianity appealed direct to the people, addressed them in their own language, and made itself comprehensible to them on their plane of thought, that it met the needs and filled the heart of the Roman world.

It is true that the Christian books and letters had to express doctrines, thought, ideas, truths, which were in a sense new. But the newness and strangeness lay in the spirit, not in the words or the metaphors or the illustrations. In the spirit lies the essence of the new thought and the new life, not in the words. This may seem to be, and in a sense it is, a mere truism. Every one says it, and has been saying it from the beginning; yet it is sometimes strangely ignored and misunderstood, and in the last few years we have had some remarkable examples of this. We have seen treatises published in which the most remarkable second-century statement of the essential doctrines and facts of Christianity, the epitaph of Avircius Marcellus,--a statement intended and declaring itself to be public, popular, before the eyes and minds of all men--has been argued to be non-Christian, because every single word, phrase and image in it is capable of a pagan interpretation, and can be paralleled from pagan books and cults. That is perfectly true; it is an interesting fact, and well worthy of being stated and proved; but it does not support the inference that is deduced. The parts, the words, are individually capable of being all treated as pagan, but the essence, the spirit, of the whole is Christian. As Aristotle says, a thing is more than the sum of its parts; the essence, the reality, the Ousia, is that which has to be added to the parts in order to make the thing.

It is therefore proposed in the present work to employ the same method as in all the writer's other investigations--to regard the Apocalypse as written in the current language familiar to the people of the time, and not as expressed in a peculiar and artificial Christian language: the term "artificial" is required, because, if the Christians used a kind of language different from that of the ordinary population, it must have been artificial.

Nor are the thoughts--one might almost say, though the expression must not be misapplied or interpreted in a way different from what is intended--nor are the thoughts of the Christian books alien from and unfamiliar to the period when they were written. They stand in the closest relation to the period. They are made for it: they suit it: they are determined by it.

We take the same view about all the books of the New Testament. They spring from the circumstances of their period, whatever it was in each case; they are suited to its needs; in a way they think its thoughts, but think them in a new form and on a higher plane; they answer the questions which men were putting, and the answers are expressed in the language which was used and understood at the time. Hence, in the first place, their respective dates can be assigned with confidence, provided we understand the history and familiarise ourselves with the thoughts and ways of the successive periods. No one, who is capable of appreciating the tone and thought of different periods, could place the composition of any of the books of the New Testament in the time of the Antonines, unless he were imperfectly informed of the character and spirit of that period; and the fact that some modern scholars have placed them (or some of them) in that period merely shows with what light-hearted haste some writers have proceeded to decide on difficult questions of literary history without the preliminary training and the acquisition of knowledge imperatively required before a fair judgment could be pronounced.

From this close relation of the Christian books to the time in which they originated, arises, e.g., the marvellously close resemblance between the language used about the birth of the divine Augustus and the language used about the birth of Christ. In the words current in the Eastern Provinces, especially in the great and highly educated and "progressive" cities of Asia, shortly before the Christian era, the day of the birth of the (Imperial) God was the beginning of all things; it inaugurated for the world the glad tidings that came through him; through him there was peace on earth and sea: the Providence, which orders every part of human life, brought Augustus into the world, and filled him with the virtue to do good to men: he was the Saviour of the race of men, and so on. Some of these expressions became, so to say, stereotyped for the Emperors in general, especially the title "Saviour of the race of men," and phrases about doing good to mankind; others were more peculiarly the property of Augustus.

All this was not merely the language of courtly panegyric. It was in a way thoroughly sincere, with all the sincerity that the people of that overdeveloped and precocious time, with their artificial, highly stimulated, rather feverish intellect, were capable of feeling. But the very resemblance--so startling, apparently, to those who are suddenly confronted with a good example of it--is the best and entirely sufficient proof that the idea and narrative of the birth of Christ could not be a growth of mythology at a later time, even during the period about A.D. 60-100, but sprang from the conditions and thoughts, and expressed itself in the words, of the period to which it professes to belong. It is to a great extent on this and similar evidence that the present writer has based his confident and unhesitating opinion as to the time of origin of the New Testament books, ever since he began to understand the spirit and language of the period. Before he began to appreciate them, he accepted the then fashionable view that they were second century works.

But so far removed are some scholars from recognising the true bearing of these facts, and the true relation of the New Testament to the life and thought of its own time, that probably the fashionable line of argument will soon be that the narrative of the Gospels was a mere imitation of the popular belief about the birth of Augustus, and necessarily took its origin during the time when that popular belief was strong, viz., during the last thirty years of his reign. The belief died with him, and would cease to influence thought within a few years after his death: he was a god only for his lifetime (though a pretence was made of worshipping all the deceased Emperors who were properly deified by decree of the Senate): even in old age it is doubtful if he continued to make the same impression on his people, but as soon as he died a new god took his place. New ideas and words then ruled among men, for the new god never was heir to the immense public belief which hailed the divine Augustus. With Tiberius began a new era, new thoughts, and new forms: he was the New Caesar, Neos Kaisar.

There are already some signs that, as people begin to learn these facts, which stand before us on the stones engraved before the birth of Christ, this line of argument is beginning to be developed. It will at least have this great advantage, that it assigns correctly the period when the Christian narrative originated, and that it cuts away the ground beneath the feet of those who have maintained that the Gospels are the culmination of a long subsequent growth of mythology about a more or less historical Jesus. The Gospels, as we have them, though composed in the second half, and for the most part in the last quarter, of the first century, are a faithful presentation in thought and word of a much older and well-attested history, and are only in very small degree affected by the thoughts and language of the period when their authors wrote, remaining true to the form as fixed by earlier registration.

Similarly, the Seven Letters are the growth of their time, and must be studied along with it. They belong to the last quarter of the first century; and it is about that time that we may look for the best evidence as to the meaning that they would bear to their original readers.

Chapter 6: The Symbolism of the Seven Letters

In attempting to get some clear idea with regard to the symbolism involved in the Seven Letters, it is not proposed to discuss the symbolism of the Apocalypse as a whole, still less the religious or theological intention of its author. The purpose of this chapter is much more modest--merely to try to determine what was the meaning which ordinary people in the cities of Asia would gather from the symbolism: especially how would they understand the Seven Stars, the Lamps and the Angels. That is a necessary preliminary, if we are to appreciate the way in which Asian readers would understand the book and the letters addressed to them.

In the Seven Letters symbolism is less obtrusive and more liable to be unnoticed than in the visions that follow; and it will best show their point of view to take first a simple example of the figures which march across the stage of the Apocalypse itself in the later chapters. Those figures are to be interpreted according to the symbols which they bear and the accompaniments of their progress before the eyes of the seer. It is the same process of interpretation as is applied in the study of Greek art: for example a horseman almost identical in type and action appears on the two coins represented in chapter 23. In one this horseman is marked by the battle-axe which he carries as the warlike hero of the military colony Thyatira. The other shows a more peaceful figure, the Emperor Caracalla visiting Thyatira.

Similarly, in 6:2 the bowman sitting on a white horse, to whom a crown was given, is the Parthian king. The bow was not a Roman weapon: it was not used in Roman armies except by a few auxiliaries levied among outlying tribes, who carried their national weapon. The Parthian weapon was the bow; the warriors were all horsemen; and they could use the bow as well when they were fleeing as when they were charging. The writers of that period often mention the Parthian terror on the East, and their devastating incursions were so much dreaded at that time that Trajan undertook a Parthian war in 115. Virgil foretells a Roman victory: the bow and the horse have been useless:--

With backward bows the Parthians shall be there,
And, spurring from the fight, confess their fear.

Colour was also an important and significant detail. The Parthian king in 6:2 rides on a white horse. White had been the sacred colour among the old Persians, for whom the Parthians stood in later times; and sacred white horses accompanied every Persian army. The commentators who try to force a Roman meaning on this figure say that the Roman general, when celebrating a Triumph, rode on a white horse. This is a mistake; the general in a Triumph wore the purple and gold-embroidered robes of Jupiter, and was borne like the god in a four-horse car. (See chapter 26.)

The use of colour here as symbolical is illustrated by the custom of Tamerlane. When he laid siege to a city, he put up white tents, indicating clemency to the enemy. If resistance was prolonged forty days, he changed the tents, and put up red ones, portending a bloody capture. If obstinate resistance was persisted in for other forty days, black tents were substituted: the city was to be sacked with a general massacre. The meaning of the colours differs; there was no universal principle of interpretation; significance depended to some extent on circumstances and individual preference.

It is not to be supposed that St. John consciously modelled his descriptions on works of art. He saw the figures march across the heavens. But such ideas and symbolic forms were in the atmosphere and in the minds of men at the time; and the ideas with which he was familiar moulded the imagery of his visions, unconsciously to himself. It is quite in the style of Greek art that one monster in 13 should rise from the sea and the other appear out of the earth (as we shall see in chapter 7); but those ideas are used with freedom. The shapes of the monsters are not of Greek art; they are modifications of traditional apocalyptic devices; but the seer saw them in situations whose meaning we interpret from the current ideas and forms of art. Hence, e.g., in the Pergamenian letter, the white stone is not to be explained as an imitation of a precisely similar white stone used in ordinary pagan life (as most recent commentators suppose); it is a free employment of a common form in a new way to suit a Christian idea. The current forms are used in the Apocalypse, not slavishly, but creatively and boldly; and they must not be interpreted pedantically. A new spirit has been put into them by the writer.

Thus to refer to the Parthian king of 6:2: the type of the archer-horseman was familiar to the thought of all in the eastern Provinces; but if we look at the most typical representations, those which occur on coins, we find the various elements separately, but not united. The regular reverse type on Parthian coins shows the founder of the race, Arsaces, deified as Apollo, sitting on the holy omphalos, and holding the bow, the symbol of authority based on military power (see Fig. 1). A rarer type, though common on coins of King Vonones (83-100 A.D.) and of Artabanus III (42-65), shows the monarch on horseback welcomed by the genius of the State: Fig. 2 gives the type of Artabanus: the king wears Oriental attire with characteristic full trousers. The coins of Vonones have a type similar, but complicated by the addition of a third figure.

In Greek and Roman art the Parthian appears, not as victor, but as vanquished. The coins of Trajan show two Parthian captives, a man and a woman, under a trophy of Roman victory. St. John describes the Parthian king as seen by Roman apprehension, followed by Bloodshed, Scarcity and Death; but that point of view was naturally alien to art, except the art practised in Parthia. The spirit of the artist, or of the seer of the visions, gives form to the pictures, and they must be interpreted by the spirit.

As to the letters, we notice that there are two pairs of ideas mentioned in 1:20, "the seven stars are the angels of the Seven Churches; and the seven lamps are Seven Churches." Of these, the second pair stand on the earth; and in the first pair, since the stars belong to heaven, the angels also must belong to heaven. There is the earthly pair, the Churches and the lamps that symbolise them; and there is the corresponding heavenly pair, the angels and the stars which symbolise them.

A similar correspondence between a higher and a lower embodiment of Divine character may frequently be observed in the current religious conceptions of that time. We find amid the religious monuments of Asia Minor certain reliefs, which seem to represent the Divine nature on two planes, expressed by the device of two zones in the artistic grouping. There is an upper zone showing the Divine nature on the higher, what may be called the heavenly plane; and there is a lower zone, in which the God is represented as appearing, under the form of his priest and representative, among the worshippers who come to him on earth, to whom he reveals the right way of approaching him and serving him, and whom he benefits in return for their service and offering duly completed. One of the best examples of this class of monuments, dated A.D. 100, and belonging to the circuit of Philadelphia, is published here for the first time after a sketch made by Mrs. Ramsay in 1884. The lower zone is a scene representing, according to a type frequent in late art, an ordinary act of public worship. At the right hand side of an altar, which stands under the sacred tree, a priest is performing on the altar the rite by means of which the worshippers are brought into communication with the god. The priest turns towards the left to face the altar, and behind him are five figures in an attitude nearly uniform (the position of the left hand alone varies slightly), who must represent the rest of the college of priests attached to the sanctuary. Their names are given in the inscription which is engraved under the relief. There was always a college of priests, often in considerable numbers, attached to the great sanctuaries or hiera of Anatolia; those priests must be distinguished from the attendants, ministers, and inferiors, of whom there were large numbers (in some cases several thousands).

The existence of such colleges gives special importance to the Bezan text of Acts 14:13 in which the priests of the shrine of Zeus "Before-the-City," at Lystra, are mentioned--whereas the accepted text mentions only a single priest. Professor Blass in his note rejects the Bezan reading on the ground that there was only one priest for each temple; but his argument is founded on purely Greek custom and is not correct for Anatolian temples, like the one at Lystra, where there was always a body or college of priests. In the relief which we are now studying the mutilation of the inscription makes the number of the priests uncertain; but either seven or eight were mentioned. At the Milyadic hieron of the same god, Zeus Sabazios, the college numbered six: at Pessinus the college attached to the hieron of the Great Mother contained at least ten.

On the left side of the altar stand seven figures looking towards the altar and the priest. These represent the crown of worshippers.

In the upper zone the central action corresponds exactly to the scene in the lower zone: the god stands on a raised platform on the right hand side of an altar, on which he performs the same act of ritual which his priest is performing straight below him on the lower plane, probably pouring out a libation over offerings which lie on the altar. In numerous reliefs and coins of Asia Minor a god or goddess is represented performing the same act over an altar. That one act stands symbolically for the whole series of ritual acts, just as in Revelation 2:13 Antipas stands for the entire body of the martyrs who had suffered in Asia. The deity has revealed to men the ritual whereby they can approach him in purity, and present their gifts and prayers with assurance that these will be favourably received: thus the god is his own first priest, and later priests were regarded by the devout as representatives of the god on earth, wearing his dress, acting for him and performing before his worshippers on earth the life and actions of the god on his loftier plane of existence. In this relief the intention is obvious: as a sign and guarantee that he accepts the sacred rite, the god is doing in heaven exactly the same act that his priest is performing on earth.

On the right of the raised platform stand three figures, with the right hand raised in adoration. These represent the college of priests, headed by the chief priest; and all must be understood to make the same gesture, though the right hands of the second and third are hidden. The action of the priests who stand in the lower zone behind the chief priest must be interpreted in the same way.

On the left of the platform another scene in the ritual and life of the god is represented. He drives forth in his car to make his annual progress through his own land to receive the homage of his people. He is marked as Zeus by the eagle which sits on the reins or the trappings of the horses, and as Sabazios by the serpent on the ground beneath their feet. Beside the horses walks his companion god, regarded as his son in the divine genealogy, and marked as Hermes by the winged caduceus which he carries, and as Men by the crescent and the pointed Phrygian cap. The divine nature regarded as male was commonly conceived in this double form as father and son; and when these Anatolian ideas were expressed under Greek forms and names, they were described sometimes as Zeus and Hermes (so in Acts 14:10, and in this relief), sometimes as Zeus and Apollo or Dionysus. When the deity in his male character was conceived as a single impersonation, he was called in Greek sometimes by one, sometimes by another of those four names. The Greek names were used in this loose varying way, because none of them exactly corresponded to the nature of the Anatolian conception; and sometimes one name, sometimes another, seemed to correspond best to the special aspect of the Anatolian god which was prominent at the moment.

The god on the car is here represented as beardless, but the god on the platform is bearded; and yet the two are presentments of the same divine power. But this relief is a work of symbolism, not a work of art: it aims not at artistic or dramatic truth, but at showing the divine nature in two of the characters under which it reveals itself to man: the object of the artist was to express a meaning, not to arrive at beauty or consistency.

The interpretation which has just been stated of this symbolical relief would be fairly certain from the analogy of other monuments of the same class; but it is placed beyond doubt by the inscription which occupies the broad lower zone of the stone: "in the year 185 (A.D. 100-101), the thirtieth of Daisios (22nd May), when Glykon was Stephanephoros, the people of Koloe consecrated Zeus Sabazios, the priests being Apollonius," etc. (probably seven others were named).

The people consecrated Zeus Sabazios either by building him a temple, or simply by erecting a statue in his honour: in either case the action was a stage in the gradual Hellenising of an Anatolian cult in outward show by making it more anthropomorphic. The original Anatolian religion was much less anthropomorphic; it had holy places rather than temples, and worshipped "the God" rather than individualised and specialised embodiments of him. Under the influence of Greek and other foreign examples, temples and statues were introduced into that simple old religion. It is impossible to get back to a stage in which it was entirely imageless and without built temples; but certainly in its earlier stages images and temples played a much smaller part than in the later period.

The symbolism of this monument is so instructive with regard to the popular religious views in Anatolia that a detailed study of it forms the best introduction to this subject. The monument is now built into the inner wall of a house at Koula, a considerable town in Eastern Lydia; but it was brought there from a place about twenty-five miles to the north. It originates therefore from a secluded part of the country, where Anatolian religious ideas were only beginning to put on an outward gloss of Hellenism, though their real character was purely Asian. Greek however was the language of the district.

It is fundamentally the same idea of a higher and a lower plane of existence that is expressed in the symbolism of the Angels and the Stars in heaven, corresponding to the Churches and the Lamps on earth. The lamp, which represents the Church, is a natural and obvious symbol. The Church is Divine: it is the kingdom of God among men: in it shines the light that illumines the darkness of the world.

The heavenly pair is more difficult to express precisely in its relation to the earthly pair. There seems to be involved here a conception, common in ancient time generally, that there are intermediate grades of existence to bridge over the vast gap between the pure Divine nature and the earthly manifestation of it. Thus the star and the angel, of whom the star is the symbol, are the intermediate stage between Christ and His Church with its lamp shining in the world. This symbolism was taken over by St. John from the traditional forms of expression in theories regarding the Divine nature and its relation to the world.

Again, we observe that, in the religious symbolic language of the first century, a star denoted the heavenly existence corresponding to a divine being or divine creation or existence located on earth. Thus, in the language of the Roman poets, the divine figure of the Emperor on earth has a star in heaven that corresponds to it and is its heavenly counterpart. So the Imperial family as a whole is also said to have its star, or to be a star. It is a step towards this kind of symbolic phraseology when Horace (Odes, i, 12) speaks of the Julian star shining like the moon amid the lesser fires; but probably Horace was hardly conscious of having advanced in this expression beyond the limits of mere poetic metaphor. But when Domitian built a Temple of the Imperial Flavian family, the poet Statius describes him as placing the stars of his family (the Flavian) in a new heaven (Silvae, v, I, 240f). There is implied here a similar conception to that which we are studying in the Revelation: the new Temple on earth corresponds to a new heaven framed to contain the new stars; the divine Emperors of the Flavian family (along with any other member of the family who had been formally deified) are the earthly existences dwelling in the new Temple, as the stars, their heavenly counterparts, move in the new heaven. The parallel is close, however widely separate the theological ideals are; and the date of Statius' poem is about the last year of Domitian's reign, A.D. 95-96.

The star, then, is obviously the heavenly object which corresponds to the lamp shining on the earth, though superior in character and purity to it; and, as the lamp on earth is to the star in heaven, so is the Church on earth to the angel. Such is the relation clearly indicated. The angel is a corresponding existence on another and higher plane, but more pure in essence, more closely associated with the Divine nature than the individual Church on earth can be.

Now, what is the angel? How shall he be defined or described? In answer to this question, then, one must attempt to describe what is meant by the angels of the Churches in these chapters, although as soon as the description is written, one recognises that it is inadequate and hardly correct. The angel of the Church seems to embody and gather together in a personification the powers, the character, the history and life and unity of the Church. The angel represents the Divine presence and the Divine power in the Church; he is the Divine guarantee of the vitality and effectiveness of the Church.

This seems clear; but the difficulty begins when we ask what is the relation of the angel to the faults and sins of his Church, and, above all, to the punishment which awaits and is denounced against those sins. The Church in Smyrna or in Ephesus suffers from the faults and weaknesses of the men who compose it: it is guilty of their crimes, and it will be punished in their person. Is the angel, too, guilty of the sins? Is he to bear the punishment for them?

Undoubtedly the angel is touched and affected by the sins of his Church. Nothing else is conceivable. He could not be the counterpart or the double of a Church, unless he was affected in some way by its failings. But the angels of the Churches are addressed, not simply as touched by their faults, but as guilty of them. Most of the angels have been guilty of serious, even deadly sins. The angel of Sardis is dead, though he has the name of being alive. The angel of Laodicea is lukewarm and spiritless, and shall be rejected. Threats, also, are directed against the angels: "I will come against thee," "I will spit thee out of my mouth," "I will come to thee" (or rather "I will come in displeasure at thee" is the more exact meaning, as Professor Moulton points out). Again, the angel is regarded as responsible for any neglect of the warning now given, "and thou shalt not know what hour I will come upon thee": "thou art the wretched one, and poor, and miserable, and blind, and naked."

These expressions seem to make it clear that the angel could be guilty, and must suffer punishment for his guilt. This is certainly surprising, and, moreover, it is altogether inconsistent with our previous conclusion that the angel is the heavenly counterpart of the Church. He who is guilty and responsible for guilt cannot stand anywhere except on the earth.

The inconsistency, however, is due to the inevitable failure of the writer fully to carry out the symbolism. It is not so difficult to follow out an allegory perfectly, so long as the writer confines himself to the realm of pure fancy; but, if he comes into the sphere of reality and fact, he soon finds that the allegory cannot be wrought out completely; it will not fit the details of life. When John addresses the angels as guilty, he is no longer thinking of them, but of the actual Churches which he knew on earth. The symbolism was complicated and artificial; and, when he began to write the actual letters, he began to feel that he was addressing the actual Churches, and the symbolism dropped from him in great degree. Nominally he addresses the Angel, but really he writes to the Church of Ephesus or of Sardis; or rather, all distinction between the Church and its angel vanishes from his mind. He comes into direct contact with real life, and thinks no longer of correctness in the use of symbols and in keeping up the elaborate and rather awkward allegory. He writes naturally, directly, unfettered by symbolical consistency.

The symbolism was imposed on the writer of the Apocalypse by the rather crude literary model, which he imitated in obedience to a prevalent Jewish fashion. He followed his model very faithfully, so much so that his work has by some been regarded as a purely Jewish original, slightly modified by additions and interpolations to a Christian character, but restorable to its original Jewish form by simple excision of a few words and paragraphs. But we regard the Jewish element in it as traditional, due to the strong hold which this established form of literature exerted on the author. That element only fettered and impeded him by its fanciful and unreal character, making his work seem far more Jewish than it really is. Sometimes, however, the traditional form proves wholly inadequate to express his thoughts; and he discards it for the moment and speaks freely.

It is therefore vain to attempt to give a rigidly accurate definition of the meaning which is attached to the term "angel" in these chapters. All that concerns the angels is vague, impalpable, elusive, defying analysis and scientific precision. You cannot tell where in the Seven Letters, taken one by one, the idea "angel" drops and the idea "Church" takes its place. You cannot feel certain what characteristics in the

Seven Letters may be regarded as applying to the angels, and what must be separated from them. But the vague description given in preceding paragraphs will be sufficient for use; and it may be made clearer by quoting Professor J. H. Moulton's description of angels: "Spiritual counterparts of human individuals or communities, dwelling in heaven, but subject to changes depending on the good or evil behaviour of their complementary beings on earth."

How far did St. John, in employing the symbolism current at the time, accept and approve it as a correct statement of truth? That question naturally arises; but the answer seems inevitable. He regards this symbolism merely as a way of making spiritual ideas intelligible to the ordinary human mind, after the fashion of the parables in the life of Christ. He was under the influence of the common and accepted ways of expressing spiritual, or philosophical, or theological truth, just as he was under the influence of fashionable forms in literature. He took these and made the best he could of them. The apocalyptic form of literature was far from being a high one; and the Apocalypse of John suffers from the unfortunate choice of this form: only occasionally is the author able to free himself from the chilling influence of that fanciful and extravagant mode of expression. The marked difference in character and power between the Apocalypse and the Gospel of St. John is in great measure due to the poor models which he followed in the former.

It is interesting that one of the most fashionable methods of expressing highly generalised truths or principles--the genealogical method--is never employed by John (except in the universally accepted phrases, "son of man," "Son of God"). The contempt expressed by Paul for the "fables and endless genealogies" of current philosophy and science seems to have been shared by most of the Christian writers; and it is true that no form of veiling ignorance by a show of words was ever invented more dangerous and more tempting than the genealogical. An example of the genealogical method may be found in Addison's 35th Spectator, an imitation of the old form, but humorous instead of pedantic.

Chapter 7: Authority of the Writer of the Seven Letters

In what relation did the writer of the Seven Letters stand to the Asian Churches which he addressed? This is an important question. The whole spirit of the early development of law and procedure and administration in the early Church is involved in the answer. That the writer shows so intimate a knowledge of those Churches that he must have lived long among them, will be proved by a detailed examination of the Seven Letters, and may for the present be assumed. But the question is whether he addressed the Churches simply as one who lived among them and knew their needs and want, who was qualified by wisdom and age and experience, and who therefore voluntarily offered advice and warning, which had its justification in its excellence and truth; or whether he wrote as one standing in something like an official and authoritative relation to them, charged with the duty of guiding, correcting and advising those Asian Churches, feeling himself directly responsible for their good conduct and welfare.

The question also arises whether he was merely a prophet according to the old conception of the prophetic mission, coming, as it were, forth from the desert or the field to deliver the message which was dictated to him by God, and on which his own personality and character and knowledge exercised no formative influence; or whether the message is full of his own nature, but his nature raised to its highest possible level through that sympathy and communion with the Divine will, which constitutes, in the truest and fullest sense, "inspiration." The first of these alternatives we state only to dismiss it as bearing its inadequacy plainly written on its face. The second alone can satisfy us; and we study the Seven Letters on the theory that they are as truly and completely indicative of the writer's character and of his personal relation to his correspondents as any letters of the humblest person can be.

Probably the most striking feature of the Seven Letters is the tone of unhesitating and unlimited authority which inspires them from beginning to end. The best way to realise this tone and all that it means is to compare them with other early Christian letters: this will show by contrast how supremely authoritative is the tone of the Seven Letters.

The letter of Clement to the Church of Corinth is not expressed as his own (though undoubtedly, and by general acknowledgment, it is his letter, expressing his sentiments regarding the Corinthians), but as the letter of the Roman Church. All assumption or appearance of personal authority is carefully avoided. The warning and advice are addressed by the Romans as authors, not to the Corinthians only, but equally to the Romans themselves. "These things we write, not merely as admonishing you, but also as reminding ourselves." The first person plural is very often used in giving advice: "let us set before ourselves the noble examples"; and so on in many other cases. Rebuke, on the other hand, is often expressed in general terms. Thus, e.g., a long panegyric on the Corinthians in sect. 2: "Ye had conflict day and night for all the brotherhood...Ye were sincere and simple and free from malice one towards another. Every sedition and every schism was abominable to you, etc.," is concluded in sect. 3 with a rebuke and admonition couched in far less direct terms: "that which is written was fulfilled; my beloved ate and drank, and was enlarged and waxed fat and kicked; hence come jealousy and envy, strife and sedition, etc." The panegyric is expressed in the second person plural, but the blame at the end is in this general impersonal form.

A good example of this way of expressing blame in perfectly general, yet quite unmistakable, terms is found in sect. 44. Here the Corinthians are blamed for having deposed certain bishops or presbyters; but the second personal form is never used. "Those who were duly appointed...these men we consider to be unjustly thrust out from their ministration. For it will be no light sin for us if we thrust out those who have offered the gifts of the bishop's office unblamably and holily." It would be impossible to express criticism of the conduct of others in more courteous and modest form, and yet it is all the more effective on that account: "if we do this, we shall incur grievous sin."

The most strongly and directly expressed censure is found in sect. 47. It is entirely in the second person plural; but here the Romans shelter themselves behind the authority of Paul, who "charged you in the Spirit...because even then ye had made parties." On this authority the direct address continues to the end of the chapter: "it is shameful, dearly beloved, yes, utterly shameful and unworthy of your conduct in Christ, that it should be reported that the very steadfast and ancient Church of the

Corinthians, for the sake of one or two persons, maketh sedition against its presbyters, etc." But the next sentence resumes the modest form: "let us therefore root this out quickly."

An example equally good is found in the letters of Ignatius; and this example is even more instructive than that of Clement, because Ignatius' letters were addressed to several of the Seven Churches not many years after the Revelation was written. Here we have letters written by the Bishop of Antioch, the mother Church of all the Asian Churches, and by him when raised through the near approach of death to a plane higher than mere humanity. He was already marked out for death--in the estimation of Christians the most honourable kind of death--as the representative of his Church; and he was on his way to the place of execution. He was eager to gain the crown of life. He had done with all thought of earth. If there was any one who could speak authoritatively to the Asian Churches, it was their Syrian mother through this chosen representative. But there is not, in any of his letters, anything approaching, even in the remotest degree, to the authoritative tone of John's letters to the Seven Churches, or of Paul's letters, or of Peter's letter to the Churches of Anatolia.

The Ephesians especially are addressed by Ignatius with profound respect. He ought to "be trained by them for the contest in faith." He hopes to "be found in the company of the Christians of Ephesus." He is "devoted to them and their representatives." He apologises for seeming to offer advice to them, who should be his teachers; but they may be schoolfellows together--a touch which recalls the tone of Clement's letter; he does not give orders to them, as though he were of some consequence. The tone throughout is that of one who feels deeply that he is honoured in associating with the Ephesian Church through its envoys.

There is not the same tone of extreme respect in Ignatius' letters to Magnesia, Tralleis, Philadelphia, and Smyrna, as in his letter to Ephesus. It is apparent that the Syrian bishop regarded Ephesus as occupying a position of loftier dignity than the other Churches of the Province; and this is an important fact in itself. It proves that already there was the beginning of a feeling, in some minds at least, that the Church of the leading city of a Province was of higher dignity than those of the other cities, a feeling which ultimately grew into the recognition of metropolitan bishoprics and exarchates, and a fully formed and graded hierarchy.

But even to those Churches of less splendid history, his tone is not that of authority. It is true that he sometimes uses the imperative; but in the more simple language of the Eastern peoples, as in modern Greek and Turkish (at least in the conversational style), the imperative mood is often used, without any idea of command, by an inferior to a superior, or by equal to equal; and in such cases it expresses no more than extreme urgency. In Magn. sect. 3 the tone is one of urgent reasoning, and Lightfoot in his commentary rightly paraphrases the imperative of the Greek by the phrase "I exhort you." In sect. 6 the imperative is represented in Lightfoot's translation by "I advise you." In sect. 10 the advice is expressed in the first person plural (a form which we found to be characteristic of Clement), "let us learn to live," "let us not be insensible to His goodness." Then follows in sect. 11 an apology for even advising his correspondents, "not because I have learned that any of you are so minded, but as one inferior to you, I would have you be on your guard betimes." When in Trall. sect. 3 he is tempted to use the language of reproof, he refrains: "I did not think myself competent for this, that being a convict I should give orders to you as though I were an Apostle."

It is needless to multiply examples. The tone of the letters is the same throughout. Ignatius has not the right, like Paul or Peter or an Apostle, to issue commands to the Asian Churches. He can only advise, and exhort, and reason--in the most urgent terms, but as an equal to equals, as man to men, or, as he modestly puts it, as inferior to superiors. He has just the same right and duty that every Christian has of interesting himself in the life of all other Christians, of advising and admonishing and entreating them to take the course which he knows to be right.

The best expression of his attitude towards his correspondents is contained in a sentence which he addresses to the Romans, in which he contrasts his relation to them with the authority that belonged to the Apostles: "I do not give orders to you, as Peter and Paul did: they were Apostles, I am a convict: they were free, but I am a slave to this very hour."

But John writes in an utterly different spirit, with the tone of absolute authority. He carries this tone to an extreme far beyond that even of the other Apostles, Paul and Peter, in writing to the Asian Churches. Paul writes as their father and teacher: authority is stamped on every sentence of his letters. Peter reviews their circumstances points out the proper line of conduct in various situations and relations, addresses them in classes--the officials and the general congregation--in a tone of authority and responsibility throughout: he writes because he feels bound to prepare them in view of coming trials.

St. John expresses the Divine voice with absolute authority of spiritual life and death in the present and the future. Such a tone cannot be, and probably hardly ever has been, certainly is not now by any scholar, regarded as the result of mere assumption and pretence. Who can imagine as a possibility of human nature that one who can think the thoughts expressed in these letters could pretend to such authority either as a fanciful dreamer deluding himself or as an actual impostor? Such suggestions would be unreal and inconceivable.

It is a psychological impossibility that these Letters to the Asian Churches could have been written except by one who felt himself, and had the right to feel himself, charged with the superintendence and oversight of all those Churches, invested with Divinely given and absolute authority over them, gifted by long knowledge and sympathy with insight unto their nature and circumstances, able to understand the line on which each was developing, and finally bringing to a focus in one moment of supreme inspiration--whose manner none but himself could understand or imagine--all the powers he possessed of knowledge, of intellect, of intensest love, of gravest responsibility of sympathy with the Divine life, of commission from his Divine Teacher.

Moreover, when we consider how sternly St. Paul denounced and resented any interference from any quarter, however influential, with the conduct of his Churches, and how carefully he explained and apologised for his own intention of visiting Rome, that he might not seem to "build on another's foundation," and again when we take into consideration the constructive capacity of the early Church and all that is implied therein, we must conclude that St. John's authority was necessarily connected with his publicly recognised position as the head of those Asian Churches, and did not arise merely from his general commission as an Apostle.

In a word, we must recognise the authoritative succession in the Asian Churches of those three writers: first and earliest him who speaks in the Pauline letters; secondly, him who wrote "to the Elect who are sojourners of the Dispersion in...Asia" and the other Provinces; lastly, the author of the Seven Letters.

Chapter 8: The Education of St. John in Patmos

Closely related to this authority claimed and exercised by the writer of the Apocalypse over the Church--so closely related that it is merely another aspect of that authority--is the claim which he makes to speak in the name of Christ. He writes in a book what he has seen and heard. The words of the letter are given him to set down. It is the Divine Head of the Church Himself, from whom all the letters and the book as a whole originate. The writer is distinguished from the Author; though the distinction is not to be regarded as carried through the book with unbroken regularity, and must not be pressed too closely. The one idea melts into the other with that elusive indefiniteness which characterises the book as a whole.

On his credentials as a legate or messenger is founded the authority which the writer exercise over the Church. Over the Church God alone has authority; and no man may demand its obedience except in so far as he is been directly commissioned by God to speak. Only the messenger of God has any right to obedience: other men can only offer advice.

Let us try to understand this attitude and this claim by first of all understanding more clearly the situation in which the writer was placed, and the circumstances in which the work originated. Only in that way can the problem be fairly approached. It may prove insoluble. In a sense it must prove insoluble. At the best we cannot hope to do more than state the conditions and the difficulties clearly in a form suited to the mind and thoughts of our own time. But a clear understanding of the difficulties involved is a step towards the solution. The solution however must be reached by every one for himself: it is a matter for the individual mind, and depends on the degree to which the individual can even in a dim vague way comprehend the mind of St. John. It involves the personal element, personal experience and personal opinion; and he who tries to express the solution is exposed to subjectivity and error. The solution is to be lived rather than spoken.

St. John had been banished to Patmos, an unimportant islet, whose condition in ancient times is little known. In the Imperial period banishment to one of the small rocky islands of the Aegean was a common and recognised penalty, corresponding in some respects (though only in a very rough way and with many serious differences) to the former English punishment of transportation. It carried with it entire loss of civil rights and almost entire loss of property; usually a small allowance was reserved to sustain the exile's life. The penalty was life-long; it ended only with death. The exile was allowed to live in free intercourse with the people of the island, and to earn money. But he could not inherit money nor bequeath his own, if he saved or earned any: all that he had passed to the State at his death. He was cut off from the outer world, though he was not treated with personal cruelty or constraint within the limits of the islet, where he was confined.

But there are serious difficulties forbidding the supposition that St. John was banished to Patmos in this way.

In the first place this punishment was reserved for persons of good standing and some wealth. Now it seems utterly impossible to admit that St. John could have belonged to that class. In Ephesus he was an obscure stranger of Jewish origin; and under the Flavian Emperors the Jews of Palestine were specially open to suspicion on account of the recent rebellion. There is no evidence, and no probability, that he possessed either the birth, or the property, or the civic rights, entitling him to be treated on this more favoured footing. He was one of the common people, whose punishment was more summary and far harsher than simple banishment to an island.

In the second place, even if he had been of sufficiently high standing for that form of punishment, it is impossible to suppose that the crime of Christianity could have been punished so leniently at that period. If it was a crime at all, it belonged to a very serious class; and milder treatment is unknown as a punishment for it. In its first stages, before it was regarded as a crime, some Christians were subjected to comparatively mild penalties, like scourging; but in such cases they were punished, not for the crime of Christianity, not for "the name," but for other offences, such as causing disorder in the streets. But St. John was in Patmos for the word of God and the testimony of Jesus, partaker with you in the tribulation and kingdom and patience which are in Jesus. His punishment took place at a time when the penalty for Christianity was already fixed as death in the severer form (i.e. fire, crucifixion, or as a public spectacle at games and festivals) for persons of humbler position and provincials, and simple execution for Roman citizens. Nor is it possible to suppose that St. John was banished at an early stage in the persecution, before the procedure was fully comprehended and strictly carried out. The tradition that connects his punishment with Domitian is too strong.

The conclusion seems inevitable: St. John was not punished with the recognised Roman penalty of banishment to an island (deportatio in insulam): the exile to Patmos must have been some kind of punishment of a more serious character.

There was such a penalty. Banishment combined with hard labour for life was one of the grave penalties. Many Christians were punished in that way. It was a penalty for humbler criminals, provincials and slaves. It was in its worst forms a terrible fate: like the death penalty it was preceded by scourging, and it was marked by perpetual fetters, scanty clothing, insufficient food, sleep on the bare ground in a dark prison, and work under the lash of military overseers. It is an unavoidable conclusion that this was St. John's punishment. Patmos is not elsewhere mentioned as one of the places where convicts of this class were sent; but we know very little about the details and places of this penalty; and the case of St. John is sufficient proof that such criminals were in some cases sent there. There were no mines in Patmos. Whether any quarries were worked there might be determined by careful exploration of the islet. Here, as everywhere in the New Testament, one is met by the difficulty of insufficient knowledge. In many cases it is impossible to speak confidently, where a little exploration by a competent traveller would probably give certainty.

Undoubtedly, there were many forms of hard labour under the Roman rule, and these varied in degree, some being worse than others. We might wish to think that in his exile St. John had a mild type of punishment to undergo, which permitted more leisure and more ease; but would any milder penalty be suitable to the language of 1:9, your brother and partaker with you in the tribulation? It is possible perhaps to explain those words as used by an exile, though subjected only to the milder penalty inflicted on persons of rank. But how much more meaning and effect they carry, when the penalties of both parties are of the same severe character. Now it is a safe rule to follow, that the language of the New Testament is rarely, if ever, to be estimated on the lower scale of effectiveness. The interpretation which gives most power and meaning is the right one. St. John wrote to the Churches in those words of 1:9, because he was suffering in the same degree as themselves.

Banished to Patmos, St. John was dead to the world; he could not learn much about what was going on in the Empire and in the Province Asia. It would be difficult for him to write his Vision in a book, and still more difficult to send it to the Churches when it was written. He could exercise no charge of his Churches. He could only think about them, and see in the heavens the process of their fate. He stood on the sand of the seashore, and saw the Beast rise from the sea and come to the land of Asia: and he saw the battle waged and the victory won. Just as the Roman supreme magistrate or general was competent to read in the sky the signs of the Divine will regarding the city or the army entrusted to his charge, so St. John could read in the heavens the intimation of the fortunes and the history of his Churches.

In passing, a remark on the text must be made here. It is unfortunate that the Revisers departed from the reading of the Authorised Version in 13:1; and attached the first words to the preceding chapter, understanding that the Dragon "stood upon the sand of the sea." Thus a meaningless and unsuitable amplification--for where is the point in saying that the Dragon waxed wroth with the Woman, and went away to war with the rest of her seed; and he stood upon the sand of the sea? the history breaks off properly with his going away to war against the saints (the conclusion of that war being related in 19:19-21), whereas it halts and comes to a feeble stop, when he is left standing on the seashore--was substituted for the bold and effective personal detail, I stood upon the sand of the shore of Patmos, and saw a Beast rise out of the sea.

St. John could see all this; and through years of exile, with rare opportunities of hearing what happened to his Churches, he could remain calm, free from apprehension, confident in their steadfastness on the whole and their inevitable victory over the enemy. In that lonely time the thoughts and habits of his youth came back to him, while his recently acquired Hellenist habits were weakened in the want of the nourishment supplied by constant intercourse with Hellenes and Hellenists. His Hellenic development ceased for the time. The head of the Hellenic Churches of Asia was transformed into the Hebrew seer. Nothing but the Oriental power of separating oneself from the world and immersing oneself in the Divine could stand the strain of that long vigil on the shore of Patmos. Nothing but a Vision was possible for him; and the Vision, full of Hebraic imagery and the traces of late Hebrew literature which all can see, yet also often penetrated with a Hellenist and Hellenic spirit so subtle and delicate that few can appreciate it, was slowly written down, and took form as the Revelation of St. John.

Most men succumb to such surroundings, and either die or lose all human nature and sink to the level of the beasts. A few can live through it, sustained by the hope of escape and return to the world. But St. John rose above that life of toil and hopeless misery, because he lived in the Divine nature and

35

had lost all thought of the facts of earth. In that living death he found his true life, like many another martyr of Christ. Who shall tell how far a man may rise above earth, when he can rise superior to an environment like that? Who will set bounds to the growth of the human soul, when it is separated from all worldly relations and trammels, feeding on its own thoughts and the Divine nature, and yet is filled not with anxiety about its poor self, but with care, love and sympathy for those who have been constituted its charge?

When he was thus separated from communication with his Churches, St. John was already dead in some sense to the world. The Apocalypse was to be, as it were, his last testament, transmitted to the Asian Churches from his seclusion when opportunity served, like a voice coming to them from the other world.

Those who can with sure and easy hand mark out the limits beyond which the soul of man can never go, will be able to determine to their own satisfaction how far St. John was mistaken, when he thought he heard the Divine voice and listened to a message transmitted through him to the Churches and to the Church as a whole. But those who have not gauged so accurately and narrowly the range of the human soul will not attempt the task. They will recognise that there is in these letters a tone and a power above the mere human level, and will confess that the ordinary man is unable to keep pace with the movement of this writer. It is admitted that the letters reveal to us the character and the experiences of the writer, and that they spring out of his own nature. But what was his nature? How far can man rise above the human level? How far can man understand the will and judgment of God? We lesser men who have not the omniscient confidence of the critical pedant, do not presume to fix the limits beyond which St. John could not go.

But we know that from the Apocalypse we have this gain, at least. Through the study of it we are able in a vague and dim way to understand how that long drawn-out living death in Patmos was the necessary training through which he must pass who should write the Fourth Gospel. In no other way could man rise to that superhuman level, on which the Fourth Gospel is pitched, and be able to gaze with steady unwavering eyes on the eternal and the Divine and to remain so unconscious of the ephemeral world. And they who strive really to understand the education of Patmos will be able to understand the strangest and most apparently incredible fact about the New Testament, how the John who is set before us in the Synoptic Gospels could ever write the Fourth Gospel.

The Revelation, which was composed in the circumstances above described, must have been slow in taking form. It was not the vision of a day; it embodied the contemplation and the insight of years. But its point of view is the moment when the Apostle was snatched from the world and sent into banishment. After that he knew nothing; his living entombment began then; and if the Revelation is quoted as an historical authority about the Province, its evidence applies only to the period which he knew.

At last there came the assassination of the tyrant, the annulling of all his acts, and the strong reaction against his whole policy. The Christians profited by this. The persecution, though not first instituted by him, was closely connected with his name and his ideas, and was discredited and made unpopular by the association. For a time it was in abeyance.

In particular, the exile pronounced against St. John was apparently an act of the Emperor, and ceased to be valid when his acts were declared invalid. The Apostle was now free to return to Asia. He may have brought the Apocalypse with him. More probably an opportunity had been found of sending it already. But it reached the Churches, and began to be effective among them, in the latter part of Domitian's reign; and hence Irenaeus says it was written at that time. But while his account is to be regarded as literally true, yet the composition was long and slow, and the point of view is placed at the beginning of the exile.

There grew up later the belief that his exile had only been short; and that he was banished about two years before the end of Domitian's reign. But this seems to rest on no early or good evidence: all that can be reckoned as reasonably certain (so far as certainty can be predicated of a time so remote and so obscure) is that St. John was banished to Patmos and returned at the death of Domitian.

Antoninus Pius (138-161), indeed, laid down the rule that criminals might be released from this penalty after ten years on account of ill-health or old age, if relatives took charge of them. But this amelioration cannot be supposed to have been allowed in the Flavian time for an obscure Christian. No other end for the punishment of St. John seems possible except the fall of Domitian; and in that case he must have been exiled by Domitian, for if he had been condemned by another Emperor, his fate would not have been affected by the annulment of Domitian's acts.

There arose also in that later time a misconception as to the character of the Flavian persecution. It was regarded as an act of Domitian alone, and was supposed to be, like all the other persecutions except the last, a brief but intense outburst of cruelty: this misconception took form before the last persecution, and was determined by the analogy of all the others.

But the Flavian persecution was not a temporary flaming forth of cruelty: it was a steady, uniform application of a deliberately chosen and unvarying policy, a policy arrived at after careful consideration, and settled for the permanent future conduct of the entire administration. It was to be independent of circumstances and the inclination of individuals. The Christians were to be annihilated, as the Druids had been; and both those instances of intolerance were due to the same cause, not religious but political, viz., the belief that each of them endangered the unity of the Empire and the safety of the Imperial rule. Domitian was not a mere capricious tyrant. He was an able, but gloomy and suspicious, ruler. He applied with ruthless logic the principle which had apparently been laid down by his father Vespasian, and which was confirmed a few years later by Trajan. But the more genial character of Vespasian interfered in practice with the thorough execution of the principle which he had laid down; and the clear insight of Trajan recognised that in carrying it out methods were required which would be inconsistent with the humaner spirit of his age, and he forbade those excesses, while he approved the principle. But the intellect of Domitian perceived that the proscription of the Christians was simply the application of the essential principles of Roman Imperialism, and no geniality or humanity prevented him from putting it logically and thoroughly into execution. His ability, his power to grasp general principles, and his narrow intensity of nature in putting his principles into action, may be gathered from his portrait, Fig. 5, taken from one of his coins.

Chapter 9: The Flavian Persecution in the Province of Asia as Depicted in the Apocalypse

The shadow of the Roman Empire broods over the whole of the Apocalypse. Not merely are the Empire and the Emperors and the Imperial city introduced explicitly and by more or less clear descriptions among the figures that bulk most largely in the Visions: an even more important, though less apparent, feature of the book is that many incidental expressions would be taken by the Asian readers as referring to the Empire. Their minds were filled with the greatness, the majesty, the all-powerful and irresistible character of the Roman rule; and, with this thought in their minds, they inevitably interpreted every allusion to worldly dignity and might as referring to Rome, unless it were at the outset indicated by some marked feature as not Roman. One such exception is the Horseman of 6:1, who rides forth accompanied by Bloodshed, Scarcity and Death: he is marked by the bow that he carries as the Parthian terror (chapter 6, Figs. 1, 3), which always loomed on the eastern horizon as a possible source of invasion with its concomitant trials.

Those incidental allusions can be brought out only by a detailed study and scrutiny of the Apocalypse, sentence by sentence. But it will facilitate the understanding of the Seven Letters to notice here briefly the chief figures under which the power of Rome appears in the Apocalypse. Some of these are quite correctly explained by most modern commentators; but one at least is still rather obscure. Almost every interpreter rightly explains the Dragon of 12:3ff, the Beast of 13:1ff, and the Woman of 17:3ff; but the monster in 13:18ff is not quite properly explained, and this is the one that most intimately concerns the purpose of the present work.

The Dragon of 12:1, the supreme power of evil, acts through the force of the Empire, when he waited to devour the child of the Woman and persecuted the Woman and proceeded to make war on the rest of her seed; and his heads and his horns are the Imperial instruments by whom he carries on war and persecution. The Beast of 13:1, with his ten diademed horns and the blasphemous names on his seven heads, is the Imperial government with its diademed Emperors and its temples dedicated to human beings blasphemously styled by Divine names.

The Woman of 17:1, sitting on a scarlet-coloured beast with seven heads and ten horns and names of blasphemy, decked in splendour and lapped in luxury and drunk with the blood of the saints and the blood of the martyrs, is the Imperial city, which attracted to her allurements and her pomp the kings of the nations, the rich and distinguished men from all parts of the civilised world. The term "kings" was commonly used in the social speech of that period to indicate the wealthy and luxurious. The kings of the client-states in Asia Minor and Syria, also, visited Rome from time to time. Epiphanes of Cilicia Tracheia was there in A.D. 69, and took part in the Civil War on the side of Otho.

To Rome go the saints and the martyrs to be tormented, that the woman and her guests may be amused on festivals and State occasions. She sits upon the Imperial monster, the beast with its heads and its horns and its blasphemous names and its purple or scarlet hue (for the ancient names of colours pass into one another with little distinction), because Rome had been raised higher than ever before by the Imperial government. Yet the same Beast and the ten horns, by which she is exalted so high, shall hate her, and shall make her desolate and naked, and shall eat her flesh, and shall burn her utterly with fire: for the Emperors were no true friends to Rome, they feared it, and therefore hated it, curtailed its liberties, deprived it of all its power, murdered its citizens and all its leading men, wished (like Caligula) that the whole Roman People had one single neck, and (like Nero) burned the city to the ground.

In a more veiled, and yet a clearly marked way the Province Asia appears as a figure in the Vision. It must be understood, however, what "the Province" was in the Roman system and the popular conception. The Province was not a tract of land subjected to Rome: as a definite tract of the earth "Asia" originally had no existence except in the sense of the whole vast continent, which is still known under that name. A "Province" to the Roman mind meant literally "a sphere of duty," and was an administrative, not a geographical, fact: the Province of a magistrate might be the stating of law in Rome, or the superintendence of a great road, or the administration of a region or district of the world; but it was not and could not be (except in a loose and derivative way) a tract of country. From the Asian point of view the Province was the aspect in which Rome manifested itself to the people of Asia. Conversely, the Province was the form under which the people of Asia constituted a part of the Empire.

Rome appeared to the Asians in a double aspect, and so the Province had a double character, i.e. two horns.

In the first place the Province of Asia was the entire circle of administrative duties connected with that division of the Empire, which stood before the minds of the people of Asia (and among them of the writer of the Apocalypse) as the whole body of officials, who conducted the administration, especially the Senate in Rome acting through its chosen agent on the spot, the individual Senator whom the rest of the Senate delegated to represent it and to administer its power in Asia for the period of a year, residing in official state as Proconsul in the capital or making his official progress through the principal cities.

In the second place the Province was the whole circle of religious duties and rites, which constituted the ideal bond of unity holding the people of Asia together as a part of the Imperial realm; and this ritual was expressed to the Asian mind by the representative priests, constituting the Commune (or, as it might almost be called, the Parliament) of Asia: the one representative body that spoke for the "Nation," i.e. the Province, Asia.

Again, the Province meant the status which a certain body of persons and cities occupied in the Roman Empire. They possessed certain privileges in the Empire, in virtue of being provincials, and their rights and duties were determined by "the Law of the Province," which was drawn up to regulate the admission of the Province in the Empire. Thus, e.g., a Phrygian occupied a place in the Empire, not as a Phrygian, but as an Asian or a Galatian (according as he belonged to the Asian or the Galatian part of Phrygia). A Phrygian was a member of a foreign conquered race. An Asian or a Galatian was a unit in the Empire, with less privileges indeed than a Roman Citizen, but still honoured with certain rights and duties. These rights and duties were partly civil and partly religious: as an Asian, he must both act and feel as part of the Empire--he must do certain duties and feel certain emotions of loyalty and patriotism--loyalty and patriotism were expressed through the Provincial religion, i.e. the State cult of the majesty of Rome and of the Emperor, regulated by the Commune.

The Province of Asia in its double aspect of civil and religious administration, the Proconsul and the Commune, is symbolised by the monster described 13:11ff. This monster had two horns corresponding to this double aspect; and it was like unto a lamb, for Asia was a peaceful country, where no army was needed. Yet it spake as a dragon, for the power of Rome expressed itself quite as sternly and haughtily, when it was unsupported by troops, as it did when it spoke through the mouth of a general at the head of an army.

The monster exerciseth all the authority of the first Beast in his sight; for the provincial administration exercised the full authority of the Roman Empire, delegated to the Proconsul for his year of office.

It maketh the earth and all that dwell therein to worship the first Beast, for the provincial administration organised the State religion of the Emperors. The Imperial regulation that all loyal subjects must conform to the State religion and take part in the Imperial ritual, was carried out according to the regulations framed by the Commune, which arranged the ritual, superintended and directed its performance, ordered the building of temples, and the erection of statues, fixed the holidays and festivals, and so on--saying to them that dwell on the earth that they should make an image to the Beast.

At this point occurs a remarkable series of statements, constituting the one contemporary account of the Flavian persecution of the Christians in Asia. They are to the effect that the Commune attempted to prove the truth and power of the Imperial religion by means of miracles and wonders: the monster "doeth great signs, that he should even make fire to come down out of heaven upon the earth in the sight of men; and he deceiveth them that dwell on the earth by reason of the signs which it was given him to do in the sight of the Beast; saying to them that dwell on the earth that they should make an image to the Beast. And it was given him to give breath to the statue of the Beast, that the statue of the Beast should both speak and cause that as many as should not worship the statue of the Beast should be killed." The last statement is familiar to us; it is not directly attested for the Flavian period by pagan authorities, but it is proved by numerous Christian authorities, and corroborated by known historical facts, and by the interpretation which Trajan stated about twenty-five years later of the principles of Imperial procedure in this department. It is simply that straightforward enunciation of the rule as to the kind of trial that should be given to those who were accused of Christianity. The accused were required to prove their loyalty by performing an act of religious worship of the statue of the Emperor, which (as Pliny mentioned to Trajan) was brought into court in readiness for the test: if they performed the ritual, they were acquitted and dismissed: if they refused to perform it, they were condemned to death. No other proof was sought; no investigation was made; no accusation of any specific crime or misdeed was made, as had been the case in the persecution of Nero, which is described by Tacitus. That short and simple procedure was legal, prescribed by Imperial instructions, and complete.

No scholar now doubts that the account given in these words of the Apocalypse represents quite accurately the procedure in the Flavian persecution. Criticism for a time attempted to discredit the unanimous Christian testimony, because it was unsupported by direct pagan testimony; and signally failed. The attempt is abandoned now.

Quite correct also is the statement that "the Province" ordered the inhabitants of Asia to make a statue in honour of the Beast. The Commune ordered the construction of statues of the Imperial gods, and especially the statue of the Divine Augustus in the temple at Pergamum.

But the other statements in this remarkable passage are entirely uncorroborated: not even indirect evidence supports them. It is nowhere said or hinted, except in this passage, that the State cultus in Asia, the most civilised and educated part of the Empire, recommended itself by tricks and pseudo-miracles, such as bringing down fire from heaven or making the Imperial image speak. With regard to these statements we are reduced to mere general presumptions and estimate of probabilities.

Are we then to discredit them as inventions, or as mere repetitions of traditional apocalyptic ideas and images, not really applicable to this case? By no means. This is the one contemporary account that has been preserved of the Flavian procedure: the one solitary account of the methods practised then by the Commune in recommending and establishing the State religion. It is thoroughly uncritical to accept from it two details, which are known from other sources to be true, and to dismiss the rest as untrue, because they are neither corroborated nor contradicted by other authorities. This account stands alone: there is no other authority: it is corroborated indirectly in the main facts. The accessory details, therefore, are probably true: they are not entirely unlikely, though it is rather a shock to us to find that such conduct is attributed to the Commune in that highly civilised age--highly civilised in many respects, but in some both decadent and barbarous.

It must, also, be remembered that the people of the Province Asia were not all equally educated and civilised: many of them had no Greek education, but were sunk in ignorance and the grossest Oriental superstition. There is no good reason apparent why this contemporary account should be disbelieved; and we must accept it.

The attempt was made under the authority of the Commune, by one or more of its delegates in charge of the various temples and the ritual practised at them, to impress the populace with the might of the Imperial divinity by showing signs and miracles, by causing fire to burst forth without apparent cause, and declaring that it came down from heaven, and by causing speech to seem to issue from the statue in the temple. The writer accepts those signs as having really occurred: the monster was permitted by God to perform those marvels, and to delude men for a time. None of the details which this contemporary account mentions is incredible or even improbable. A Roman Proconsul in Cyprus had a Magian as his friend and teacher in science: the Magian probably showed him the sign of spontaneous fire bursting forth at his orders. In a Roman Colony at Philippi a ventriloquist, a slave girl, earned large sums for her owners by fortune-telling (Acts 16:16). Why should we refuse to believe that ventriloquism was employed in an Asian temple at this time of excited feeling among both persecutors and persecuted?

It is not necessary to suppose that the Commune of Asia encouraged and practised everywhere such methods. It would be sufficient justification for the statements in this passage, if the methods were practised by any of its official representatives in any of the Asian temples of the Imperial religion, without condemnation from the Commune. There is no reason to think that the shrine of the Sibyl at Thyatira was alien to such impostures, or that the people in Ephesus, who were impressed by the magical powers of the sons of Sceva (Acts 19:13f) and duped by other fraudulent exhibitors, were unlikely to be taken in by such arts, when practised with official sanction.

That these marvels and signs were connected more particularly with one individual, and not so much with the Commune as a body, is suggested by the only other reference to them, vis. 19:20, when the Beast and the kings of the earth and their armies gathered together to make ar against Him that sat upon the horse and against His army; and the Beast was taken, and with him the false prophet that wrought the signs in his sight, wherewith he deceived them that had received the mark of the Beast and them that worshipped his image. We must understand that these words refer to some definite person, who exercised great influence in some part of Asia and was the leading spirit in performing the marvels and signs. He is as real as the prophetess of Thyatira, 2:20. He had been prominent in deceiving the people for the benefit of the Imperial government, and is associated with its approaching destruction. This association in ruin would be all the more telling, if the prophet had visited Rome and been received by some of the Flavian Emperors.

A personage like Apollonius of Tyana would suit well the allusions in the Apocalypse. He lived and exercised great influence in Asia, especially at Ephesus, where after his death he enjoyed a special cult as "the averter of evil" (Alexikakos), because he had taught the city how to free itself from a pestilence by detecting the human being under whose form the disease was stalking about in their midst, and putting to death the wretched old man on whom (like an African wizard smelling out the criminal) he fixed the guilt.

Apollonius enjoyed widely the reputation of a magician. He had been well received in Rome, and was the friend of Vespasian, Titus and Nerva. His biographer Philostratus defends him from the charge of magic, but represents him as a worker of signs and wonders; and it must be remembered that St. John does not regard the prophet as an impostor, but as one to whom it was given to perform marvels. Philostratus, it is true, does not represent him as an upholder of the Imperial cultus, and rather emphasises his opposition to Domitian; but the aim of the biographer is not to give an exact history of Apollonius as he was, but to place an ideal picture before the eyes of the world. There is every reason to think that a man like Apollonius would use all his influence in favour of Vespasian and Titus, and no reason to think that he would discountenance or be unwilling to promote the Imperial cultus. While he was opposed to Domitian, it does not appear that the mutual dislike had come to a head early in the reign of that Emperor, when according to our view the Apocalypse was written, though Philostratus represents Apollonius as for seeing everything and knowing intuitively the character of every man.

It seems, then, quite possible that Apollonius may actually be meant by this prophet associated with the Beast; but, even if that be not correct, yet it is certain that there were other magicians and workers of wonders in the Asian cities; and it is in no way improbable that one of them may have been employed as an agent, even as a high-priest, of the Imperial religion. The over-stimulated, cultured yet morbid society of the great cities of Asia Minor furnished a fertile soil for the development of such soothsayers, fortune-tellers and dealers in magic: Lucian's account of Alexander of Abonoteichos in Paphlagonia may be taken as a good example in the second century. The existence of many such impostors in the Province Asia during the first century is attested, not merely by the passages already quoted from the Acts, but also by an incident recorded by Philostratus in the biography of Apollonius. The Asian cities by the Hellespont, dreading the recurrence of earthquakes, contributed ten talents to certain Egyptians and Chaldeans for a great sacrifice to avert the danger. Apollonius encountered and drove away the impostors--the circumstances of the contest are not recorded--discovered the reason why Earth and Sea were angry, offered the proper expiatory sacrifices, averted the danger at a small expense, and the earth stood fast.

The monster, who stands for the Province, is described s coming up out of the earth. He is contrasted with the Beast which came up out of the sea. They are thus described as native and as foreign: the one belongs to the same land as the readers of the Apocalypse, the other comes from across the sea, and seems to rise out of the sea as it comes. This form of expression was usual, both in language and in art. Foreign products and manufactures were described as "of the sea": we use "sea-borne" in the same sense: the goddess who came in with the Phoenicians, as patroness and protectress of the Sidonian ships, was represented as "rising from the sea." Beings native to the country, or closely connected with the earth, were represented in art as reclining on the ground (e.g., river- or mountain-gods, as chapter 19), or emerging with only half their figure out of the ground (as the goddess of the earth).

Thus the Beast was marked clearly to the readers having a home beyond the sea, while the monster was closely connected with their own soil, and had its home in their own country.

The monster causeth all, the small and the great, and the rich and the poor, and the free and the bond, that there be given them a mark on their right hand or upon their forehead; and that no man should be able to buy or to sell, save he that hath the mark, the name of the Beast or the number of his name.

This refers to some unknown, but (as will be shown) not in itself improbable attempt, either through official regulation or informal "boycott," to injure the Asian Christians by preventing dealings with traders and shopkeepers who had not proved their loyalty to the Emperor. That such an attempt may have been made in the Flavian persecution seems quite possible. It is not described here as an Imperial, but only as a provincial regulation; now it is absolutely irreconcilable with the principles of Roman administration that the Proconsul should have issued any order of the kind except with Imperial authorisation; therefore we must regard this as a recommendation originating from the Commune of Asia. The Commune would have no authority to issue a command or law; but it might signalise its devotion to the Emperor by recommending that the disloyal should be discountenanced by the loyal, and that all loyal subjects should try to restrict their custom to those who were of proved loyalty. Such a recommendation might be made by a devoted and courtly body like the Commune; and it was legal to do this, because all who refused to engage in the public worship of the Emperors were proscribed by Imperial act as traitors and outlaws, possessing no rights.

Only some enactment of this kind seems adequate to explain this remarkable statement of 13:16f. In a very interesting section of his Biblical Studies, p. 241f, Dr. Deissmann describes the official stamp impressed on legal deeds recording and registering the sale of property; and maintains that this whole passage takes its origin from the custom of marking with the Imperial stamp all records of sale. This seems an inadequate explanation. The mark of the Beast was a preliminary condition, and none who wanted it were admitted to business transactions. But the official stamp was merely the concomitant guarantee of legality; it was devoid of religious character; and there was no reason why it should not be used by Christians as freely as by pagans.

That the mark of the Beast must be impressed in the right hand or the forehead is a detail which remains obscure: we know too little to explain it with certainty. If it had been called simply the mark on the forehead, it might be regarded as the public proof of loyalty by performance of the ritual: this overt, public proof might be symbolically called "a mark on the forehead." But the mention of an alternative place for the mark shows that a wider explanation is needed. The proof of loyalty might be made in two ways; both were patent and public; they are symbolically described as the mark on the right hand or on the forehead; without one or the other no one was to be dealt with by the loyal provincials.

That something like a "boycott" might be attempted in the fervour of loyal hatred for the disloyal Christians seems not impossible. That "strikes" occurred in the Asian cities seems established by an inscription of Magnesia; and where "strikes" occur, an attempted "boycott" seems also possible. But the character attributed to this mark of the Beast extends far beyond the operation of a mere restriction on trading transactions. It must be remembered that the age was the extremest and worst period of "delation," i.e. of prosecution by volunteer accusers on charges of treason. The most trifling or the most serious actions were alike liable to be twisted into acts of personal disrespect to the Emperor, and thus to expose the doer of them to the extremest penalty of the law; a falsehood told, a theft committed, a wrong word spoken, in the presence of any image or representation of the Emperor, might be construed as disrespect to his sacred majesty: even his bust on a coin constituted the locality an abode of the Imperial god, and made it necessary for those who were there to behave as in the Divine presence. Domitian carried the theory of Imperial Divinity and the encouragement of "delation" to the most extravagant point; and thereby caused a strong reaction in the subsequent Imperial policy. Precisely in that time of extravagance occurs this extravagant exaggeration of the Imperial theory: that in one way or another every Asian must stamp himself overtly and visibly as loyal, or be forthwith disqualified from participation in ordinary social life and trading. How much of grim sarcasm, how much of literal truth, how much of exaggeration, there lies in those words,--that no man should be able to buy or sell, save he that hath the mark of the Beast on his right hand or upon his forehead,--it is impossible for us now to decide. It is probably safe to say that there lies in them a good deal of sarcasm, combined with so much resemblance to the real facts as should ensure the immediate comprehension of the readers. But that there is an ideal truth in them, that thy give a picture of the state of anxiety and apprehension, of fussy and over-zealous profession of loyalty which the policy of Domitian was producing in the Roman world, is certain.

This is the description given by St. John of the Flavian persecution. It shows that persecution to have been an organised attempt to combine many influences so as to exterminate the Christians, and not a mere sporadic though stern repression such as occurred repeatedly during the second century. But it is already certain that the Flavian persecution was of that character. Trajan, while admitting the same principle of State, that the Christians must be regarded as outlaws and treated like brigands, deprived persecution of its worst characteristics by forbidding the active search after Christians and requiring a formal accusation by a definite accuser. Under the Flavian Emperors we see an extremely cruel and bitter public movement against the Christians, an attempt to enlist religious feeling on the side of the Empire, and a zealous participation of the Asian provincial bodies, beginning from the Commune, in the persecution as a proof of their loyalty.

A recent writer on this subject expresses doubt as to "the degree to which the worship of the Emperor had become the normal test applied to one accused of being a Christian." How any doubt can remain in face of this passage, even were it alone, it is hard to see. It is difficult to devise a more effective and conclusive declaration that the religion of Christ and the religion of the Emperor were now explicitly and professedly ranged against one another, and that the alternative presented to every individual Christian was to "worship the image of the Beast" or death.

It furnishes no argument against this view of the character of the Flavian persecution that, during the persecutions of the second century, no attempt seems to have been made actively to stimulate religious feeling among the populace as an ally against the new religion. The attempt was made in the last great persecution, during the times of Diocletian and his successors. Then again the Imperial government attempted to seek out and exterminate the Christians. It "took advantage of and probably stimulated a philosophical religious revival, characterised by strong anti-Christian feeling; and employed for its own ends the power of a fervid emotion acting on men who were often of high and strongly religious motives. Christianity had to deal with a reinvigorated and desperate religion, educated and spiritualised in the conflict with the Christians. The Acta of St. Theodotus of Ancyra furnishes an instance of the way in which the devoted fanaticism of such men made them convenient tools for carrying out the purposes of the government; the approach of the new governor of Galatia and the announcement of his intentions struck terror into the hearts of the Christians; his name was Theotecnus, the child of God,' a by-name assumed by a philosophic pagan reactionary in competition with the confidence of the Christians in their Divine mission and the religious names which their converts assumed at baptism." This description gives some idea of the state of things in the Province Asia which prompted the words of St. John. We need not doubt that Theotecnus and others like him also made use of signs and marvels for their purposes. Theotecnus seems to have been the author of the Acts of Pilate, an attack on the Christian belief. A remarkable inscription found near Acmonia in Phrygia is the epitaph

W. M. Ramsay

of one of those pagan philosophic zealots, not an official of the Empire, but a leading citizen and priest in the Province. He is described in his epitaph as having received the gift of prophecy from the gods. His very name Athanatos Epitynchanos, son of Pius, Immortal Fortunate, son of Religious, quite in the style of the Pilgrim's Progress, marks his character and part in the drama of the time. His pretensions to prophetic gift were supported, we may be sure, by signs and marvels.

Less is known about the second last persecution, 249-51 A.D., in which Decius attempted in a similar way to seek out and exterminate the Christians. But another inscription of Acmonia is the epitaph of a relative, perhaps the grandfather or uncle of Athanatos Epitynchanos. His name was Telesphoros, Consummator, and he was hierophant of a religious association in Acmonia; and his wife and his sons Epitynchanos and Epinikos (Victorious) made his grave in company with the whole association. This document is a proof that a similar religious pagan revival accompanied the persecution of Decius in Acmonia; and Acmonia may be taken as a fair example of the provincial spirit in the persecutions. It is evident that, in those great persecutions, a strong public feeling against the Christians stimulated the Emperors to action, and that the Emperors, in turn, tried to urge on the religious feeling of the public into fanaticism, as an aid in the extermination of the sectaries.

In the two last persecutions official certificates of loyalty were issued to those who had complied with the law and taken part in the ritual of the Imperial religion. These certificates form an apt parallel to the "mark of the Beast," and prove that that phrase refers to some real feature of the Flavian persecution in Asia.

Those three persecutions stand apart from all the rest in a class by themselves. The intermediate Emperors shrank from thoroughly and logically putting in practice the principle which they all recognised in theory--that a Christian was necessarily disloyal and outlawed in virtue of the name and confession. All three are characterised by the same features and methods, which stand clearly revealed in the Apocalypse for the first of them and in many documents for the last.

The analogy of the official certificates in the time of Diocletian suggests that in the Flavian period the mark of the Beast on the right hand may have been a similar official certificate of loyalty. A provincial who was exposed to suspicion must carry in his hand such a certificate, while one who was notoriously and conspicuously loyal might be said to carry the mark on his forehead. In the figurative or symbolic language of the Apocalypse hardly anything is called by its ordinary and direct name, but things are indirectly alluded to under some other name, and words have to be understood as implying something else than their ordinary connotation; and therefore it seems a fair inference that the mark on the forehead is the apocalyptic description of a universal reputation for conspicuous devotion to the cult of the Emperor.

The shadow of the Imperial religion lies deep over the whole book. But the remarkable feature of the book--the feature which gave it its place in the New Testament in spite of some undeniable defects, which for a time made its place uncertain, and which still constitute a serious difficulty in reading it as an authoritative expression of the Christian spirit--is that the writer is never for a moment affected by the shadow. He was himself a sufferer, not to death, but to what he would feel as a worse fate: he was debarred from helping and advising his Churches in the hour of trial. But there is no shadow of sorrow or discouragement or anxiety as to the issue. The Apocalypse is a vision of victory. The great Empire is already vanquished. It has done its worst; and it has already failed. Not all the Christians have been victors; but those who have deserted their ranks and dropped out of the fight have done so from inner incapacity, and not because the persecuting Emperor is stronger than they. Every battle fought to the end is a defeat for the Empire and a Christian victory. Every effort that the Emperor makes is only another opportunity for failing more completely. The victory is not to gain: it already is. The Church is the only reality in its city: the rest of the city is mere pretence and sham. The Church is the city, heir to all its history and its glories, heir too to its weaknesses and its difficulties and sometimes succumbing to them.

The most dangerous kind of error that can be made about the Apocalypse is to regard it as a literal statement and prediction of events. Thus, for example 18:1-19:21 is not to be taken as a prophecy of the manner in which, or the time at which, the downfall of the great Empire and of the great City was to be accomplished; it is not to be understood as foreshadowing the Papacy, according to the foolish imaginings, "philosophy and vain deceit" as St. Paul would have called them (Col 2:8) of one modern school; it is not to be tortured by extremists on any side into conformity with their pet hatreds. Those are all idle fancies, which do harm to no one except those who waste their intellect on them. But it becomes a serious evil when the magnificent confidence and certainty of St. John as to the speedy accomplishment of all these things is distorted into a declaration of the immediate Coming of the Lord and the end of the world. Time was not an element in his anticipation. He was gazing on the eternal, in which time has no existence. Had any Asian reader asked him at what time these things should be accomplished, he would assuredly have answered in the spirit of Browning's Grammarian:--

What's time? Leave "now" to dogs and apes;
Man has forever.

43

Moreover, it is declared in the plainest language which the Apocalypse admits that the series of the Emperors is to continue yet for a season. The Beast himself is the eighth king (i.e. Emperor, according to the strict technical usage of the Greek word): he is the incarnation and climax of the whole seven that precede: he is Domitian himself as the visible present embodiment of the Imperial system. But the beast has also ten horns: these are ten Emperors, which have not been invested with Imperial power as yet; but they receive authority as Emperors with the Beast (i.e. as units in the Imperial system) for one hour: these shall war against the Lamb, and the Lamb shall overcome them: 17:12, 14.

The number ten is here to be interpreted as in 2:10, where the Church of Smyrna is to be exposed to persecution for ten days. It merely denotes a finite number as contrasted with infinity: the series of Emperors is limited and comes to an end in due season. Rome shall perish. In one sense Rome is perishing now in every failure that it makes, in the victory of every martyr. The Beast was and is not. In another sense the end is not yet. But there is an end. The power of every Emperor is for one hour: he shall live his little span of pomp and pride, of power and failure, and he shall go down to the abyss, like his predecessors.

Chapter 10: The Province of Asia and the Imperial Religion

The Roman Province of Asia included most of the western half of Asia Minor, with the countries or regions of Caria, Lydia, Phrygia, Mysia, and the coast-lands of the Troad, Aeolis and Ionia. It was the earliest Roman possession on the continent of Asia. Conquered by the Romans in the war against Antiochus the Great, it was given by them to their ally Eumenes, King of Pergamum, at the peace which was concluded in 189 B.C.; and in 133 B.C. it was bequeathed by his nephew and adopted son Attalus III to the great conquering people. The real existence of this will, formerly suspected to be a mere invention of the Romans, is now established by definite testimony. The King knew that the illegitimate Aristonicus would claim the Kingdom, and that there was no way of barring him out except through the strength of Rome.

Thus Asia had been a Roman Province for more than two hundred years when the Seven Letters were written. Its history under Roman rule had been chequered. It was the wealthiest region of the whole Roman Empire, and was therefore peculiarly tempting to the greed of the average Roman official. Amid the misgovernment and rapacity that attended the last years of the Republic, Asia suffered terribly. The Asiatics possessed money; and the ordinary Roman, whose characteristic faults were greed and cruelty, shrank from no crime in order to enrich himself quickly during his short tenure of office in the richest region of the world. Hence the Province welcomed with the enthusiasm of people brought back from death to life the advent of the Empire, which inaugurated an era of comparative peace, order, and respect for property. In no part of the world, probably, was there such fervent and sincere loyalty to the Emperors as in Asia. Augustus had been a saviour to the Asian peoples, and they deified him as the Saviour of mankind, and worshipped him with the most whole-hearted devotion as the God incarnate in human form, the "present deity." He alone stood between them and death or a life of misery and torture. They hailed the birthday of Augustus as the beginning of a new year, and worshipped the incarnate God in public and in private.

In order to understand rightly the position of Christianity in Asia and the spirit of the Seven Asian Letters, it is necessary to conceive clearly the means whereby the Imperial policy sought to unify and consolidate the Province. There can be little doubt that several of the features of Christianity were determined in Asia. Roman Provincial unity, founded in a common religion, was the strongest idea in Asia, and it must inevitably influence, whether directly or through the recoil from and opposition to it, the growth of such an organisation as the Church in Asia, for the Christian Church from the beginning recognised the political facts of the time and accommodated itself to them.

Meetings of representatives of the Asian cities were held at least as early as 95 B.C., and probably date from the time of the Pergamenian kings. Doubtless the kings tried to make their kingdom a real unity, with a common feeling and patriotism, and not merely an agglomeration of parts tied together under compulsion and external authority; and, if so, they could attain this end only by instituting a common worship. In the case of the Asian Commune a Pergamenian origin seems proved by the name of the representatives in the official formula "it seemed good to the Hellenes in Asia." It appears improbable that an assembly which had been formed by the Romans for diffusing Roman ideas would have borne officially the name of "the Hellenes in Asia." But the Pergamenian kings counted themselves the champions of Hellenism against Asiatic barbarism; and their partisans in the cities were "the Hellenes."

Such common cults had always the same origin, viz., in an agreement among the persons or cities concerned to unite for certain purposes, and to make certain deities witnesses and patrons of their union. Thus every treaty between two cities had its religious side, and involved the common performance of rites by representatives of both sides: these rites might be performed either to the patron gods of the two cities (which was usual), or to some god or gods chosen by common consent. The same process was applied when a larger body of cities agreed (of course first of all by negotiations and treaty) to form a union. Every such union of cities had its religious side and its religious sanction in rites performed by representatives of all the cities. These representatives, as being chosen to perform a religious duty, were priests of the common worship.

It is an easy step, though not a necessary one, to institute also city temples of the same worship, so that the city may itself carry on the same ritual on its own behalf. All that is necessary for the common worship is one sacred place where the meetings can be held.

In the Pergamenian time the common cult was probably the worship of the typically Pergamenian deities (whose worship also spread to some of the Asia cities, as is pointed out later). The policy of Rome allowed free play to this religion, as it always did to any social institution which was not disloyal and dangerous. But the Asian assembly soon began to imitate the example set by Smyrna in 195 B.C. of worshipping the power of Rome; and from 95 B.C. onwards there occur cases of Asian cults of beneficent Roman officers (Scaevola, Q. Cicero, etc.), as well as of similar municipal cults. Such an Asian cult could be instituted only by an assembly of representatives of the Asian cities, and the old Pergamenian institution thus served a Roman purpose. The name Commune occurs first in a letter sent by M. Antony in 33 B.C. to "the Commune of the Hellenes of Asia"; the older references give various names, implying always an assembly of Asian representatives. It was Augustus who constituted the Commune finally, using its loyalty to Rome and himself for an Imperial end.

In that agglomeration of various countries and nations, differing in race and in speech, the one deep-seated unifying feeling arose from the common relation in which all stood to the Emperor and to Rome. There was nothing else to hold the Province together in a unity except the enthusiastic loyalty which all felt to the Roman Imperial government. There was not then in any of the races that inhabited the Province a strong national feeling to run counter to the Roman loyalty. It does not appear that Lydian or Phrygian patriotism and national feeling had much power during the first two centuries of the Province. Circumstances had long been such that national patriotic feeling could hardly be called into existence. There was plenty of strong feeling and true loyalty among the inhabitants of each city towards their own city. But Greek life and the Greek spirit, while favourable to the growth of that municipal feeling, did not encourage a wider loyalty. It remained for the Roman organisation and unifying power to widen the range of loyalty; and the first important stage in this process came through that intense personal devotion to Augustus as the Saviour of the civilised world and bearer of the Majesty of Rome.

In the condition of human thought and religious conceptions that then prevailed, such an intense feeling must take a religious form. Whatever deeply affected the minds of a body of men, few or many, inevitably assumed a religious character. No union or association of any kind was then possible except in a common religion, whose ritual expressed the common feelings and purpose. Thus the growth of an Asian Provincial religion of Rome and the Emperor was natural.

The Imperial policy took advantage of this natural growth, guided it, and regulated it, but did not call it into existence. Augustus at first rather discouraged it--doubtless because he dreaded lest its anti-republican character might offend Roman sentiment. But it was too strong for him; and after a time he perceived the advantages that it offered, and proceeded to utilise it as a political device, binding together the whole Province in a common religious ceremonial, and a common strong feeling. The one and only Asian unity was the Imperial cult. It was directed and elaborated by the Commune or Common Council of Asia, a body which seems to have had more of the "representative" character than any other institution of ancient times, and thus was the prototype of a Parliament. Asia was divided into districts, apparently, and a certain number of cities had the title of metropolis; but the details regarding the representation of the districts or the metropoles in the Commune are unknown.

The relation of the Christian organisation in Asia to the Commune, or rather to the tendency towards consolidation which took an Imperial form in the Commune, is brought out in striking relief by several facts. The Commune was the common assembly of the Hellenes of Asia. The tendency towards consolidation was a fact of Hellenism, not of the native Anatolian spirit. Now it has been elsewhere shown that Christianity was at first far more strenuously opposed to the native spirit than to the Hellenic. The one reference to the Commune in the New Testament outside of the Apocalypse is in Acts 19:31, where certain members of that body, "chief officers of Asia," are mentioned as friends of St. Paul, and took his side against the mob of worshippers of Ephesian Artemis, a typically Anatolian goddess.

Again Christianity in Asia expressed itself in Greek, not in any of the native languages. Although the majority, probably, of the people of Phrygia spoke the Phrygian language and a large number of them were entirely ignorant of Greek in the first century, yet there is no evidence and no probability that Christianity ever addressed itself to them in Phrygian. St. Paul avoided Phrygia, with the exception of the two cities in the Phrygian Region of the Roman Province Galatia, viz., Antioch and Iconium (Acts 16:6). The Church in Asia was Greek-speaking, and had become, by the fourth century, the most powerful agent in making a knowledge of Greek almost universal, even in the rural parts of the Province. The Greek character of the entire Church in its earlier stages--for even the Church in Rome was mainly Greek in language until the middle of the second century--was chiefly determined by the character of the Province Asia. The relation of the Province to the Greek language therefore needs and deserves attention.

The Province of Asia included the most civilised and educated regions of the Asiatic continent, ancient and famous Greek cities like Cyme, Colophon and Miletus, the realms of former lines of monarchs like the Lydian kings at Sardis, the Attalid kings at Pergamum, and the Carian kings at Halicarnassus. It was the most thoroughly Hellenised part of all Anatolia or Asia Minor. The native languages had died out in its western parts, and been replaced by Greek; Lydian had ceased to be spoken or known in Lydia, when Strabo wrote about A.D. 20; Carian was then probably unknown in the western parts of Caria, though the central and eastern districts were not so far advanced. Mysia, the northwestern region of the Province, was probably in a similar condition to Caria, the west and the coasts entirely Greek-speaking, the inner parts less advanced. Most thoroughly Anatolian in character, and least affected by Greek civilisation, was Phrygia. West Phrygia and especially the parts adjoining Lydia were most affected by Hellenism; whereas in the centre and east the Greek language seems to have been hardly known outside the great cities until the late second or the third century after Christ. Even in the western parts, it is proved that in the rustic and rough region of Motella, not far from the Lydian frontier, Greek was strange to many of the country people at least as late as the second century. In the extreme southwest of Phrygia, in the district of Cibyra, Strabo mentions that four languages were spoken in the first century, viz., Greek, Pisidian, Solymian and Lydian. The last had died out in Lydia, but survived in the speech of a body of Lydian colonists in Cibyra, just as Gaelic is more widely preserved and more exclusively spoken in parts of Canada today than it is in the Highlands of Scotland.

But the great cities of the Province Asia (as distinguished from the rural parts), except a few of the most backward Phrygian towns, were pretty thoroughly Greek in the first century after Christ; and everywhere throughout the Province all education was Greek, and there was probably no writing except in Greek. It seems to have been only in the second century that the native Anatolian feeling revived, and writing began to be practised in the native tongues; at least all inscriptions in the Phrygian language (except those of the ancient kingdom, before the Persian conquest) seem to be later than about A.D. 150.

Religion, too, was in outward appearance Hellenised in the cities; and the Anatolian deities were there commonly called by Greek names. But this was only a superficial appearance; the ritual and the character of the religion continued Anatolian even in the cities, while in the rural districts there was not even an outward show of Hellenisation.

Thus, in the Province Asia, there was a great mixture of language, manners and religion. Apart form the Roman unity, the various nations were as far from being really uniform in character and customs and thought, as they were from being one in blood. The Imperial Government did not attempt to compel the various peoples to use Latin or any common language: it did not try to force Roman law or habits and ways on the Province, still less to uproot the Greek civilisation. It was content to leave the half-Greek or Graeco-Asiatic law and civilisation of Asia undisturbed. But it discouraged the national distinctions and languages; it recognised Greek, but not Phrygian or Pisidian or Carian; it tried to make a unified Graeco-Roman Asia Provincia out of that agglomeration of countries. The attempt failed ultimately; but it was made; it was the ruling feature of administration in the first century; and the whole trend of Roman feeling and loyalty in all the provinces of Asia Minor during the first century was in favour of the Provincial idea and against the old national divisions. The term which Strabo uses to represent in Greek the Latin Asia Provincia expressed the true Roman point of view. He speaks of the Province as "the nation of Asia": i.e., the Roman Province took the place of any national divisions: loyalty considered that there was only one nation in Asia, that the Province was the nation.

As time went on and the past pre-Imperial miseries were forgotten, the fervour of loyalty, which had for a time given some real strength to the Imperial religion, began to cool down; and there was no longer strength in it to hold the Province together, while there was a growth in the strength of national feeling. Polemon the Sophist of the time of Hadrian and Pius was called "the Phrygian," because he was born of a Laodicean family; and when Ionians were using such a nickname, Phrygians naturally began to retort by assuming it as a mark of pride. It was Hadrian probably who saw that the Roman ideal was not strong enough in itself without support from local and old national feeling; and from his time onwards the Imperial policy ceased to be so hostile to the old national distinctions. He did not try to break up the vast Roman Provinces; but there are traces of an attempt to recognise national divisions: e.g., the new Province of the Tres Eparchiae was left in fact and name a loose aggregate of three countries, Cilicia, Isauria, Lycaonia, which kept their national names and had probably three distinct Communes or Councils. The union of Asia was already old; but he tried to strengthen it in a way characteristic of ancient feeling, viz., by giving it a support in Anatolian religion as well as in the Imperial religion.

During the first century the State religion was simply the worship of the Emperor or of Rome and the Emperor. But that was only a sham religion, a matter of outward show and magnificent ceremonial. It was almost devoid of power over the heart and will of man, when the first strong sense of relief from misery had grown weak, because it was utterly unable to satisfy the religious needs and cravings of human nature. From a very early time there seems to have existed in the Eastern Provinces a tendency to give more reality to this Imperial religion by identifying the Divine Emperor with the local god, whatever form the latter had: thus the religious feelings and habits of the people in each district were associated to some extent with the Imperial divinity and the State religion. Perhaps it was Domitian who first saw clearly that the Imperial religion required to be reinforced by enlisting in its service the deep-seated reverence of men for their local god. In the second century the custom of associating the Emperor with the local deity in a common religious ritual seems to have spread much more widely, and the old tendency to make certain local gods into gods of the Province became more marked. Under Hadrian a silver coinage for the whole of Asia was struck with the types, not merely of the Pergamenian temple of Augustus, but also of the Ephesian Diana, the two Smyrnaean goddesses Nemesis, the Sardian Persephone, etc., thus giving those deities a sort of Provincial standing. This class of coins was struck under the authority of the Commune. But it was in the Flavian persecution that this approximation between the native religions and the Imperial worship began first to be important. This approximation put an end to the hope, which St. Paul had cherished, that the conquest of the Empire by the new faith might be accomplished peacefully. It now became apparent that war was inevitable, and its first stage was the Flavian persecution.

In Asia the Ephesian religion of Artemis was the only native cultus which had by its own natural strength spread widely through the Province. Before the Roman period the royal character of Pergamum had given strength to its deities, especially Asklepios the Saviour and Dionysos the Guide (Kathegemon). The latter was the royal god, and the royal family was regarded as sprung from him, and the reigning king was his representative and incarnation. Asklepios, on the other hand, was the god of the city Pergamum. Hence in several cities even in distant Phrygia the worship of those two deities was introduced; and after the Roman period had begun, the respect felt for the capital of Asia was expressed by paying honour to its god. This is very characteristic of ancient feeling. The patron god is the representative of his city, just as the angel in the Seven Letters stands for his Church. Municipal patriotism was expressed by worshipping the god of the city; and other parts of Asia recognised the superior rank of Pergamum by worshipping Asklepios the Saviour.

In Roman time, also, the natural advantages of Ephesus had full play. Ephesus was brought into trading relations with many cities; many strangers experienced the protection and prayed for the favour of the Ephesian goddess. Thus, for example, she is recognised alongside of the native god Zeus and the Pergamenian Asklepios in the last will and testament of a citizen of Akmonia, dated A.D. 94. Many cities of Asia made agreements with each other for mutual recognition of their cults and festivals and common rights of all citizens of both cities at the festivals; and such agreements were usually commemorated by striking what are called "alliance-coins," on which the patron deities of the two cities are represented side by side. The custom shows a certain tendency in Asia towards an amalgamation and fusing of local religions; and Ephesus concluded more "alliances" of this kind than any other city of Asia. Hence in A.D. 56 the uneducated devotees of Artemis of Ephesus spoke of their goddess, "whom all Asia and the civilised world worshippeth."

The machinery of Roman government in the Province--the Proconsul (who resided mostly in the official capital, though he landed and embarked at Ephesus and often made a progress through the important cities of the Province) and other officers--does not directly affect the Seven Letters, and need not detain us.

More important is the Provincial religious organisation, directed by the Commune. The one original temple of the Asian cultus at Pergamum was soon found insufficient to satisfy the demonstrative loyalty of the Asians. Moreover, the jealous rivalry of other great cities made them seek for similar distinctions. Asian temples were built in Smyrna (Tiberius), Ephesus, Sardis, etc. Each temple was a meeting-place of the Commune; and where the Commune met, games "common to Asia" were celebrated (such as those at which Polycarp suffered in Smyrna). The Commune was essentially a body charged with religious duties, but religion was closely interwoven with civil affairs, and the Commune had other work: it had control of certain revenues, and must therefore have had an annual budget, it struck coins, etc.

The most interesting side of Imperial history is the growth of ideas, which have been more fully developed later. Universal citizenship, universal religion, a universal Church, were ideas which the Empire was slowly, sometimes quite unconsciously, working out or preparing for. The Commune contained the germ on one side of a Parliament of representatives, on another side of a religious hierarchy.

Chapter 11: The Cities of Asia as Meeting-Places of the Greek and the Asiatic Spirit

The marked and peculiar character of the society and population of the great Asian cities, amid which the local Churches were built up, is present in the writer's mind throughout the Seven Letters; and it is necessary to form some conception of this subject. Disregarding differences, we shall try to describe briefly the chief forces which had been at work in those cities during the last three centuries, and the prominent features that were common to them all about A.D. 90. Some of them were ancient Greek colonies, like Smyrna and Ephesus, some were old Anatolian cities, like Pergamum and Sardis; but all these had recently experienced great changes, and many new cities, like Laodicea, Philadelphia, Thyatira, had been founded by the kings.

The successors of Alexander the Great were Greek kings, ruling Oriental lands and peoples. To maintain their hold on their dominions it was necessary to build up a suitable organisation in the countries over which they ruled. Their method everywhere was similar: it was to make cities that should be at once garrisons to dominate the country and centres of Graeco-Asiatic manners and education, which the kings were desirous of spreading among their Oriental subjects. The rather pedantic adjective Graeco-Asiatic is used to describe the form which Greek civilisation was forced to assume, as it attempted to establish itself in Oriental lands: it did not merely change the cities, it was itself much altered in the attempt. Sometimes those kings founded new cities, where previously there seem to have been only villages. Sometimes they introduced an accession of population and change of constitution in already existing cities, a process which may be described as re-founding. In both cases alike a new name, connected with the dynasty, was almost invariably substituted for the previous name of the village or city, though in many cases the old name soon revived, e.g., in Ephesus and in Tarsus. Commonest among them were the Seleucid names Antioch and Laodicea, and the Macedonian Alexandria.

The new population consisted generally of colonists brought from foreign countries, who were considered intruders and naturally not much liked by the older population. The colonists were granted property and privileges in their new cities; and they knew that the continuance of their fortunes and rights depended on the permanence of the royal government which had introduced them. Thus those strangers constituted a loyal garrison in every city where they had been planted. With them were associated in loyalty the whole party that favoured the royal policy, or hoped to profit by it. It would appear that these constituted a powerful combination in the cities. They were in general the active, energetic, and dominating party.

How important in the New Testament writings those Asian foundations of the Greek kings were, is brought out very clearly by a glance over the list of cities. Laodicea and Thyatira were founded or refounded by Seleucid kings: the Ionian Greek cities in general were profoundly modified by them. Ephesus, Smyrna, Troas, Pergamum and Philadelphia were refounded by other Greek kings in the same period and under similar circumstances.

Two classes of settlers were specially required and encouraged in the Seleucid colonies. In the first place, of course, soldiers were needed. These were found chiefly among the mercenaries of many nations--but mostly of northern race, Macedonians, Thracians, etc.--who made up the strength of the Seleucid armies. The harsh, illiterate, selfish, domineering tone of those soldier-citizens was often satirised by the Greek writers of the third and second centuries before Christ, who delighted to paint them as braggarts, cowards at heart, boasting of false exploits; and the boastful soldier, the creation of Greek wit and malice, has been perpetuated since that time on the Roman and the Elizabethan stage in traits essentially the same.

But the Greek kings knew well that soldiers alone were not enough to establish their cities on a permanent basis. Other colonists were needed, able to manage, to lead, to train the rude Oriental peasantry in the arts on which civilised life must rest, to organise and utilise their labour and create a commercial system. The experience of the present day in the cities of the east Mediterranean lands shows where such colonists could best be found. They were Greeks and Jews. Nowadays Armenians also would be available; but at that time Armenia had hardly come within reach of even the most elementary civilisation. Only among the Greeks and the Jews was there that familiarity with ideals, that power and habit of thinking for themselves and of working for a future and remote end, which the kings needed in their colonists. Modern students do not as a rule conceive the Jews as an educated race, and some can hardly find language strong enough to describe their narrowness and deadness of intellect. But when compared with the races that surrounded them, the Greeks excepted, the Jews stood on a far higher intellectual platform: they knew one book (or, rather, one collection of books) well, and it was a liberal education to them.

One might hardly expect to find that the Greeks were loyal subjects of Seleucid kings. They were apt to be democratic and unruly; but it is as true of ancient as it is of modern times that the Greeks are "better and more prosperous under almost any other government than they are under their own." They accommodated themselves with their usual dexterity and pliancy to their position; and circumstances, as we have seen, made them dependent on the kings. The stagnant and unprogressive Oriental party looked askance at and disliked the Greek element; and the latter must regard the kings as their champions, even though the Seleucid kings were far too autocratic and too strongly tinged with the Oriental fashions for the Greek colonists to feel in thorough sympathy with them. But settlers and kings alike had the common interest that they must dominate the uneducated mass of the ancient population. Thus the constitution of the new cities was a compromise, a sort of limited monarchy, where democratic freedom and autocratic rule tempered and restrained each other; and the result was distinctly favourable to the development and prosperity of the cities.

It may seem even stranger that the Jews should be found by Seleucid kings their best and most loyal subjects outside of Palestine, for those kings were considered by the Jews of Palestine to be the most deadly enemies of their race and religion. But the Jew outside of Palestine was a different person and differently situated from the Jew in his own land. Abroad he was resigned to accept the government of the land in which he lived, and to make the best of it; and he found that loyalty was by far the best policy. He could be useful to the government; and the government was eager to profit by and ready to reward his loyalty. Thus their interest were identical. Moreover, the Jewish colonies planted by the Seleucid kings in Asia Minor and Cilicia were all older than the Maccabean rising, when the Jewish hatred for the Seleucid kings came to a head.

Their moral scruples divided the Jews from their neighbours in the cities, and thereby made them all the more sensible of the fact that it was the royal favour which maintained them safe and privileged in the places where they lived as citizens. In Palestine their ritual kept the Jews aloof from and hostile to the Seleucid kings, and fed their national aspirations. But in the Graeco-Asiatic cities their ritual actually bound them more closely to the king's service.

Through similar causes, at a later time, the Jews in Palestine hated the Roman government and regarded it as the abominable thing, and they were subdued only after many rebellions and the most stubborn resistance. And yet, through that troubled period, the Jews outside Palestine were loyal subjects of the Empire, distinguished by their special attachment to the side of the Emperors against the old Roman republican party.

Moreover, the Jews, an essentially Oriental race, found the strong Oriental tinge in the policy of the Seleucid kings far more congenial to them than the Greek colonists could do. The "grave Hebrew trader," if one may imitate the words of Matthew Arnold, was by nature essentially opposed to "the young, light-hearted master of the wave." Hence the Jewish settlers formed a counterpoise against the Greek colonists in the Seleucid cities, and, wherever the Greek element seemed too strong, the natural policy of the kings was to plant Jews in the same city.

That remarkable shifting and mixing of races was, of course, not produced simply by arbitrary acts of the Greek kings, violently transporting population hither and thither at their caprice. The royal policy was successful, because it was in accordance with the tendencies of the time as described in chapter 1. The Graeco-Asiatic cities between 300 and 100 B.C. were in process of natural growth through the settling in them of strangers; and the strangers came for purposes of trade, eager to make money. The kings interfered only to regulate and to direct to their own advantage a process which they had not originated and could not have prevented. What they did for those strangers was to give them the fullest rights in the cities where they settled. The strangers and their descendants would have always remained aliens; but the kings made them citizens, gave them a voice in the government and a position in the city as firm and influential as that of the best, increased their numbers by assisting immigrants, and presented them with lands.

Even the Jews, though introduced specially by the Seleucid kings, and always most numerous in the Seleucid colonies, were spread throughout the great cities of the Greek world, and especially in the chief centres of trade and finance (as might be expected).

The result of that free mixture of races in the Graeco-Asiatic cities was to stimulate a rapid and precocious development. There was great ease of intercourse and freedom of trade, a settled and sound coinage and monetary system, much commerce on a considerable scale, much eagerness and opportunity to make money by large financial operations. There was also a notable development on the intellectual side. Curiosity was stimulated in the meeting of such diverse races. The Oriental came into relations with the European spirit: each tried to understand and to outwit the other.

Thus an amalgamation of Oriental and European races and intellect, manners and law, was being worked out practically in the collision and competition of such diverse elements. It was an experiment in a direction that is often theorised about and discussed at the present day. Can the east take on the western character? Can the Asiatic be made like a European? In one sense that is impossible: in another sense it was done in the Graeco-Asiatic cities, and can be done again. It was done in them, not by Europeanising the Asiatic, but by profoundly modifying both; each learned from the other; and that is the only treatment of the problem that can ever be successful.

This great experiment in human development was conducted on a small scale and in a thin soil, but as all the more precocious on that account, and also the more short-lived. It was a hot-house growth, produced in circumstances which were evanescent; and it was unnatural and unhealthy.

The smallness of scale on which all Greek history was conducted is one of its most remarkable features. In Greece proper, as contrasted with the big countries and the large masses of modern nations, the scale was quite minute. In the Graeco-Asiatic States the scale seemed much greater; but development was really confined to a number of spots here and there, showing only as dots on a map, small islets in the great sea of stagnant, unruffled, immovable Orientalism. The Greek political and social system demanded a small city as its scene, and broke down when the attempt was made to apply it on a larger scale. But no more stimulating environment to the intellect could be found than was offered in the Graeco-Asiatic cities, and the scanty glimpses which we get into the life of those cities reveal to us a very quick, restless, intelligent society, keenly interested in a rather empty and shallow kind of philosophic speculation, and almost utterly destitute of any vivifying and invigorating ideal.

The interest and importance to us of this moment in society lies in the fact that Pauline Christianity arose in it and worked upon it. In every page of Paul's writings that restless, self-conceited, morbid, unhealthy society stands out in strong relief before the reader. He knew it so well, because he was born and brought up in its midst. He conceived that his mission was to regenerate it, and the plan which he saw to be the only possible one was to save the Jew from sinking down to the pagan level by elevating the pagan to the true Jewish level. The writer of the Seven Letters also, though a Jew from Palestine, had learned to know the Asian cities by long residence.

The noblest feature of Greek city life was its zeal and provision for education. The minute carefulness with which those Asian-Greek cities legislated and provided for education--watching over the young, keeping them from evil, graduating their physical and mental training to suit their age, moving them on from stage to stage--rouses the deepest admiration in the scholar who laboriously spells out and completes the records on the broken stones on which they are written, and at the same time convinces him how vain is mere law to produce any healthy education. It is pathetic to think how poor was the result of all those wise and beautiful provisions.

The literature of the age has almost utterly perished; but the extremely scanty remains, along with the Roman imitations of it, do not suggest that there was anything really great in it, though much cleverness, brilliance, and sentimentality. Perhaps Theocritus, who comes at the beginning of the age, might rank higher; but the great master of bucolic poetry, the least natural form of poetic art, can hardly escape the charge of artificiality and sentimentality. In the realm of creative literature, the spirit of the age is to be compared with that of the Restoration in England, and partakes of the same deep-seated immorality.

The age was devoted to learning: it investigated antiquities, studied the works of older Greek writers, commented on texts; and the character of the time, in its poorness of fibre and shallowness of method, is most clearly revealed in this department. It is hardly possible to find any trace of insight or true knowledge in the fragments of this branch of literature that have come down to us. Athenodorus of Tarsus was in many respects a man of ability, courage, education, high ideas and practical sense; but take a specimen of his history of his own city: "Anchiale, daughter of Japetos, founded Anchiale (a city near Tarsus): her son was Cydnus, who gave his name to the river at Tarsus: the son of Cydnus was Parthenius, from whom the city was called Parthenia: afterwards the name was changed to Tarsus." This habit of substituting irrational "fables and endless genealogies" (1 Tim 1:4) for the attempt really to understand nature and history was engrained in the spirit of the time, and shows how superficial and unintelligent its learning was. Out of it could come no real advance in knowledge, but only frivolous argumentation and "questionings" (1 Tim 1:4).

Only in the department of moral philosophy did the age sometimes reach a lofty level. A touch of Oriental sympathy with the Divine nature enabled Athenodorus and others to express themselves with singular dignity and beauty on the duty of man and his relation to God. But the "endless genealogies" frequently obtruded themselves in their finest speculations.

The Christian letters need to be constantly illustrated from the life of those cities, and to be always read in the light of a careful study of the society in them. It was, above all, the philosophical speculation in which they excelled and delighted that Paul detested. He saw serious danger in it. Not only was it useless and resultless in itself, mere "empty deceit" (Col 2:8), but, far worse, it led directly to superstition. Vain speculation, unable to support itself in its lofty flight, unable to comprehend the real unity of the world in God, invented for itself silly genealogies (1 Tim 1:4), in which nature and creation were explained under the empty fiction of sonship, and a chain of divine beings in successive generations was made and worshipped; and human nature was humbly made subservient to these fictitious beings, who were described as "angels" (Col 2:18ff).

This philosophical speculation cannot be properly conceived in its historical development without bearing in mind the mixed population and the collision of Jewish and Greek thought which belonged to those great Graeco-Asiatic cities. It united Greek and Jewish elements in arbitrary eclectic systems. The mixture of Greek and Jewish thought is far more conspicuous in Asia Minor than in Europe. Hence there is not much trace of it in the Corinthian letters (though some writers try to discover it, and lay exaggerated stress on it): the Corinthian philosophers were of a different kind. But in the cities of Asia, Phrygia, South Galatia, and Cilicia--all along the great roads leading east and west across Asia Minor-- the minds of men were filled with crude attempts at harmonising and mingling Oriental (especially Jewish) and Greek ideas. Their attempts took many shapes, from mere vulgar magical formulae and arts to the serious and lofty morality of Athenodorus the Tarsian in his highest moments of philosophy.

When we think of the intellectual skill, the philosophic interest, and the extreme cleverness of the age, we feel the inadequacy of those arguments--or rather those unargued assertions--according to which the Epistle to the Colossians reveals a stage of philosophic speculation, as applied to Christian doctrines, so advanced that it could not have been reached earlier than the second century. How long would it take those clever and subtle philosophic inquirers in those cities to achieve the slight feat of intellectual gymnastics presupposed in the Epistle?

Such then was the motley population of the numerous Seleucid colonies which were planted in Lydia, Phrygia, Pisidia, and Lycaonia during the third century, and in Cilicia during the second century B.C. The language of the settlers was Greek, the language of trade and education; and it was through these cities that a veneer of Greek civilisation was spread over the Asiatic coasts.

The jealousies and rivalries of those great cities are a quaint feature of their history in the Roman period. The old Greek pride in their patris, their father-land--which to them was simply their city--had no longer the opportunity of expressing itself in the field of politics. No city could have a foreign policy. Even in municipal matters, while the Empire nominally allowed home rule, yet in practice it discouraged it: the management of city business was more and more taken out of the hands of the cities: the Emperor was there to think for all and provide for all better than they could for themselves. Municipal pride expressed itself in outward show, partly in the healthier direction of improving and beautifying the cities, partly in the vainglorious invention of names and titles. In every Province and district there was keen competition for the title first of the Province or the district. Every city which could pretend to the first place in respect of any qualification called itself "first," and roused the jealousy of other cities which counted themselves equally good. Smyrna was "first of Asia in size and beauty," Ephesus first of Asia as the landing-place of every Roman official, Pergamum first as the official capital, and Sardis boldly styled itself "first metropolis of Asia, of Lydia, of Hellenism" on the arrogant coin. Similarly in the Province Bithynia Nicomedia and Nicaea competed for the primacy. So again in Cilicia Tarsus and Anazarba, in one district of Macedonia Philippi and Amphipolis (see chapter 14), disputed with one another about those empty titles. A temporary agreement between the three chief cities of Asia, implying a lull in their rivalry, is attested by the coin shown in chapter 14.

The prosperity, both material and intellectual, of the cities was very great under the kings. As the dynasties decayed, the Romans took over their power, and during the disintegration of the Roman Republic and the long Civil Wars the cities suffered severely from misgovernment and extortion. But prosperity was restored by the triumph of the new Empire, which was welcomed with the utmost enthusiasm by the Graeco-Asiatic cities. The Roman Empire did not, as a rule, need to found cities and introduce new population in order to maintain its hold on Asia Minor. It stood firmly supported by the loyalty of the city population. Only on the South-Galatian frontier was a line of Coloniae--Antioch, Lystra, etc.--needed to protect the loyal cities from the unsubdued tribes of Mount Taurus. The two Roman Coloniae in Asia, Troas and Parium, were founded for sentimental and economic reasons, not to hold a doubtful land.

But the history of those cities, and the letters of the New Testament, show that a very high degree of order, peace and prosperity may result in a thoroughly unhealthy life and a steady moral deterioration, unless the condition of the public mind is kept sound by some salutary idea. The salutary idea which was needed to keep the Empire sound and the cities healthy was what Paul preached; and that idea was the raising of the Gentiles to equality with the Jews in religion and morality.

An amalgamation of Oriental and Hellenic religious ideas had been sought by many philosophers, and was practised in debased forms by impostors who traded on the superstitions of the vulgar. It was left for Christianity to place it before the world accomplished and perfected.

Chapter 12: The Jews in the Asian Cities

In chapter 11 we recognised how important an element the Jewish colonists were in the cities which the Seleucid kings founded or re-founded as strongholds of their power, and as centres of the Graeco-Asiatic civilisation amid the dreary ocean of Oriental monotony; and we also saw what were the reasons which made them trusty supporters of the Seleucid regime and specially useful to counterbalance the Greek element in those cities, all the more trusty and useful because they were unpopular, and even hated by their fellow-citizens.

Considering how important a part the Jewish Christians must have played in the Asian Churches (Acts 18:20, 19:1-8, 20:21), it is necessary to examine their position in the cities more closely. The point of view taken in the Apocalypse is that the Christians were the true Jews (just as they constitute the real element in the city where they dwell), and the national Jews who clung to the old Hebrew ideas were not the true Jews but merely the synagogue of Satan. The Palestinian Jew who could express such a view had travelled far along the Pauline path of development.

The Jews were too clever for their fellow-townsmen. They regarded with supreme contempt the gross obscene ritual and the vulgar superstitions of their neighbours; but many of them were ready to turn those superstitions to their own profit; and a species of magic and soothsaying, a sort of syncretism of Hebrew and pagan religious ideas, afforded a popular and lucrative occupation to the sons of Sceva in Ephesus and to many another Jew throughout the Asiatic Greek cities. It was probably an art of this kind that was practised in the Chaldean's holy precinct at Thyatira, which is mentioned in an inscription of the Roman period (see chapter 23).

There were among those Jews, of course, persons of every moral class, from the destined prophet, Saul of Tarsus, whose eyes were fixed on the spiritual future of his people, down to the lowest Jew who traded on the superstitions and vices of those pagan dogs whom he despised and abhorred, while he ministered to the excesses from which in his own person he held aloof. But among them all there was, in contrast to the pagan population around them, a certain unity of feeling and aspiration bred in them by their religion, their holy books, the Sabbath meetings and the weekly lessons and exhortations, the home training and the annual family meal of the Passover. These made an environment which exercised a strong influence even on the most unworthy.

Of their numbers we can form no estimate, but they were very great. In preparing for the final struggle in western Asia Minor about 210 B.C., Antiochus III moved 2,000 Jewish families from Babylonia into Lydia and Phrygia, and that was a single act of one king, whose predecessors and successors carried out the same policy on a similar scale. The statistics which Cicero gives, when he describes how a Roman Governor in 66 B.C. arrested the half-shekel tribute which the Jews sent to Jerusalem, show a very large Jewish population in Phrygia and a large Jewish population in Lydia.

Except in a few such references history is silent about that great Jewish population of Asia Minor. But inscriptions are now slowly revealing, by here a trace and there a trace, that nobles and officers under the Roman Empire who have all the outward appearance of ordinary Roman provincial citizens were really part of the Phrygian Jewish population. The original Jews of Asia Minor seem to have perished entirely, for the Turkish Jews of the present day are Spanish-speaking Jews, whose ancestors were expelled from Spain by the most famous of Spanish sovereigns and sheltered in Turkey by Mohammedan Sultans. In the dearth of evidence one can only speculate as to their fate. Reasons have elsewhere been stated showing that a considerable part of that original Jewish population adopted Christianity, and thus lost their isolation and cohesion, and became merged in the Christian Empire of the fourth and following centuries after Christ.

As to those Jews, very many in number, who clung unfalteringly to their own faith, what was likely to be their fate in the Christian Empire? The Eastern Empire was largely Greek in language and in spirit alike; and any one who has become familiar with the intensity and bitterness of the hatred that separates the Greek from the Jew, will recognise that in general the alternative of extermination or expulsion was presented to them. There was no place and no mercy for the Jew in the Greek Christian Empire. The barbarous lands of Europe and the steppes and villages of Russia were a gentler home to them than the most civilised of lands.

When one thinks of the character of the Hellenic cities, one must ask how and on what conditions the Jews were able to live in them.

When the Jews were present in such a city merely as resident aliens, their position is easier to understand. It was quite usual for strangers to reside in a Greek city for purposes of trade, and even to become permanent inhabitants with their families. But, as has been already pointed out, there was no ordinary way by which such inhabitants could attain the citizenship. They and their descendants continued to rank only as resident aliens. It was easy for them to retain and practise their own religious rites. Strangers naturally brought their religion with them; and their regular custom was to form an association among themselves for the common practice of their own rites. Such religious associations were numerous and recognised by law and custom; and Jewish residents could carry their religion with them under this legal form.

It was in this way as a rule that foreign religions spread in the Greek cities. The foreign Asiatic rites, by their more impressive and enthusiastic character, attracted devotees, especially among the humbler and less educated Greeks. Thus Oriental cults spread in such cities as Corinth, Athens, and other trading centres, in spite of the fact that those pagan cults were essentially non-proselytising, and preferred to keep their bounds narrow and to restrict the advantages of their religion to a small number.

Similarly the Jewish association, with its synagogue or place of prayer by sea-shore or river bank, attracted attention and proselytes, though it repelled and roused the hatred of the majority, because it was "so strange and mysterious and incomprehensible to the ordinary pagan, with its proud isolation, its lofty morality, its superiority to pagan ideas of life, its unhesitating confidence in its superiority." Thus the Jews became a power even where they ranked only as aliens.

It is much more difficult to understand the position of the Jews in those Hellenic cities where they possessed the rights of citizenship. Now, as a rule, in the cities founded by the Seleucid kings, the Jews were actually citizens. But it was to the ancient mind an outrage and an almost inconceivable thing, that people could be fellow-citizens without engaging in the worship of the same city gods. The bond of patriotism was really a religious bond. The citizen was encompassed by religious duties from his cradle to his grave. It was practically impossible for the Jew to be a citizen of a Greek city in the ordinary way. Some special provision was needed.

That special provision was made by the Seleucid kings in founding their cities. It was a noteworthy achievement, and a real step in the history of human civilisation and institutions, when they succeeded in so widening the essential theory of the Greek city as to enable the Jew to live in it as an integral part of it. The way in which this result was attained must be clearly understood, as it throws much light on the position of the Jews in the Graeco-Asiatic cities.

The Greek city was never simply an aggregation of citizens. The individual citizens were always grouped in bodies, usually called "Tribes," and the "Tribes" made up the city. This was a fundamental principle of Greek city organisation, and must form the starting-point of all reasoning on the subject. The city was an association of groups, not of individuals. It is generally admitted that the groups were older than the institution of cities, being a survival of a more primitive social system. As Mr. Greenidge says, Roman Public Life, p. 66: "Simple membership of a State, which was not based on membership of some lower unit, was inconceivable to the Graeco-Roman world." In the Seleucid City-States that "lower unit" was generally called the "Tribe."

The "Tribe" was united by a religious bond (as was every union or association of human beings in the Graeco-Roman world): the members met in the worship of a common deity (or deities), and their unity lay in their participation in the same religion. It was, therefore, as utterly impossible for a Jew to belong to an ordinary Tribe, as it was for him to belong to an ordinary Hellenic city.

But, just as it was possible for a group of Jewish aliens to reside in a Greek city and practise their own religious rites in a private association, so it was possible to enroll a body of Jewish citizens in a special "Tribe" (or equivalent aggregation), which was united without any bond of pagan religion. That this must have been the method followed by the Seleucid kings is practically certain (so far as certainty can exist in that period of history), though the fact cannot everywhere be demonstrated in the absence of records. Josephus mentions that in Alexandria the "Tribe" of the Jews was called "Macedonians," i.e. all Jews who possessed the Alexandrian citizenship were enrolled in "the Tribe Macedones": this "Tribe" consisted of Jews only, as Josephus' words imply, and as was obviously necessary (for what Greek would or could belong to a Tribe which consisted mainly of the multitude of Jews with whom the rest of the Alexandrian population was almost constantly at war?).

The example of Alexandria may be taken as a proof that, by a sort of legal fiction, an appearance of Hellenism was given to the Jewish citizens in a Greek City-State. It was of the essence of both Ptolemaic and Seleucid cities that they should be centres of Hellenic civilisation and education. In the period of which we are treating the term "Hellenes" did not imply Greek blood and race, but only language and education and social manners. The Jews could never be, in the strict sense, Hellenes, for their manners and ways of thinking were too diverse from the Greek; but by enrolling them in a "Tribe," and giving this "Tribe" a Greek name and outward appearance, the Seleucid and Ptolemaic kings made them members of a city of Hellenes.

But the other difficulty remained. There was a religious bond uniting the whole city. The entire body of citizens was knit together by their common religion; and the Jews stood apart from this city cultus, abhorring and despising it.

The Seleucid practice trampled under foot this religious difficulty by creating an exception to the general principle. The Jews were simply declared by the founder of the dynasty, Seleucus, and his successors to be citizens, and yet free to disregard the common city cultus. They were absolved from the ordinary laws and regulations of the city, if these conflicted with the Jewish religion: especially, they could not be required to appear in court, or take any part in public life, on the Sabbath. Certain regulations were modified to suit Jewish scruples. When allowances of oil were given to the citizens, the royal law ordered that an equivalent in money should be given to the Jewish citizens, whose principles forbade them to use oil that a Gentile had handled or made. Their Hellenic fellow-citizens were never reconciled to this. It seemed to them an outrage that members of the city should despise and reject the gods of the city. This rankled in their minds, a wound that could not be healed. Time after time, wherever a favourable opportunity seemed to offer itself, they besought their masters--Greek king or Roman emperor--to deprive the Jews of their citizenship: for example, their argument to Agrippa in 15 B.C. was that fellow-citizens ought to reverence the same gods.

Therein lay the sting of the case to the Greeks or Hellenes. The Jews never merged themselves in the Hellenic unity. They always remained outside of it, a really alien body. In a time when patriotism was identified with community of religion, it was not possible to attain true unity in those mixed States. A religious revolution was needed, and to be effective it must take the direction of elevating thought. Then one great man, with the true prophet's insight, saw that unity could be introduced only by raising the Gentiles to a higher level through their adoption of the Jewish morality and religion; and to that man's mind this was expressed as the coming of the Messiah, an idea which was very differently conceived by different minds. Elsewhere we have attempted to show the effect upon St. Paul of this idea as it was forced on him in his position at Tarsus, which was pre-eminently the meeting-place of East and West.

It follows inevitably from the conditions, that there can never have been a case of a single and solitary Jewish citizen in a Hellenic city. It was impossible for a Jew to face the religious difficulty in an ordinary Greek city. He could not become a member of an ordinary "Tribe": he could become a member of a Hellenic city only where the act of some superior power had altered the regular Greek constitution in favour of the Jews as a whole. It may be set aside as impossible, as opposed to all evidence and reasonable inference, either that an ordinary Hellenic city would voluntarily set aside its own fundamental principles in order to welcome its most hated enemies and most dangerous commercial rivals, or that the superior power would or could violate the constitution of the city in favour of a single individual. Where Jews are proved or believed to have been citizens of a Hellenic city, the origin of their right must lie in a general principle laid down by a superior power, accompanied by the introduction of a body of Jewish citizens sufficiently strong to support one another and maintain their own unity and religion.

But might not a Jew occasionally desire the Hellenic citizenship for the practical advantages it might offer in trade? He might desire those advantages in some or many cases; but they could not be got without formal admission to a "Tribe," and if he were admitted to an ordinary Hellenic Tribe through a special decree, he must either participate in its religion or sacrifice the advantages which he aimed at. In fact, it may be doubted whether any person who avoided the meetings and ceremonies of the tribesmen could have retained the membership. The Jew must either abandon his nation and his birthright absolutely, or he must stand outside of the Hellenic citizenship, except in those cities whose constitution had been widened by the creation of a special "Tribe" or similar body for Jews.

The case may be set aside as almost inconceivable that any Jew in the pre-Roman period, except in the rarest cases, absolutely disowned his birthright and was willing to merge himself in the ordinary ranks of Hellenic citizenship. Professor E. Schurer has emphasised the thoroughly Hebraic character even of the most Hellenised Jews who had settled outside Palestine; and there can be no doubt that he is right. They were a people of higher education and nobler views than the Gentiles; and they could not descend entirely to the Gentile level. Even the lowest Jew who made his living out of Gentile superstitions or vices usually felt, as we may be sure, that he was of a higher stock, and was not willing to become a Gentile entirely.

Moreover, the race hatred was too strong. The Greeks would not have permitted it, even if a Jew had desired it. The Greeks had no desire to assimilate the Jews to themselves; they only desired to be rid of them.

The position of the Jews in the Ionian cities is illustrated by an incident that occurred in 15 B.C. There was a body of Jews in Ephesus; and the other citizens, i.e. the Hellenes, tried to induce Agrippa to expel these on the ground that they would not take part in the religion of the city. Their argument is instructive. They appealed to the settlement of the Ephesian constitution by Antiochus II, 261-246 B.C., as authoritative; and this proves that there had been no serious change in the principles of the Ephesian constitution since that time.

That body of Jews in Ephesus did not consist simply of non-citizens, resident (perhaps for many generations) in the city for purposes of trade. That there were Ephesian citizens among them is clearly implied in the pleading of their fellow-citizens: the Hellenes of Ephesus made no charge against Jewish strangers: in the forefront of their case they put their claim that the Hellenes alone had any right to the citizenship, which was the gift of Antiochus II. These words are useless and unnecessary, unless there was a body of Jews claiming to be citizens of Ephesus, whom the Greeks desired to eject from the citizenship. They came to Agrippa asking permission, not to expel Jewish strangers from the town, but to deprive the Jews of their participation in the State.

Moreover, the next words quoted from the argument of the Hellenes are even stronger: they put the case that the Jews are kinsmen and members of the same race with themselves, "If the Jews are kinsmen to us, they ought to worship our gods." The only conceivable kinship between Jews and Greeks was that which they acquired through common citizenship. The idea that common citizenship implies and produces kingship is very characteristic of ancient feeling and language. We note in passing that this idea occurs in St. Paul, Romans 16:7, 11, where the word "kinsmen" will be understood as denoting Tarsian Jews by those who approach the Epistles from the side of ordinary contemporary Greek thought. It can hardly mean Jews simply (as "kinsmen according to the flesh" does in Romans 9:3); for many other persons in the same list are not so called, though they are Jews. Andronicus and a few others are characterised as members of the same city and "Tribe" as Paul.

The Jewish rights, therefore, must have originated from Antiochus II. Now, throughout his reign, that king was struggling with Ptolemy King of Egypt for predominance in the Ionian cities; and the constitution which he introduced in Ephesus must have been intended to attach the city to his side, partly by confirming its rights and freedom, partly by introducing a new body of colonists whose loyalty he could depend upon; and among those colonists were a number of Jews.

This conclusion seems inevitable; and Professor E. Schurer has rightly held it. But the common view has been hitherto that Antiochus II merely gave freedom to the Ionian cities, including Ephesus; and even so competent an authority as Professor Wilcken adopts the prevalent view. What Antiochus gave was not mere freedom in our vague sense, but a definite constitution. The ancients knew well that freedom among a large body of men is impossible without a constitution and written laws.

It is not likely to be suggested by any scholar that some Jews might have been made Ephesian citizens, when the resident aliens who had helped in the war against Mithridates were granted citizenship by the Ephesian State. No new Tribes were then instituted; the constitution remained undisturbed; and those aliens would have to accept enrollment in one of the pagan groups or "Tribes," out of which the city was constituted; and this we have seen that Jews could not accept. If there was a body of Jewish citizens in Ephesus (as seems certain), they must have been placed there by some external authority; and, as we have seen, the constitution was permanently settled by Antiochus II, so that no new Tribes had been instituted and no modification by external authority had been made.

It is pointed out in chapter 17 that a new Tribe, whose name is unknown (because it was changed afterwards to Sebaste), was instituted at this time for the new settlers whom Antiochus introduced. He doubtless brought colonists of several nationalities, and avoided any pagan religious bond of Tribal unity. The Jews constituted a special division (Chiliastys) in this Tribe.

Antiochus acted similarly in several of the Ionian cities, possibly even in them all. His changes are recorded to have been made in the Ionian cities, and not to have been confined to Ephesus. The case of Ephesus may be taken as typical of many other Asian cities; yet there are few cities in which it can be proved conclusively that there was a body of Jewish citizens. As a rule, the individual Jews escape our notice: only general facts and large numbers have been recorded.

A little more is known about the Jews of the Lycus Valley through the extremely important inscriptions preserved at Hierapolis. Laodicea and Hierapolis, lying so near one another, in full view across the valley, must be taken as a closely connected pair, and all that is recorded about the Jews of Hierapolis may be taken as applying to those of Laodicea (apart from certain differences in the constitution of the two cities). The subject will therefore find a more suitable place in chapter 29.

In each city where a body of Jewish citizens was formed, it was necessary to frame a set of rules safeguarding their peculiar position and rights; for no rights could exist in a Greek city without formal enactment in a written law. This body of law is called in an inscription of Apameia in Phrygia "the Law of the Jews"; and the character of the reference shows beyond question that municipal regulations, and not the Mosaic Law, are meant under that name. Apameia, therefore must have contained a class of Jewish citizens; and its character and history have been investigated elsewhere. A similar law and name must have existed in the other cities where there was a body of Jewish citizens.

The Jews had come, or been brought, into Asia Minor during the time when Palestine was growing Hellenised in the warmth of Seleucid favour. In their new homes they were even more kindly treated, and all the conditions of their life were calculated to strengthen their good feeling to the kings, and foster the Hellenising tendency among them, at least in externals. They necessarily used the Greek language; they became accustomed to Greek surroundings; they learned to appreciate Greek science and education; and doubtless they did not think gymnastic exercises and sports such an abomination as the authors of First and Second Maccabees did.

But, as Professor E. Schurer and others have rightly observed, there is not the slightest reason to think that the Jews of Asia Minor ceased to be true to their religion and their nation in their own way: they really commanded a wider outlook over the world and a more sane and balanced judgment on truth and right than their brethren in Palestine. They looked to Jerusalem as their centre and the home of their religion. They contributed to maintain the Temple with unfailing regularity. They went on pilgrimage in great numbers, and the pilgrim ships sailed regularly every spring from the Aegean harbours for Caesaria. They were in patriotism as truly Jews as the straitest Pharisee in Jerusalem. Doubtless Paul was far from being the only Jew of Asia Minor who could boast that he was "a Pharisee sprung from Pharisees." Yet they were looked at with disfavour by their more strait-laced Palestinian brethren, and regarded as little better than backsliders and Sadducees. They had often, we may be sure, to assert their true Pharisaism and spirituality, like Paul, in answer to the reproach of being mere Sadducees with their Greek speech and Greek ways.

In truth, there was great danger lest they should forget the essence of their Hebrew faith. Many of them undoubtedly did so, though they still remained Jews in name and profession, and in contempt for the Gentiles, even while they learned from them and cheated them and made money by pandering to their superstitions. Many such Jews were, in very truth, only "a Synagogue of Satan" (as at Smyrna and Philadelphia), but still they continued to be "a Synagogue." The national feeling was sound, though the religious feeling was blunted and degraded.

In such surroundings was Saul of Tarsus brought up, a member of a family which moved both in the narrow and exclusive circle of rich Tarsian citizenship and in the still more proud and aristocratic circle of Roman citizenship. In his writings we see how familiar he was with the Graeco-Asiatic city life, and how readily illustrations from Greek games and Roman soldiers and triumphs suggest themselves to him. In him are brought to a focus all the experiences of the Jews of Asia Minor. He saw clearly from childhood that the Maccabean reaction had not saved Palestine, that the Pharisaic policy of excluding Gentile civilisation and manners had failed, and that the only possible salvation for his nation was to include the Gentiles by raising them to the Jewish level in morality and religion. Judaism, he saw, must either lose its vigour amid the sunshine of prosperity in Asia Minor, and gradually die, or it must conquer the Gentiles by assimilating them. The issue was, however, certain. The promise of God had been given and could not fail. This new prophet saw that the time of the Messiah and His conquest of the Gentiles had come.

And amid such surroundings the Jew that wrote the Apocalypse had lived for years. He had come much in contact both with the Hellenist Jews of the Diaspora and with the Christianised pagans in the Asian cities. He had been all the more influenced by those surroundings, because his whole outlook on the world had long ago been modified by the ardent spirit of St. Paul. He was still bound to Jewish models and literary forms in composing the Apocalypse; but sometimes the spirit and the thought which he expresses in those forms are essentially non-Judaic though their wider character is concealed from most of the commentators under the outward show of Judaism. His growing mind was on the point of bursting the last Jewish fetters that still contained it, the reverence for traditional Jewish literary forms; it had not yet done so, but in the composition of this book it was working towards full freedom.

Chapter 13: The Pagan Converts in the Early Church

In one respect Ignatius is peculiarly instructive for the study of the early Asian Churches, in which the converts direct from Paganism must have been a numerous and important body. This peculiar position and spirit of Pagan converts (coming direct from Paganism), as distinguished from Jews or those Pagans who had come into the Church through the door of the Jewish synagogue, must engage our attention frequently during the study of the Seven Letters; and Ignatius will prove the best introduction.

The Pagan converts had not the preliminary education in Jewish thoughts and religious ideas which a previous acquaintance with the service of the synagogue had given those Gentiles who had been among "the God-fearing" before they came over to Christianity. The direct passage from Paganism to Christianity must have left a different mark on their nature. Doubtless, some or even many of them came from a state of religious indifference or of vicious and degraded life. But others, and probably the majority of them, must have previously had religious sensibility and religious aspirations. Now what became of those early religious ideas during their later career as Christians? If they had previously entertained any religious aspirations and thoughts, these must have sought expression, and occasionally met with stimulus and found partial satisfaction in some forms of Pagan worship or speculation. Did these men, when they as Christians looked back on their Pagan life, regard those moments of religious experience as being merely evil and devilish; or did they see that such actions had been the groping and effort of nature towards God, giving increased strength and vitality to their longing after God, and that those moments had been really steps in their progress, incomplete but not entirely wrong?

To this inevitable question Ignatius helps us to find an answer, applicable to some cases, though not, of course, to all. That he had been a convert from Paganism is inferred with evident justification by Lightfoot from his letter to the Romans. He was born into the Church out of due time, imperfect in nature, by an irregular and violent birth, converted late, after a career which was to him a lasting cause of shame and humiliation in his new life. That feeling might be considered as partly a cause of the profound humility which he afterwards felt towards the long-established Ephesian Church. Hence he writes to the Romans: "I do not give orders to you as Peter and Paul did: they were Apostles, I am a convict; they were free, but I am a slave to this very hour." In the last expression we may see a reference, not to his having been literally a slave (as many do), but to his having been formerly enslaved to the passions and desires of Paganism; from this slavery he can hope to be set free completely only through death; death will give him liberty, and already even in the journey to Rome and the preparation to meet death, "I am learning to put away every desire."

The remarkable passage in Eph. sect. 9 must arrest every reader's attention: "Ye are all companions in the way, God-bearers, shrine-bearers, Christ-bearers, and bearers of your holy things, arrayed from head to foot in the commandments of Jesus Christ; and I, too, taking part in the festival, am permitted by letter to bear you company." The life of the Ephesian Christians is pictured after the analogy of a religious procession on the occasion of a festival; life for them is one long religious festival and procession. Now at this time it is impossible to suppose that public processions could have formed part of their worship. Imperial law and custom, popular feeling, and the settled rule of conduct in the Church, all alike forbade such public and provocative display of Christian worship. Moreover it is highly improbable that the Church had as yet come to the stage when such ceremonial was admitted as part of the established ritual: the ceremonies of the Church were still of a very simple and purely private character. It was only when the ceremonial could be performed in public that it grew in magnificence and outward show.

Yet the passage sets before the readers in the most vivid way the picture of such a festal scene, with a troop of rejoicing devotees clad in the appropriate garments, bearing their religious symbols and holy things in procession through the streets. That is exactly the scene which was presented to the eyes of all Ephesians several times every year at the great festivals of the goddess; and Ignatius had often seen such processions in his own city of Antioch. He cannot but have known what image his words would call up in the minds of his readers, and he cannot but have intended to call up that image, point by point, and detail after detail. The heathen devotees were dressed for the occasion, mostly in white garments, with garlands of the sacred foliage (whatever tree or plant the deity preferred), while many of the principal personages wore special dress of a still more sacred character, which marked them as playing for the time the part of the god and of his attendant divine beings, and some were adorned with the golden crown either of their deity or of the Imperial religion. But the Ephesian Christians wear the orders of Christ. The heathen devotees carried images of their gods, both the principal deities and many associated beings. The Christian Ephesians in their life carry God and carry Christ always with them, for, as Ignatius has said in the previous sentence, their conduct in the ordinary affairs of life spiritualised those affairs, inasmuch as they did everything in Christ. Many of the heathen devotees carried in their processions small shrines containing representations of their gods; but the body of every true right-living Christian is the temple and shrine of his God. The heathen carried in the procession many sacred objects, sometimes openly displayed, sometimes concealed in boxes (like the sacred mystic things which were brought from Eleusis to Athens by one procession in order that a few days later they might be carried back by the great mystic procession to Eleusis for the celebration of the Mysteries); and at Ephesus an inscription of the period contains a long enumeration of various objects and ornaments which were to be carried in one of the great annual processions. But the Christians carry holiness itself with them, wherever they go and whatever they do.

How utterly different is the spirit of this passage from the Jewish attitude towards the heathen world! Every analogy that Ignatius here draws would have been to the Jews an abomination, the forbidden and hateful thing. It would have been loathsome to them to compare the things of God with the things of idols or devils. Ignatius evidently had never passed through the phase of Judaism; he had passed straight from Paganism to Christianity. He very rarely quotes from the Old Testament, and when he does his quotations are almost exclusively from Psalms and Isaiah, the books which would be most frequently used by Christians.

Hence he places his new religion directly in relation with Paganism. Christianity spiritualises and enlarges and ennobles the ceremonial of the heathen; but that ceremonial was not simply rejected by him as abominable and vile, for it was a step in the way of religion.

The point of view is noble and true, and yet it proved to be the first step in the path that led on by insensible degrees, during the loss of education in the Church, to the paganising of religion and the transformation of the Pagan deities into saints of the Church, Demeter into St. Demetrius, Achilles Pontarches into St. Phocas of Sinope, Poseidon into St. Nicolas of Myra, and so on. From these words of Ignatius it is easy to draw the moral, which assuredly Ignatius did not dream of, that the Church should express religious feeling in similar processions; and, as thought and feeling deteriorated, the step was taken.

The same true and idealised spirit is perceptible in other parts of Ignatius' letters. In Eph. sect. 10 he says: "Pray continually for the rest of mankind (i.e. those who are not Christians, and specially the Pagans), for there is in them a hope of repentance. Give them the opportunity of learning from your actions, if they will not hear you." The influence of St. Paul's teaching is here conspicuous: by nature the Gentiles do the things of the Law, if they only give their real nature free play, and do not degrade it (Rom 2:16).

Ignatius felt strongly the duty he owed to his former co-religionists, as Paul felt himself "a debtor both to Greeks and to Barbarians"; and just as the term "debtor" implies that Paul had received and felt himself bound to repay, such indubitably must have been the thought in the mind of Igantius. Ignatius learned the lesson from Paul, because he was prepared to learn it. Many have read him and have not learned it.

In this view new light is thrown on a series of passages in the letters of Ignatius, some of which are obscure, and one at least has been so little understood that the true reading is by many editors rejected, though Lightfoot's sympathetic feeling for Ignatius keeps him right, as it usually does; and Zahn independently has decided in favour of the same text.

One of the most characteristic and significant features in the writings of Ignatius is the emphasis that he lays on silence, as something peculiarly sacred and Divine. He recurs to this thought repeatedly. Silence is characteristic of God, speech of mankind. The more the bishop is silent, the more he is to be feared (Eph. sect. 6). The acts which Christ has done in silence are worthy of the Father; and he that truly possesses the Word of Christ is able even to hear His silence, so as to be perfect, so that through what he says he may be doing, and through his silence he may be understood (Eph. sect. 15). And so again he is astonished at the moderation of the Philadelphian bishop, whose silence is more effective than the speech of others.

So far the passages quoted, though noteworthy, do not imply anything more than a vivid appreciation of the value of reserve, so that speech should convey the impression of a latent and still unused store of strength. But the following passages do more; they show that a certain mystic and Divine nature and value were attributed by Ignatius to Silence; and in the light of those two passages, the words quoted above from Eph. sect. 15 are seen to have also a mystic value.

In Eph. sect. 19 he speaks of the three great Christian mysteries--the virginity of Mary, the birth of her Son, and the death of the Lord, "three mysteries shouting aloud (in the world of men), which were wrought in the Silence of God." In Magn. sect. 8 he speaks of God as having manifested Himself through His Son, who is His Word that proceeded from Silence.

Now, we must ask what was the origin of this mystic power that Ignatius assigns to Silence. Personally, I cannot doubt that his mind and thought were influenced by his recollection of the deep impression that certain Pagan Mysteries had formerly made on him.

It is mentioned in the Philosophumena, lib. v., that "the great and wonderful and most perfect mystery, placed before those who were [at Eleusis] initiated into the second and higher order, was a shoot of corn harvested in silence." In this brief description a striking scene is set before us: the hushed expectation of the initiated, the contrast with the louder and more crowded and dramatic scenes of the previous Mystic acts, as in absolute silence the Divine life works itself out to an end in the growing ear of corn, which is reaped before them. There can be no doubt, amid all the obscurity which envelopes the Eleusinian ceremonial, that great part of the effect which they produced on the educated and thoughtful, the intellectual and philosophic minds, lay in the skilful, dramatically presented contrast between the earlier naturalistic life, set before them in scenes of violence and repulsive horror, and the later reconciliation of the jarring elements in the peaceful Divine life, as revealed for the benefit of men by the Divine power, and shown on the mystic stage as perfected in profound silence. Think of the hierophant, a little before, shouting aloud, "a holy son Brimos the Lady Brimo has borne," as the culmination of a series of outrages and barbarities: then imagine the dead stillness, and the Divine life symbolised to the imagination of the sympathetic and responsive mystai in the growing and garnered ear of the Divinely revealed corn which dies only to live again, which is destroyed only to be useful.

The scene which we have described is mentioned only as forming part of the Eleusinian Mysteries; and it may be regarded as quite probable that Ignatius had been initiated at Eleusis. Initiation at Eleusis (which had in earlier times been confined to the Athenian people) was widened in later times so that all "Hellenes," i.e. all persons whose language and education and spirit were Greek, were admitted. Thus, for example, Apollonius of Tyana, who had been rejected in A.D. 51 on the ground, not that he was a foreigner, but that he was suspected of magic, was admitted to initiation in A.D. 55. But it is also true that (as is pointed out in Dr. Hastings' Dictionary of the Bible, v., p. 126) "the Mysteries celebrated at different religious centres competed with one another in attractiveness," and they all borrowed from one another and "adapted to their own purposes elements which seemed to be attractive in others." Hence it may be that Ignatius had witnessed that same scene, or a similar one, in other Mysteries.

That the highest and most truly Divine nature is silent must have been the lesson of the Eleusinian Mysteries, just as surely as they taught--not by any formal dogmatic teaching (for the words uttered in the representation of the Divine drama before the initiated were concerned only with the dramatic action), but through the impression produced on those who comprehended the meaning of the drama, and (as the ancients say) it required a philosophic spirit and a reverent religious frame of mind to comprehend--that the life of man is immortal. Both those lessons were to Ignatius stages in the development of his religious consciousness; and the way in which, and the surroundings amid which, he had learned them affected his conception and declaration of the principles, the Mysteries of Christianity. Marcellus of Ancyra, about the middle of the fourth century, was influenced probably in the same way, when he declared that God was along with quietness and that, as early heretics had taught, in the beginning there was God and Silence.

The importance of Silence in the mystic ritual is fully appreciated by Dr. Dieterich in his valuable and fascinating book, Eine Mithrasliturgie (Leipzig, 1903) p. 42. Among the preparatory instructions given to the Mystes was this: "Lay thy right finger on thy mouth and say, Silence! Silence! Silence! symbol of the living imperishable God!" Silence is even addressed in prayer, "Guard me, Silence." Dr. Dieterich remarks that the capital S is needed in such an invocation.

Lightfoot considers (see his note on Trall. sect. 2) that when Ignatius speaks of the mysteries of Christianity, he has no more in his mind than "the wide sense in which the word is used by St. Paul, revealed truths." But we cannot agree in this too narrow estimate. To Ignatius there lies in the term a certain element of power. To him the "mysteries" of the Faith would have been very insufficiently described by such a coldly scientific definition as "revealed truths": such abstract lifeless terms were to him, as in Colossians 2:8, mere "philosophy and vain deceit." The "mysteries" were living, powerful realities, things of life that could move the heart and will of men and remake their nature. He uses the term, I venture to think, in a similar yet slightly different sense from Paul, who employs it very frequently. Paul, too, attaches to it something of the same idea of power; for "the mystery of iniquity" (2 Thess 2:7) is to him a real and strong enemy. But Ignatius seems to attach to the "mysteries" even more reality and objectivity than Paul does.

Surely Ignatius derived his idea of the "mysteries" partly at least from the experiences of his Pagan days. He had felt the strong influence of the grater Mysteries, to which some of the greatest thinkers among the Greeks bear testimony; and the Christian principles completed and perfected the ideas which had begun in his Pagan days.

This idea, that the religious conceptions of Paganism served as a preparatory stage leading up to Christianity, was held by many, as well as by Ignatius. Justin Martyr gave clear expression to it, and Eusebius works it out in his Praeparatio Evangelica. Those who were conscious that a real development of the religious sense had begun in their own mind during their Pagan days and experiences, and had been completed in their Christian life, must inevitably have held it; and there were many Pagans of a deeply religious nature, some of whom became Christians.

The change of spirit involved in this development through Paganism to Christianity is well expressed by a modern poet:--

Girt in the panther-fells,
Violets in my hair,
Down I ran through the woody dells,
Through the morning wild and fair,--
To sit by the road till the sun was high,
That I might see some god pass by.
>Fluting amid the thyme
I dreamed through the golden day,
Calling through melody and rhyme:
"Iacchus! Come this way,--
From harrowing Hades like a king,
Vine leaves and glories scattering."
Twilight was all rose-red,
When, crowned with vine and thorn,
Came a stranger god from out the dead;
And his hands and feet were torn.
I knew him not, for he came alone:
I knew him not, whom I fain had known.
He said: "For love, for love,
I wear the vine and thorn."
He said: "For love, for love,
My hands and feet were torn:
For love, the winepress Death I trod."
And I cried in pain: "O Lord my God."
Mrs. Rachel Annand Taylor, Poems, 1904

That the same view should be strongly held in the Asian Churches was inevitable. That often it should be pressed to an extreme was equally inevitable; and one of its extreme forms was the Nicolaitan heresy, which the writer of the Seven Letters seems to have regarded as the most pressing and immediate danger to those Churches. That writer was a Jew, who was absolutely devoid of sympathy for that whole side of thought, alike in its moderate and its extreme forms. The moderate forms seemed to him lukewarm; the extreme forms were a simple abomination.

Such was the view of one school or class in the Christian Church. The opposite view, that the Pagan Mysteries were a mere abomination, is represented much more strongly in the Christian literature. There is not necessarily any contradiction between them. Ignatius felt, as we have said, that his Pagan life was a cause of lasting humiliation and shame to him, even though he was fully conscious that his religious sensibility had been developing through it. We need not doubt that he would have endorsed and approved every word of the charges which the Christian apologists made against the Mysteries. Both views are true, but both are partial: neither gives a complete statement of the case.

The mystic meaning that lay in even the grossest ceremonies of the Eleusinian and other Mysteries has been rightly insisted upon by Miss J. E. Harrison in her Prolegomena to the Study of Greek Religion (especially chapter 8), a work well worthy of being studied. Miss Harrison has the philosophic insight which the ancients declare to be necessary in order to understand and learn from the Mysteries. Their evil side is to her non-existent, and the old Christian writers who inveighed against the gross and hideous rites enacted in the Mysteries are repeatedly denounced by her in scathing terms as full of unclean imaginings--though she fully admits, of course, the truth of the facts which they allude to or describe in detail. The authoress, standing on the lofty place of philosophic idealism, can see only the mystic meaning, while she is too far removed above the ugliness to be cognisant of it. But to shut one's eyes to the evil does not annihilate it for the world, though it may annihilate it for the few who shut their eyes. Plato in the Second Book of the Republic is as emphatic as Firmicus or Clemens in recognising the harm that those ugly tales and acts of the gods did to the mass of the people. This must all be borne in mind while studying her brilliant work.

Chapter 14: The Seven Churches of Asia

What thou seest, write in a book, and send to the Seven Churches;
unto Ephesus, and unto Smyrna, and unto Pergamum, and unto Thyatira,
and unto Sardis, and unto Philadelphia, and unto Laodicea.

Some manuscripts read in this passage "the Seven Churches which are in Asia"; but the added words are certainly an interpolation from the introduction, verse 4, "John to the Seven Churches which are in Asia." The addition states correctly the limits of the area from which the Seven Churches were selected; but it loses the emphasis implied in the simple phrase "The Seven Churches." From the context it is clear that they all belonged to Asia, i.e., to the Roman province called by that name; but here, in the very beginning of John's vision, the Seven are mentioned as a recognised number, already to the hearer and the readers.

This remarkable expression, "The Seven Churches," must arrest the attention of every reader. At the first glance one might gather that only those Seven Churches existed in the Province Asia, and that the Revelation had been composed at an early date when there were no more Churches than the Seven. But that is impossible. There never was a time when those Seven Churches existed, and no others. Their situation shows that they could not well be the first seven to be founded: several other unnamed Churches certainly must have been formed before Thyatira and Philadelphia. Moreover, references in the New Testament prove beyond question the existence of various other Churches in the Province before the earliest date at which the composition of the Apocalypse of John has ever been placed. A survey of the chief facts regarding those other Churches will prove instructive for the present investigation.

(1.) Already during the residence of St. Paul in Ephesus, A.D. 54 to 56, "all they which dwelt in Asia heard the word" (Acts 19:10). That would never have been recorded, except as an explanation of the rapid spread of the new religion and the growth of numerous Churches.

(2.) Already in A.D. 61 the Church of Colossae was the recipient of a letter from St. Paul; he asks the Colossians to cause that his letter be read in the Church of the Laodiceans, and that "ye also read the letter from Laodicea" (Col 4:16); and he mentions a body of Christians, who must have constituted a Church, at Hierapolis (Col 4:13). In this case it is evident that the three Churches of the Lycus Valley were considered by every one to stand in close relation to one another. They are very near, Hierapolis being about six miles north, and Colossae eleven miles east, from Laodicea, and they are grouped together as standing equal in the affection and zeal of the Colossian Epaphras. Any letter addressed to one of them was regarded apparently by St. Paul as common to the other two. This did not require to be formally stated about Laodicea and Hierapolis, which are in full view of one another on opposite sides of the glen; but Colossae lay in the higher glen of the Lycus. It has been suggested that Hierapolis and Colossae perhaps ceased to be Churches, because those cities may have been destroyed by an earthquake between A.D. 61 and 90. Such a supposition cannot be entertained. There is not the slightest reason to think that those cities were annihilated about that time. On the contrary Hierapolis continued to grow steadily in wealth and importance after this hypothetical destruction; and, if Colossae rather dwindled than increased, the reason lay in its being more and more overshadowed by Laodicea. The earthquakes of Asia Minor have not been of such a serious nature, and seem rarely if ever to have caused more than a passing loss and inconvenience. There was nothing in such an event likely either to kill or to frighten away the Christians of those two Churches.

(3.) Troas was the seat of a Church in A.D. 56 (2 Cor 2:12) and A.D. 57 (Acts 20:7ff). It was then considered by St. Paul to be "a door," through which access was opened to a wide region that lay behind in the inner country: its situation in respect of roads and communication made it a specially suitable and tempting point of departure for evangelisation; it was a link in the great chain of Imperial postal communication across the Empire; and its importance lay in its relation to the other cities with which it was connected by a series of converging roads. The ordinary "overland" route from Rome to the East by the Appian and the Egnatian Way crossed the Aegean from Neapolis, the harbour of Philippi, to Troas, Pergamum, etc.; and there must have been continual communication, summer and winter alike, between Neapolis and Troas. Places in such a situation, where a change was made from land-travel to sea-faring, offered a peculiarly favourable opportunity for intercourse and the spread of a new system of thought and life. Troas, therefore, undoubtedly played a very important part in the development of the Asian Church; yet it is not mentioned among the Seven.

(4.) It may also be regarded as practically certain that the great cities which lay on the important roads connecting those Seven leading Cities with one another had all "heard the word," and that most of them were the seats of Churches, when the Seven Letters were written. We remember that, not long afterwards, Magnesia and Tralleis, the two important, wealthy and populous cities on the road between Ephesus and Laodicea, possessed Churches of their own and bishops; that they both sent deputations to salute, console and congratulate the Syrian martyr Ignatius, when he was conducted like a condemned criminal to face death in Rome; and that they both received letters from him. With these facts in our mind we need feel no doubt that those two Churches, and many others like them, took their origin from the preaching of St. Paul's coadjutors and subordinates during his residence in Ephesus, A.D. 54-56. Magnesia inscribed on its coins the title "Seventh (city) of Asia," referring doubtless to the order of precedence among the cities as observed in the Common Council of the Province, technically styled Commune Asiae. This seems to prove that there was some special importance attached in general estimation to a group of seven representative cities in Asia, which would be an interesting coincidence with the Seven Churches. Of the seven cities implied in the Magnesian title five may be enumerated with practical certainty, viz., the three rivals "First of Asia," Smyrna, Ephesus and Pergamum, along with Sardis and Cyzicus. The remaining two seats were doubtless keenly contested between Magnesia, Tralleis (one of the richest and greatest in Asia), Alabanda (chief perhaps in Caria), Apamea (ranked by Strabo next to Ephesus as a commercial centre of the Province) and Laodicea; but apparently at some time under the Empire a decision by the Emperor, or by a governor of the Province, or by the Council of Asia, settled the precedence to some extent and placed Magnesia seventh. Neither Thyatira nor Philadelphia, however, can have had any reasonable claim to a place among those seven leading cities of the Province.

(5.) Another city which can hardly have failed to possess an important Church when the Seven Letters were written is Cyzicus. Not merely was it one of the greatest cities of the Province (as has been mentioned in the preceding paragraph): it also lay on one of the great routes by which Christianity spread. It has been pointed out elsewhere that the early Christianisation of Bithynia and Pontus was not due (as has been commonly assumed) to missionaries travelling by land from Syria across Asia Minor to the Black Sea coasts. Those cross-country routes from south to north were little used at that period; and it was only during the last quarter of the first century that Cappadocia, which they traversed, began to be properly organised as a Province; for before A.D. 74 Cappadocia was merely a procuratorial district, i.e., it was governed in the interest of the Emperor as successor of the old native kings by his procurator, who administered it on the old native lines. Moreover, it is stated that inner Pontus was hardly affected by Christianity until the Third century, while Pontus on the coast was Christianised in the first century and the pagan ritual had almost fallen into disuse there by A.D. 112, as Pliny reported to Trajan. Those maritime regions therefore must have been Christianised by sea, in other words by passengers on ships coming from "the parts of Asia" or from Rome itself. On the route of such ships lay Cyzicus, one of the greatest commercial cities of Asia Minor, which must have attracted a certain proportion of the merchants and passengers on those ships. It was along the great routes of international communication that Christianity spread first; and Cyzicus can hardly have been missed as the new thought swept along this main current of intercourse. But Cyzicus has no place among the Seven Churches, though it was the leading city and capital of a great district in the north of the Province.

It is therefore evident that those Seven must have been selected out of a much larger number of Churches, some of them very important centres of thought and influence, for some reason which needs investigation. Now it is inconceivable that St. John should simply write to Seven Churches taken at random out of the Province which had been so long under his charge, and ignore the rest. One can understand why St. Paul wrote (so far as his letters have been preserved) to some of his Churches and not to others: apart from the fact that he doubtless sent more letters than have been preserved, he wrote sporadically, under the spur of urgent need, as a crisis occurred now in one of his Churches, now in another. But St. John is here writing a series of letters on a uniform plan, under the spur of one single impulse; and it is clearly intended that the Seven Churches should be understood as in a way summing up the whole Province. That could only be the case if each was in some way representative of a small group of Churches, so that the whole Seven taken together represented and summed up the entire Province. Similarly, it is clear that the Church of Asia taken as a whole is in its turn representative of the entire Catholic Church.

Thus we can trace the outline of a complicated and elaborate system of symbolism, which is very characteristic of this book. There are seven groups of Churches in Asia: each group is represented by one outstanding and conspicuous member: these representatives are the Seven Churches. These Seven representative Churches stand for the Church of the Province; and the Church of the Province, in its turn, stands for the entire Church of Christ. Corresponding to this sevenfold division in the Church, the outward appearance and envisagement of the Divine Author of the Seven Letters is divided into seven groups of attributes; and one group of attributes is assumed by Him in addressing each of the Seven Churches, so that the openings of the Seven Letters, put together, make up his whole outward and visible character.

But how was this selection of the Seven Churches accomplished? There are only two alternatives; either the selection was made on this occasion for the first time, or it had in some way or other come into existence previously, so that there were already Seven recognised and outstanding Churches of Asia. The first alternative seems generally to have been accepted, but apparently without any serious consideration. It seems to have been thought that the sacred number, Seven, had a fascination for one who was so much under the dominion of symbolism as the writer of the Apocalypse evidently was. On this view, being presumably fascinated by the charm of that number, he chose those Seven from the whole body of the Asian Churches, and treated them as representative in the first place of the Province and ultimately of the entire Catholic church. But it is impossible to acquiesce contentedly in this supposition. There is no way of escaping the obvious implication in 1:4 and 1:11, that those Seven were already known to the world and established in popular estimation as "the Seven Asian Churches," before the Vision came to St. John.

It is therefore necessary to adopt the second alternative. As the Church of the great Province Asia gradually consolidated and completed its organisation, there came into existence seven groups, and at the head or the centre of each stood one of the Seven Churches. This process had been completed up to this point before St. John wrote, and affected the imagery of his vision.

The genesis of one of those groups can be traced at the very beginning of the Christian history of the Province. Already in A.D. 61 the letter to Laodicea and the letter to Colossae were, as has been indicated above, treated as common to a group of three Churches in the Lycus Valley. But, although the Colossian letter was intended to be circulated, it was written to the Church of Colossae immediately and directly. In writing that letter St. Paul had not in mind the group of Churches: there stood before his imagination the Church of Colossae, and to it he addressed himself. In the primary intention it is a letter to Colossae; in a secondary intention it was made common to the whole group. The same may be presumed to have been the character of the unknown Laodicean letter.

The opinion has been advocated by some scholars that the Laodicean letter was the one which is commonly known as the Epistle to the Ephesians, and that it ought to be regarded as a circular letter, copies of which were sent to all the Asian Churches; though in that cast it might be expected that the Colossians would receive a copy direct. But Professor Rendel Harris has thrown serious doubt on the view that Ephesians was a circular letter, by his very ingenious argument that it must have been written as an answer to a question (see Expositor, 1898, Dec., p. 401ff): in that case it would be addressed to the Church which had proposed the question to St. Paul.

In the facts just stated it seems to be implied that the chief Churches of the Lycus Valley were already in A.D. 61 regarded as practically common recipients of a letter addressed to one. Their interests and needs were known to one another, and were presumed to be very similar; they were in constant intercourse with one another, and especially Laodicea and Hierapolis were not far removed from being really a single city; and evidently it was the aim and policy of St. Paul to encourage them to bear vividly in mind their common character and sisterhood.

Now, starting from this situation in A.D. 61, and taking into consideration the creative and constructive capacity which the Christian Church showed from the beginning, we must infer that the consolidation of the three Churches into a recognised group had been completed before the Seven Letters were written. In a vigorous and rapidly growing body like the Church of the Province Asia, a fact was not likely to lie for a long time inactive, and then at last begin actively to affect the growth of the whole organism. Rather we must conceive the stages in the Christian history of the Lycus Valley as being three: first, the natural union and frequent intercommunication of three separately founded, independent and equal Churches, as appears in A.D. 61; secondly, the equally natural growing pre-eminence before the eyes of the world of the leading city, Laodicea, so that letters which were addressed to one city were still intended equally for all, but Laodicea was the one that was almost inevitably selected as the representative and outstanding Church; thirdly, the predominance and presidency of Laodicea as the administrative head and centre amid a group of subordinate Churches.

How far this development had proceeded when the Seven Letters were written it is hardly possible to say with certainty. We can, however, feel very confident that the third stage had not yet been completely attained. The Seven Letters afford no evidence on this point, except that, by their silence about any other Churches, they suggest that Laodicea was already felt to stand for and therefore to be in a way pre-eminent in its group; while, on the other hand, the spirit of the early Church seems to be inconsistent with the view that Laodicea had as yet acquired anything like headship or superiority. But the whole question as to the growth of a fixed hierarchy and order of dignity among the Churches is obscure, and needs systematic investigation.

The case of the Lycus Valley Churches must be regarded as typical. It was the result of circumstances common to the entire Province. Hence, the inference must be drawn that a series of similar groups was formed throughout Asia; that the Seven Churches stood forth as in a certain degree pre-eminent, though certainly not predominant, in their respective groups; and that thus each in the estimation of the Asian world carried with it the thought of the whole group of which it formed a centre.

The subject, however, is not yet complete. The character of that first group in the Lycus Valley would suggest that the groups were territorial, marked off by geographical limits. But a glance at the rest of the Seven shows that this is not the case: there is here evidently nothing like a division of Asia into geographical groups: the Seven Churches are a circle of cities round the west-central district of the Province, while south, east, and north are entirely unrepresented.

Again, the classification is not made according to rank or dignity or importance in the Province. It is true that the first three, Ephesus, Smyrna and Pergamum, are the greatest and outstanding cities of the Province, which vied with one another for the title, which all claimed and used and boasted about, "First of Asia": there were three cities "First of Asia," just as there were two First of Cilicia and two First of Bithynia; and Acts 16:11 shows that Philippi claimed to be "First of that division of Macedonia," refusing to acknowledge Amphipolis, the official capital, as superior to itself. This might suggest that they, as the three greatest and most important cities of the Province, were selected as centres of three groups of Churches. Also it is true that among the remaining four, two, viz., Sardis and Laodicea, were, like the first three, the heads of conventus (i.e., governmental districts for legal purposes). But this principle breaks down completely in the case of Thyatira and Philadelphia, which were secondary and second-rate cities, the latter in the conventus of Sardis, the former in that of Pergamum. The Seven Churches, therefore, were not selected because they were planted in the most important and influential cities--had that been the case, Cyzicus, Alabanda, and Apameia could hardly have been omitted--nor is the order of enumeration, beginning with Ephesus, Smyrna, and Pergamum, due to the fact that those were the three most important cities of Asia.

In order to complete this investigation, we must try to reach some clearer conception of the almost wholly unknown process by which the Church of the Province Asia gradually worked out its internal organisation during the first century. At the beginning of that process all those Churches of Asia, apparently, stood side by side, equal in standing, fully equipped with self-governing authority, except in so far as they looked up to St. Paul as their founder (either immediately or through his subordinate ministers) and parent, director and counsellor: their relation to one another was in some degree analogous to a voluntary union of States in a federal republic. Before the end of the century, the Province was divided into districts with representative cities, and Asia was advancing along a path that led to the institution of a regularly organised hierarchy with one supreme head of the Province.

Now let us try to imagine the situation in which this process occurred. The purpose which was being worked out in the process was--unity. The Christian Church was bent on consolidating itself in its struggle for the spiritual lordship of the Empire. The means whereby it attained that purpose, as has been shown in chapter 3, lay in constant intercommunication, partly by travel, but still more by letter. The result which was brought about could not fail to stand in close relation to the means by which it had been worked out. And a glance at the map shows that there was some relation here between the means and the result. Travelling and communication, of course, are inextricably involved in the road system: they are carried out, not along the shortest lines between the various points, but according to the roads that connect them. And all the Seven Cities stand on the great circular road that bound together the most populous, wealthy, and influential part of the Province, the west-central region.

It is only fair to observe that that great scholar, the late Dr. Hort, pointed the way to the true principle of selection in an excursus to his fragmentary, posthumously published edition of First Peter. In that excursus, which is a model of scientific method in investigation, he points out that the reason for the peculiar order in which the Provinces are enumerated at the beginning of the Epistle lies in the route along which the messenger was to travel, as he conveyed the letter (perhaps in so many distinct copies) to the central cities of the various Provinces. We now find ourselves led to a similar conclusion in the case of Asia: the gradual selection of Seven representative Churches in the Province was in some way connected with the principal road-circuit of the Province.

So far the result which we have reached is unavoidable and undeniable: it merely states the evident fact. But, if we seek to penetrate farther, and to trace the process of development and consolidation more minutely, it is necessary to enter upon a process of imaginative reconstruction. We have given to us as the factors in this problem, the state of the Asian Church about A.D. 60, and again its state about A.D. 90: we know that the process whereby the one was transformed into the other within those thirty years took place along that road circuit, and was connected with correspondence and intercourse. The details have to be restored; and as this necessarily involves an element of hypothesis, it ought to be treated in a special chapter.

Chapter 15: Origin of the Seven Representative Cities

The analogous case, quoted from Dr. Hort in the conclusion of the preceding chapter, must not be pressed too closely or it might prove misleading. The fact from which we have to start is that the First Epistle of Peter enumerates the Provinces in the order in which a messenger sent from Rome would traverse them, and that, similarly, the Seven Churches are enumerated in the order in which a messenger sent from Patmos would reach them.

In the former case the letter was written in Rome, and the messenger would, in accordance with the regular customs of communication over the Empire, sail to the Black Sea, and land at one of the harbours on the north coast of Asia Minor. He might either disembark in the nearest Province, and make his way by land round the whole circuit, ending in the most distant; or he might choose a vessel bound for the most distant Province and make the circuit in the reverse order. There are some apparent advantages in the latter method, which he adopted. He landed at one of the Pontic harbours, Amastris or Sinope or Amisos, traversed in succession Pontus, Cappadocia, Galatia and Asia, and ended in Bithynia, at one of whose great harbours he would find frequent opportunity of sailing to Rome, or, if he were detained till navigation had ceased during the winter season, the overland Post Road, through Thrace and Macedonia, would be conveniently open to him. Such a messenger would visit in succession one or more of the leading cities of each Province, because the great Imperial routes of communication ran direct between the great cities. He would not concern himself with distributing the letter to the individual Christians in each Province; that task would be left to the local Church, which would use its own organisation to bring the knowledge of the message home to every small Church and every individual. His work would be supplemented by secondary messengers on smaller circuits in each Province and again in each city. In no other way was effective and general distribution possible.

In the latter case the letter enclosing the Apocalypse with the Seven Letters was written in Patmos, and the messenger would naturally land at Ephesus, and make his round through the Seven representative Churches as they are enumerated by the writer. The route was clearly marked out, and the messenger could hardly avoid it. He would go north along the great road through Smyrna to Pergamum (the earliest Roman road built in the Province about 133-130 B.C., as soon as Asia was organised). Thence he would follow the imperial Post Road to Thyatira, Sardis, Philadelphia and Laodicea, and so back to Ephesus, or on to the East, as duty called him, using in either case the great Central Route of the Empire. At each point, like the other messenger, he would trust to the local organisation to complete the work of divulgation.

In those two circuits--the general Anatolian circuit of First Peter, and the special Asian circuit of the Apocalypse--it is obvious that the messengers were not merely ordered to take the letter (whether in one or in several copies) and deliver it, using the freedom of their own will as to the way and order of delivery. The route was marked out for them beforehand, and was already known to the writers when composing the letters. The question then arises whether the route in those two cases was chosen expressly for the special occasion and enjoined by the writer on the messenger, or was already a recognised circuit which messengers were expected to follow in every similar case. Without going into minute detail, it may be admitted that the route indicated in First Peter might possibly have been expressly selected for that special journey by the writer, who knew or asked what was the best route; and thus it came to be stated by him in the letter. Equally possibly it might be known to the writer as the already recognised route for the Christian messengers.

But the former supposition could not be applied in the case of the Apocalypse; it is utterly inconsistent with the results established in chapter 6, since it would leave unexplained the fundamental fact in the case, viz., that the writer uses the expression "the Seven Churches" in 1:4, 11, as recognised and familiar, established in common usage, and generally understood as summing up the whole Christian Province. Moreover, the messenger in First Peter was starting on a journey to deliver a real letter; but in the Apocalypse the letter-form is assumed merely as a literary device, and the book as a whole, and the Seven Letters as part of it, are literary compositions not really intended to be despatched like true letters to the Churches to which they are addressed. The list of the Seven Churches is taken over, like the rest of the machinery of epistolary communication, as part of the circumstances to which this literary imitation has to accommodate itself.

Moreover those who properly weigh the indisputable facts stated in chapter 6 about the growth of the Laodicean district, as an example of the steady, rapid development of early Christian organisation, must come to the conclusion that the writer of the Letters cannot have been the first to make Laodicea the representative of a group of Churches, but found it already so regarded by general consent. Now what is true of Laodicea must be applied to the rest of the Seven Churches.

In short, if there were not such a general agreement as to the representative character of the Seven Churches, it is difficult to see how the writer could so entirely ignore the other Churches, and write to the Seven without a word of explanation that the letters were to be considered as referring also to the others. St. Paul, who wrote before that general agreement had been effected, carefully explained that his letter to Colossae was intended to be read also at Laodicea, and vice versa; but St. John assumes that no such explanation is needed.

Another important point to observe is that the Seven Cities were not selected simply because they were situated on the circular route above described, nor yet because they were the most important cities on that route. The messenger must necessarily pass through Hierapolis, Tralleis and Magnesia on his circular journey; all those cities were indubitably the seats of Churches at that time; yet none of the three found a place among the representative cities, although Tralleis and Magnesia were more important and wealthy than Philadelphia or Thyatira. What then was the principle of selection?

In chapter 3 we saw that the Christian Church owed its growth and its consolidation under the early Empire to its carefulness in maintaining frequent correspondence between the scattered congregations, thus preventing isolation, making uniformity of character and aims possible, and providing (so to say) the channels through which coursed the life-blood of the whole organism; and the conclusion was reached that, since no postal service was maintained by the State for the use of private individuals or trading companies, "we find ourselves obliged to admit the existence of a large organisation" for the transmission of the letters by safe, Christian hands. Just as all the great trading companies maintained each its own corps of letter-carriers (tabellarii), so the Christians must necessarily provide means for carrying their own letters, if they wanted to write; and this necessity must inevitably result, owing to the constructive spirit of that rapidly growing body, in the formation of a letter-carrying system. The routes of the letter-carriers were fixed according to the most convenient circuits, and the provincial messengers did not visit all the cities, but only certain centres, from whence a subordinate service distributed the letters or news over the several connected circuits or groups.

Thus there emerges from the obscurity of the first century, and stands out clear before our view about A.D. 80, some kind of organisation for connecting and consolidating the numerous Churches of the Province Asia. The Province had already by that date been long and deeply affected by the new religion; and it must be presumed that there existed a congregation and a local Church in almost every great city, at least in the parts most readily accessible from the west coast.

Such is the bare outline of a kind of private messenger-service for the Province, similar in many ways, doubtless, to the private postal systems which must have been maintained by every great trading corporation whose operations extended over the same parts (the wealthiest and most educated and "Hellenised" parts) of the Province. The general character of this messenger service, in so far as it was uniform over the whole Roman Empire, has been described in chapter 3. A more detailed view of the special system of the Province Asia may now be gained from a closer study of the character and origin of the Seven Churches.

When letters or information were sent round the Churches of the Province, either the same messenger must have gone round the whole Province, and visited every Church, or several messengers must have been employed simultaneously. The former method is obviously too inconvenient and slow: the single messenger would require often to go and return over part of the same road, and the difference of time in the receiving of the news by the earlier and the later Churches would have been so great, that the advantages of intercommunication would have been to a great degree lost. Accordingly, it must be concluded that several messengers were simultaneously employed to carry any news intended for general information in the Province of Asia.

Again, either those several messengers must all have started from the capital and centre of communication, viz., Ephesus, or else one must have started from the capital, and others must have started on secondary routes, receiving the message from the primary messenger at various points on his route. The former of these alternatives is evidently too cumbrous, as it would make several messengers travel simultaneously along the same road bearing the same message. It is therefore necessary to admit a distinction between primary and secondary circuits, the former starting from Ephesus, the latter from various points on the primary circuit.

Now, if we combine this conclusion with our previously established results, the hypothesis inevitably suggests itself that the Seven groups of Churches, into which the Province had been divided before the Apocalypse was composed, were seven postal districts, each having as its centre or point of origin one of the Seven Cities, which (as was pointed out) lie on a route which forms a sort of inner circle round the Province.

Closer examination of the facts will confirm this hypothesis so strongly as to raise it to a very high level of probability: in fact, the hypothesis is simply a brief statement of the obvious facts of communication, and our closer examination will be merely a more minute and elaborate statement of the facts.

The Seven Cities, as has been already stated, were situated on a very important circular route, which starts from Ephesus, goes round what may be called Asia par excellence, the most educated and wealthy and historically pre-eminent part of the Province. They were the best points on that circuit to serve as centres of communication with seven districts: Pergamum for the north (Troas, doubtless Adramyttium, and probably Cyzicus and other cities on the coast contained Churches); Thyatira for an inland district on the northeast and east; Sardis for the wide middle valley of the Hermus; Philadelphia for Upper Lydia, to which it was the door (3:8); Laodicea for the Lycus Valley, and for Central Phrygia, of which it was the Christian metropolis in later time; Ephesus for the Cayster and Lower Meander Valleys and coasts; Smyrna for the Lower Hermus Valley and the North Ionian coasts, perhaps with Mitylene and Chios (if those islands had as yet been affected).

In this scheme of secondary districts it is evident that some are very much larger than others. The whole of Western and Central Caria must be included in the Ephesian district. The Northeastern part of Caria would more naturally fall in the Laodicean district, to which also a vast region of Phrygia should belong, leaving to the Philadelphian district another large region, Northern and West-central Phrygia with a considerable part of Eastern Lydia. But it is possible, and even probable, that Ephesus was the centre from which more than one secondary circuit went off: it is not necessary to suppose that only one secondary messenger started from such a city. So also with Laodicea and possibly with Philadelphia and Smyrna and others. An organisation of this kind, while familiar to all in its results, would never be described by any one in literature, just as no writer gives an account of the Imperial Post-service; and hence no account is preserved of either. While the existence of a primary circuit, and a number of secondary circuits going off from the Seven Cities of the primary circuit, seems certain, the number and arrangement of the secondary circuits is conjectural and uncertain.

The whole of the arrangements would have to be made to suit the means of communication that existed in the Province Asia, the roads and the facilities for travel, on which chapter 3 may be consulted. It lies apart from our purpose to work it out in detail; but the system which seems most probable is indicated on the accompanying sketch-map, and those who investigate it minutely will doubtless come to the conclusion that some of the circuits indicated are fairly certain, but most can only be regarded as, at the best, reasonably probable, and some will probably be found to be wrong when a more thorough knowledge of the Asian road-system (which is the only evidence accessible) has been attained. It will, however, be useful to discuss some conspicuous difficulties, which are likely to suggest themselves to every investigator.

The first is about Troas. Considering its importance as the doorway of Northwestern Asia, one might at first expect to find that it was one of the Seven representative Churches. But a glance at the map will show that it could not be worked into the primary circuit of the provincial messenger, except by sacrificing the ease and immensely widening the area and lengthening the time of his journey. On the other hand Troas comes in naturally on that secondary circuit which has Pergamum as its origin. The Pergamenian messenger followed the Imperial Post road through Adramyttium, Assos and Troas, along the Hellespont to Lampsacus. There the Post Road crossed into Europe, while the messenger traversed the coast road to Cyzicus, and thence turned south through Poimanenon to Pergamum. This circuit is perhaps the most obvious and convincing of the whole series, as the account of the roads and towns on it in the Historical Geography of Asia Minor will bring out clearly.

The second difficulty relates to Tralleis and Magnesia. As the primary messenger had to pass through them, why are they relegated to the secondary circuit of Ephesus? Obviously, the primary messenger would reach them last of all; and long before he came to them the messenger on a secondary Ephesian circuit would have reached them. Moreover, it is probable that the primary circuit was not devised simply with a view to the Province of Asia, but was intended to be often conjoined with a further journey to Galatia and the East, so that the messenger would not return from Laodicea to the coast, but would keep on up the Lycus by Colossae eastwards.

Thirdly, Caria does not fit well in the secondary districts and circuits. It is so great that it seems to require for itself one special circuit; and if so Tralleis was the one almost inevitable point of communication with the primary circuit. Yet Tralleis was not one of the Seven Churches. But probably a distinction must be made. Western Caria (Alabanda, Stratonicea and the coast cities) probably formed a secondary circuit along with the Lower Meander Valley; and Ephesus was the starting point for it. On the other hand the eastern and southern part of Caria lay apart from any of the great lines of communication: it was on the road to nowhere: any one who went south from the Meander into the hilly country did so for the sake of visiting it, and not because it was on his best way to a more distant goal. Now the new religion spread with marvellous rapidity along the great routes; it floated free on the great currents of communication that swept back and forward across the Empire, but it was slower to make its way into the back-waters, the nooks and corners of the land: it penetrated where life was busy, though was active, and people were full of curiosity and enterprise: it found only a tardy welcome among the quieter and less educated rural districts. Hence that part of Caria was little disturbed in the old ways, when most of the rest of Asia was strongly permeated with Christianity.

Fourthly, an immense region of Northern and Eastern Phrygia seems to be quite beyond any reasonably easy communication with the primary circular route.

As to Northern Phrygia, it is extremely doubtful whether it had been much affected by the new religion when the Seven Letters were written. It was a rustic, scantily educated region, which offered no favourable opportunity for Christianity. Some, indeed, would argue that, as Bithynia was so strongly permeated with the new religion, before A.D. 111, Phrygia which lies farther south and nearer the original seats of Christianity, must have been Christianised earlier. This argument, however, ignores the way in which Christianity spread, viz., along the main roads and lines of communication. The same cause, which made Eastern Caria later in receiving the new faith (as shown above), also acted in Northern Phrygia. A study of the interesting monuments of early Christianity in that part of the country has shown that it was Christianised from Bithynia (probably not earlier than the second century), and it was therefore left out of the early Asian system, as being still practically a pagan country. Southern Phrygia lay near the main Central Route of the Empire, and its early Christian monuments show a markedly different character from the North Phrygian monuments, and prove that it was Christianised (as was plainly necessary) from the line of the great Central Highway. This part of Phrygia lay entirely in the Upper Meander Valley, and fell naturally within the Laodicean circuit.

Eastern Phrygia, on the other hand, was Christianised from Iconium and Pisidian Antioch, and was therefore not included in the early Asian system which we have described. Doubtless, during the second century, a complete provincial organisation came into existence; and all Christian Asia was then united. But, as great part of Phrygia had for a long time been outside of the Asian system of the Seven Churches, it was sometimes even in the second century thought necessary for the sake of clearness to mention Phrygia along with Asia in defining the Church of the whole Province. Hence we have the phrase "the Churches (or Brethren) of Asia and Phrygia" in Tertullian, adv. Prax 1, and in the letter of the Gallic Christians.

In the case of Laodicea it seems natural and probable that two secondary circuits must be admitted. One would include the Lycus and the Upper Meander Valleys: the messenger would go along the great Central Highway and trade route through Colossae to Apameia, and thence through the Pentapolis and back by Eumeneia to Laodicea. Hierapolis, being so close to Laodicea, would share in any Laodicean communication without any special messenger. Another secondary circuit would follow the important Pamphylian Road (to Perga and Attalia), as far as Cibyra, and then perhaps keep along the frontier of the Province to Lake Ascania; but this road was rather a rustic byway, and it is hardly probable that the frontier region was Christianised so early as the first century. The Cibyra district, on the Pamphylian Road, was more likely to be penetrated early by the new thought; and the name Epaphras in an inscription of this district may be a sign that the impulse came from Colossae.

Thus we find that the Seven Letters are directed to a well-marked district embracing the greater part of the Province Asia; and natural features, along with indubitable epigraphic and monumental evidence, make it probable that the district of the Seven Letters contained the entire Asian Church as it was organised about the end of the first century. The importance of the Seven Letters becomes evident even in such a small though interesting matter as this.

Chapter 16: Plan and Order of Topics in the Seven Letters

Each of the Seven Letters opens, as letters in ancient time always did, by stating who sends the message and to whom it is sent. But the exordium does not take the form that it would have if the sender of the message were the writer of the letter, viz., "the writer to the person addressed." In the present case the letters are written by John, who imagines himself to be only the channel through which they come from the real Author; and the exordium is altered to suit this situation. The writer does not name himself; but after naming the persons addressed--To the angel of the Church in Ephesus--he gives a brief description of the Author of the message. The seven descriptions all differ from one another; and, taken together, they make up the complete account given in Revelation 1 of One like unto a son of man. The Divine Author presents Himself in a different aspect to each individual Church; and the seven aspects make up His complete personal description, as the different Churches make up the complete and Universal Church. This expresses in another way what we have tried to show in chapter 14: the Seven Churches make up the complete Church of the Province Asia, because each of them stands in place of a group of Churches, and the Church of the Province Asia in its turn stands in place of the Universal Church of Christ.

This variation from the ordinary formula of ancient letters is connected with the fact, which has already been pointed out, that these are not true letters, but literary compositions, or rather parts of one larger composition. Although for convenience we have called them the Seven Letters, they were not to be sent separately to the Seven Churches. The Apocalypse is a book which was never intended to be taken except as a whole; and the Seven Letters are a mere part of this book, and never had any existence except in the book. The Seven Churches had established their representative position before the book was composed; and that is assumed throughout by the author. They stand to him, in their combination, for the entire Province, and the Province stands to him for the entire Church of Christ; though, when he is writing to Smyrna or Thyatira, he sees and thinks of Smyrna or Thyatira alone.

As to the brief description of the Divine Author, which is prefixed to each of the Seven Letters, there is a special appropriateness in each case to the character or circumstances of the Church which is addressed. To a certain extent we can comprehend wherein this appropriateness lies; but there is probably a good deal which escapes us, because our knowledge of the character and history of the Seven Churches is so incomplete. From this appropriateness it follows that the complete description of the Divine Author, which is made up of those seven parts, is logically later than the parts, though it comes first in the book. This appears especially in the Thyatiran letter. In the highly complex plan of the work, every detail was selected separately in view of its suitability for one or other of the Seven Churches, and was then worked into its place in the full description in the first chapter. Yet the description is complete: the writer worked up the parts into a whole before stating them separately for the Seven churches.

After the formal heading or exordium, each of the Seven Letters begins by a statement intimating that the writer possesses full knowledge of the character and position of the Church which he is addressing. In five out of the seven letters this intimation begins, I know thy works; but in the cases of Smyrna and Pergamum, the opening is different: I know thy tribulation, and I know where thou dwellest. The difference is evidently due to their peculiar circumstances. He who wishes to prove his full knowledge of the Church in Smyrna says that he knows its sufferings; because these were the striking feature in its history. And in Pergamum the most prominent and distinguishing characteristic lay in its situation, "where the throne of Satan is": by that situation its history had been strongly influenced. But in most cases what is essential to know about a Church is what it has done; and so begin all the other five.

As was stated in chapter 3, the letter to an individual church passes easily into an "Epistle General" to the whole Church, for it embodies general principles of nature, order, and government, which are applicable to all. Similarly, to apply the comparison which was there made, the Imperial Rescript addressed to a Province or to its governor embodied general principles of administration, which were afterwards regarded as applicable universally (except in so far as they were adapted to an exceptional condition of the Province addressed). But in every case, when an individual Church is addressed, as here, it is addressed in and for it itself, and its own special individual character and fortunes are clearly present before the writer's mind. He does not think of the Smyrna group when he addresses Smyrna, nor is he thinking of the Universal Church: he addresses Smyrna alone; he has it clear before his mind, with all its special qualities and individuality. Yet the group which had its centre in Smyrna, and the whole Universal Church, alike found that the letter which was written for Smyrna applied equally to them, for it was a statement of eternal truths and universal principles.

There was undoubtedly a very considerable resemblance between the Seven Cities: the surroundings in which the Seven Churches were placed were similar; and accordingly the character of all was in a superficial view similar. In every city there were doubtless Jews of the nationalist party, bitterly opposed to the Jewish Christians and through them to the Christians as a body, a source of danger and trouble to every one of the Churches; but the Jews are mentioned only in the letters to Smyrna and Philadelphia. There were Nicolaitans, beyond all question, in every Asian congregation; but they are alluded to only in the Thyatiran letters as the dominant party in that Church, in the letter to Pergamum as a strong element there, and in the Ephesian letter as disapproved and hated by the Church of Ephesus as a body. Every one of the Seven Churches was a missionary centre; but Philadelphia alone is depicted as the missionary Church.

Underneath the general similarity the writer and the Author saw the differences which determined the character, the past history, and the ultimate fate of all the Seven churches (as described in chapter 4).

But the differences should not be too much emphasised, or exclusively attended to. There are two hostile powers everywhere present, one open and declared, one secret and lurking within the camp; and the thought of these is never far from the writer's mind, even though he does not expressly mention them in every letter.

One is the Imperial power and the Imperial worship, which the writer saw plainly to be the power of Satan engaged in a determined attempt to annihilate the Church, but doomed beforehand to failure. The Church and the Imperial worship are irreconcilable; one or the other must be destroyed; and the issue is not doubtful. Since the Imperial power has now actively allied itself with the Imperial cultus in this conflict against truth and life, it has doomed itself to destruction.

The other enemy is the Nicolaitan principle. The opposition to the Nicolaitans is the chief factor in determining the character and form of the Seven Letters. But for them there would probably be no letters to the Seven Churches. The rest of the Apocalypse is occupied with the triumph over the Imperial Religion. But there was no need to warn the Churches against it: it was a sham, doomed to destruction, and already conquered in every martyrdom. The one pressing danger to the Churches was within and not without: it lay in their weaknesses of nature, and in that false teaching which was set forth with the show of authority by some prophets and leaders in the Churches. Against the Nicolaitan teachers the Seven Letters are directed in the way of warning and reproof, with strenuous opposition and almost bigoted hatred. Those teachers drew a somewhat contemptuous contrast between their highly advanced teaching, with its deep thought and philosophic insight, and the simple, uneducated, unphilosophic views which St. John championed. They gave undue emphasis to the Greek aspect of Christianity; and in its practical working out they made it their rule of life to maintain the closest possible relations with the best customs of ordinary society in the Asian cities. This attempt was in itself quite justifiable; but in the judgment of St. John (and we may add of St. Paul also) they went too far, and tried to retain in the Christian life practices that were in diametrical opposition to the essential principles of Christianity, and thus they had strayed into a syncretism of Christian and anti-Christian elements which was fatal to the growth and permanence of Christian thought.

But in his opposition to the Nicolaitans the writer does not make the mistake of going to the opposite extreme, minimising the share that Greek thought and custom might have in the Christian life, and exaggerating the opposition between Greek education and true religion. He holds the balance with a steady hand; he expresses himself in a form that should be clear and sympathetic to the Greek Churches whom he was addressing; he gives quiet emphasis to the best side of Greek education in letters which are admirable efforts of literary power; but at a certain point his sympathy stops dead; beyond that point it was fatal to go.

He saw the whole of life, and not merely one side of it; and he was not misled by indiscriminate opposition to the enemy, however strongly he hated them. He would have weakened the Church permanently, if he had made the mistake, too common in the history of religion, of condemning everything that the other side championed. He took from it all that could be taken safely, gave all that it could give to train the religious feeling to the highest, and did everything better than his enemy could.

In studying St. Paul we find ourselves forced to recognise the essential agreement of his views on this question with St. John's; and in studying St. John we find ourselves forced to the same judgment. With superficial differences they both take the same calm, sane view of the situation as a whole, and legislate for the young Church on the same lines. Up to a certain point the converted pagan should develop the imperfect, but not wholly false, religious ideas and gropings after truth of his earlier years into a Christian character; but there was much that was absolutely false and fundamentally perverted in those ideas; the pagan religions had been degraded from an originally better form by the willful sin and error of men, and all that part of them must be inexorably eradicated and destroyed. The determining criterion lay in the idolatrous element: where that was a necessary part of pagan custom or opinion, there was no justification for clinging to it: unsparing condemnation and rejection was the only course open to a true Christian.

Hence arose the one striking contrast in outward appearance between the views of the two Apostles. St. Paul clung to the hope and belief that the Church might develop within the Empire, and find protection from the Imperial government. St. John regarded the Imperial government as Antichrist, the inevitable enemy of Christianity. But in the interval between the two lay the precise formulation of the Imperial policy, which imposed on the Christians as a test of loyalty the performance of religious ritual in the worship of the Emperors. The Empire armed itself with the harness of idolatry; and the principle that St. Paul himself had laid down in the sharpest and clearest terms at once put an end to any hope that he had entertained of reconciliation and amity between the Church and the existing State.

Again, the Seven Letters repeatedly, in the most pointed way, express and emphasis the continuity of history, in the city and the local Church. The Church is not simply regarded as a separate fact, apart from the city in which it has its temporary abode; such a point of view was impossible and such a thought was inconceivable for the ordinary ancient mind. We have so grown in the lapse of centuries and the greater refinement of thought as to be able to hold apart in our minds the two conceptions; but the ancients regarded the State or the city and its religion as two aspects of one thing. So again, to the ancients every association of human beings had its religious side, and could not exist if that side were destroyed.

The literary form which beyond all others is loved by the writer of the Seven Letters is comparison and contrast. Throughout them all he is constantly striking a balance between the power which the Divine Author wields, the gifts that he gives, the promises and prospects which he holds forth to his own, and the achievements of all enemies, the Empire, the pagan cities, the Jews, and the Nicolaitans. The modern reader has almost everywhere to add one side of the comparison, for the writer only expresses one side and leaves the other to the intuition of his readers. He selects a characteristic by which the enemy prominent in his mind was, or ought to be, distinguished, and describes it in terms in which his readers could not fail to read a reference to that enemy; but he attributes it to the Divine Author or the true Church or the true Christian. Thus he describes the irresistible might that shall be given to the Thyatiran victor in terms which could not fail to rouse in every reader the thought of the great Empire and its tremendous military strength.

Examples of this rhetorical form will be pointed out in every letter; and yet it is probable that many more were apparent to the Asian readers than we can now detect. The thought that is everywhere present in the writer's mind is how much better the true Church does everything than any of its foes, open or secret.

One example may be given. The simple promise made by the Author to the Smyrnaeans, I will give you the crown of life, when compared with the address which Apollonius made to them, is seen to contain implicit allusion to a feature of the city, which was a cause of peculiar pride to the citizens: "the crown of Smyrna" was the garland of splendid buildings with the Street of Gold, which encircled the rounded hill Pagos. Apollonius in a fully expressed comparison advised the citizens to prefer a crown of men to a crown of buildings. This Author leaves one member of the figure to be understood: if we expressed his thought in full, it would be "instead of the crown of buildings which you boast of, or the crown of men that your philosophers recommend, I will give you the crown of life."

The peroration of each of the Seven Letters is modelled in the same way: all contain a claim for attention and a promise. The former is identical in all Seven Letters: he that hath an ear, let him hear what the Spirit saith to the Churches. The latter is different in every case, being adapted to the special character of each.

The claim for attention, which is made in the peroration of every letter, is perhaps to be understood as in part applying to the whole Apocalypse, but in a much greater degree it applies to the advice and reproof and encouragement contained in the individual letter and in the whole Seven Letters. There was less need to press for attention to the vision of victory and triumph, while there was serious need to demand attention to the letter, with its plain statement of the dangers to which the Church was exposed. Hence, while the claim is identical in all, it is specially needed in each letter.

The promise made to the victors at the end of every letter is to be understood as addressed partly to the Christians of the city, but still more to the true Christians of the entire Church. The idea that the individual Church is part of the Universal Church, that it stands for it after the usual symbolic fashion of the Apocalypse, is never far from the writer's mind; and he passes rapidly between the two points of view, the direct address to the local Church as an individual body with special needs of its own, and the general application and apostrophe to the entire Church as symbolised by the particular local Church.

There is a difference among the letters in regard to the arrangement of the peroration: in the first three the claim for attention comes before the promise, in the last four it comes after. It must remain doubtful whether there is any special intention in this, beyond a certain tendency in the writer towards employing variety as a literary device. Almost every little variation and turn in these letters, however, is carefully studied; and probably it is through deliberate intention that they are divided by this variation into two classes; but what is the reason for the division, and the principle involved in it, is hard to say. The first three ranked also as the three greatest cities of the Province, vying with one another for the title "First of Asia," which all three claimed. In the general estimation of the world, and in their own, they formed a group apart, while the others were second-rate. Probably there was a set of seven leading cities in public estimation, as we saw in chapter 14; and certainly there was within that set a narrower and more famous group of three. It may be that this difference almost unconsciously affected the writer's expression and produced a corresponding variation in the form, though the variation apparently conveys no difference in force or meaning, but is purely literary and formal.

An attempt has been made to explain the variation on the ground that the first three Churches are regarded as having on the whole been faithful, though with faults and imperfections; whereas the last four have been faithless for the most part, and only a "remnant" is acknowledged in them as faithful. But, while that is true of three out of the four, yet Philadelphia is praised very highly, with almost more thoroughness than any even of the first three, except Smyrna; and it is the only Church to which the Divine Author says "I have loved thee."

So far as grouping can be detected among the Seven Churches, it would rather appear that they are placed in pairs. Ephesus and Sardis go together; so again Smyrna and Philadelphia, Pergamum and Thyatira; while the distant Laodicea stands by itself, far away in the land of Phrygia. Ephesus and Sardis have both changed and deteriorated; but in Ephesus the change amounts only to a loss of enthusiasm which is still perhaps recoverable; in Sardis the deterioration has deepened into death. Smyrna and Philadelphia are praised far more unreservedly than the rest; both are poor and weak; both have suffered from the Jews; but both are full of life and vigour, now and forever. Pergamum and Thyatira have both been strongly affected by Nicolaitanism; both are compared and contrasted with the Imperial power; and both are promised victory over it. Laodicea stands alone, outcast and rejected, because it cannot make up its mind whether to be one thing or another.

This common plan on which all the Seven Letters are framed would alone furnish a sufficient proof that they are not true letters, but literary compositions which are cast in the form of letters, because that form had already established itself in usage. Now the writer certainly did not select this form merely because it was recognised in the pagan literature. He selected it because it had already become recognised as the characteristic and the best form of expression for Christian didactic literature. A philosophic exposition of truth was apt to become abstract and unreal; the dialogue form, which the Greeks loved and some of the Christian writers adopted, was apt to degenerate into looseness and mere literary display; but the letter, as already elaborated by great thinkers and artists who were his predecessors, was determined for him as the best medium of expression. In this form (as has been shown in chapter 3) literature, statesmanship, ethics, and religion met, and placed the simple letter on the highest level of practical power. Due regard to the practical needs of the congregation which he addressed prevented the writer of a letter from losing hold on the hard facts and serious realities of life. The spirit of the lawgiver raised him above all danger of sinking into the commonplace and the trivial. Great principles must be expressed in the Christian letter. And finally it must have literary form as a permanent monument of teaching and legislation.

It was a correct literary instinct that led St. John to express the message to the Seven Churches in letters, even though he had to work these letters into an apocalypse of the Hebraic style, a much less fortunate choice on pure literary grounds, though (as we have seen in chapter 8) it was practically inevitable in the position in which the writer was placed. In each letter, though it was only a literary Epistle addressed to a representative Church, the writer was obliged to call up before his mind the actual Church as he knew it; and thus he has given us seven varied and individualised pictures of different congregations.

Probably the opposition and criticism which he was sure to experience from the Nicolaitans stimulated the writer to reach the high standard of literary quality which characterises the Seven Letters in spite of the neglect of traditional rules of expression. He uses the language of common life, not the stereotyped forms of the historian or the philosophers. As Dante had the choice between the accepted language of education, Latin, and the vulgar tongue, the popular Italian, so St. John had to choose between a more artificial kind of Greek, as perpetuated from past teaching, and the common vulgar speech, often emancipated from strict grammatical rules, but nervous and vigorous, a true living speech. He chose the latter.

While one must speak about and admire the literary power of the Seven Letters, the writer did not aim at literary form. He stated his thought in the simplest way; he had pondered over the letters during the only years in Patmos, until they expressed themselves in the briefest and most direct form that great thoughts can assume; but therein lies the greatest power that the letter can attain. He reached the highest level in point of epistolary quality, because he had no thought of form, but only of effect on his reader's life.

Chapter 17: Ephesus: The City of Change

The subject of the present chapter is the early Roman city, the Ephesus of St. John and St. Paul. But as soon as we begin to examine its character and make even a superficial survey of its history, it stands out as the place that had experienced more vicissitudes than any other city of Asia. In most places the great features of nature and the relations of sea and land remain permanent amid the mutations of human institutions: but in Ephesus even nature has changed in a surprising degree. To appreciate its character as the city of change, we must observe its history more minutely than is needed in the other cities.

At the present day Ephesus has all the appearance of an inland city. The traveller who wanders among its ruins may be at first unconscious of the neighbourhood of the sea. He beholds only a plain stretching east and west, closed in on the north and south by long lines of mountain, Gallesion and Koressos. As he looks to the east he sees only ranges of mountains rising one behind another. As he looks to the west his view from most part of the city is bounded by a ridge which projects northwards from the long ridge of Koressos into the plain. This little ridge is crowned by a bold fort, called in the modern local tradition, St. Paul's Prison: the fort stands on the hill of Astyages (according to the ancient name), and the ridge contains also another peak on the west, called the Hermaion. The ridge and fort constitute the extreme western defences of the Greek city, which was built about 287 B.C. That old Greek tower, owing to its distance and isolation, has escaped intentional destruction, and is one of the best preserved parts of the old fortification. From its elevation of 450 feet it dominates the view, the most striking and picturesque feature of the Greek Ephesus.

The historian of Greece, Professor Ernst Curtius, was misled by the appearance of the city, and has described the fortunes of Ephesus as a city separated from the sea by the ridge of Astyages. This misapprehension partially distorted his view of Ephesian history and coloured his picture, which is otherwise marked by sympathetic insight and charm of expression. It is the merit of Professor Benndorf to have placed the subject in its true light, and to have shown that the history of Ephesus was determined by its original situation on the seashore and its eagerness to retain its character as a harbour in spite of the changes of nature, which left it far from the sea. The brief sketch, which follows, of the history of Ephesus is founded on Benndorf's first topographical sketch, and on the map prepared for his promised fuller study of the subject. The present writer is indebted to his kindness for a copy of the map in proof not finally corrected, and can only regret that this sketch has to be printed without access to the historical study which is to accompany it.

The most impressive view of modern Ephesus is from the western side of Mount Pion, either from the upper seats of the Great Theatre or from a point a little higher. The eye ranges westwards over the streets and buildings of the Greek and Roman city (recently uncovered by the Austrian Archaeological Institute in excavations extending over many years and conducted with admirable skill), and across the harbour to the hill of Astyages: southwest the view is bounded by the long ridge of Koressos, along the front crest of which runs the south wall of the Greek city: northwest one looks across the level plain to the sea, full six miles away, and to the rocky ridge that projects from Mount Gallesion and narrows the sea-gates of the valley: northward lie the level plain and the steep slopes of Gallesion. The mouth of the river is hidden from sight behind the hill of Astyages.

But a large and important part of ancient Ephesus is excluded from that view, and can be seen only by ascending to the top of the twin-peaked Pion, which commands the view on all sides. The view from the upper seats of the Theatre may be supplemented by looking east from the northern edge of Pion, beside the Stadium, or still better from the prominent rock (cut into an octagonal form, probably to serve a religious purpose) which stands in the plain about fifty yards in front of the northwest corner of Pion and of the Stadium. From either of these points one looks northeast and east over the valley and the site of the great Temple of Artemis to the Holy Hill of Ayassoluk, which overhung the Temple, and to the piled-up ranges of mountains beyond.

The modern visitor to Ephesus rarely finds time or has inclination to visit St. Paul's Prison: the name is traditional in the locality, but though the tower was certainly in existence at the time of St. Paul's residence in the city, there is no reason to think that he was ever imprisoned in Ephesus. It is, however, quite probable that in the Byzantine time the Apostle's name was attached to the hill and fort in place of the older name Astyages. Not merely does this western hill permit a survey over the city and valley almost equal in completeness to the view from Pion: there is also a remarkable phenomenon observable here and nowhere else in Ephesus. At the foot of the hill lies the ancient harbour, now a marsh dense with reeds. When a wind blows across the reeds, there rises to the hilltop a strange vast volume of sound of a wonderfully impressive kind; the present writer has sat for several hours alone on the summit, spellbound by that unearthly sound, until the approach of sunset and the prospect of a three hours' ride home compelled departure.

In ancient times by far the most impressive view of Ephesus was that which unfolded itself before the eyes of the voyager from the west. But the changes that time has wrought have robbed the modern traveller of that view. The ancient traveller, official or scholar, trader or tourist, coming across the Aegean Sea from the west, between Chios and Samos, sailed into Ephesus. The modern shore is a harbourless line of sandy beach, unapproachable by a ship.

The plain of Ephesus is distinctly broader near the city than it is at the present seacoast. The narrowness of the entrance, what may be called the sea-gate of the valley, has been an important factor in determining its history. Some miles above the city the valley is again narrowed by ridges projecting from the mountains of Gallesion and Koressos. In this narrow gap are the bridges by which the railway and the road from Smyrna cross the Cayster, whose banks here are now only ten feet above sea level, though the direct distance to the sea is ten kilometres and the river course is fully sixteen or twenty kilometres. Between these upper or eastern narrows and the modern seacoast lies the picturesque Ephesian plain, once the Gulf of Ephesus. The river Cayster has gradually silted up the gulf to the outer coastline beyond the ends of the mountains, and has made Ephesus seem like an inland city, whereas Strabo in A.D. 20 describes it as a city of the coast.

But about 1100 B.C. the sea extended right up to the narrows above Ephesus. Greek tradition in the valley, which can hardly have reached back farther than 1200 B.C., remembered that state of things, when the large rocky hill, two kilometres north of the Roman city, across the Cayster, was an island named Syria, and the whole Ephesian valley was an arm of the sea, dotted with rocky islets, and bordered by picturesque mountains and wooded promontories. near the southeastern end of the gulf, on the seashore, stood the shrine of the Great Goddess, the Mother, protector, teacher, and mistress of a simple and obedient people. There was no city at that time; but the people, Lelegians and Carians, dwelt after the Anatolian fashion in villages, and all looked for direction and government to the Goddess and to the priests who declared her will. Ephesus even then had some maritime interests, directed, like everything else, by the Goddess herself through her priests. Hence, even when the Temple was far distant from the receding seashore, a certain body of shipment was attached to its service, through the conservatism of a religion which let no hieratic institution die. The hill of Ayassoluk, between the Temple and the railway station, was a defensive centre close at hand for the servants of the Goddess. History shows that it was the Holy Hill, though that title is never recorded in our scanty authorities.

The sense of the holiness of this hill, and of the low ground beneath its western slope, was never wholly lost amid all the changes of religion that occurred in ancient and medieval times. On the hill Justinian's great Church of St. John Theologos was built; the medieval town was called Agios Theologos or Ayo-Thologo, the Turkish Ayassoluk; and the coins of a Seljuk principality, whose centre was at this town, bear the legend in medieval Latin Moneta Que Fit In Theologo. Between the church and the old temple of the goddess stands the splendid mosque of Isa Bey. The modern traveller, standing on the southern edge of the large hole, at the bottom of which Mr. Wood found the temple buried thirty feet deep, looks over temple and mosque to the Holy Hill and Church of Ayassoluk. All the sacred places of all the religions are close together.

The site of the temple was only found after many years of search. Those who know the spirit of Anatolian religion, and the marvellous persistence with which it clings to definite localities, would have looked for it beside the mosque, the hill and the church. But it was sought everywhere except in the right place. Professor Kiepert marked it conjecturally on his plan of Ephesus out in the open plain near the Cayster, two kilometres west of Ayassoluk; and Mr. Wood spent several years and great sums of money digging pits all over the plain. Afterwards, he went to the city, searching the public buildings for inscriptions which might by some chance allude to the temple, and at last found in the Great Theatre a long inscription which mentioned a procession going out from the Magnesian Gate to the temple. He went to the gate, and followed up the road, which lay deep beneath the ground, till he found the sacred precinct and finally the temple.

Yet this was not the earliest Ephesian sanctuary and home of the goddess. In her oldest form she was a goddess of the free wild life of nature, and her first home was in the southern mountains near Ortygia. Thence she migrated to dwell near her people in their more civilised homes on the plain, or rather she, as the Mother and the Queen-bee, guided her swarming people to their new abodes, and taught them how to adapt themselves to new conditions. But her love for her favourite wild animals, who had lived round her old home among the hills, always continued; and two stags often accompany her idol, standing one on each side of it.

But her old home among the mountains was always sacred. There were there a number of temples, ancient and recent; an annual Panegyris was held there, at which there was much competition among the young nobles of Ephesus in splendour of equipment; and Mysteries and sacred banquets were celebrated by an association or religious club of Kouretes. The myth connected the birth of Artemis with this place; and in a sense it was the birthplace of the goddess and her first Ephesian home.

In Christian times the holiness of this locality was maintained. The Mother of God was still associated with it, though the birth of God could no longer be placed there. The legend grew that she had come to Ephesus and died there; and her home and grave were known. This legend is at least as old as the Council held in Ephesus A.D. 431. After the Greek Christians of Ephesus had fled to the eastern mountains and settled in the village of Kirkindji they celebrated an annual pilgrimage and festival at the shrine of the Mother of God, the Virgin of the Gate, Panagia Kapulu. The Christian shrine was at a little distance from Ortygia; both were under the peak of Solmissos (Ala-Dagh), but Ortygia was on the west side, while the Panagia was on the north side higher up the mountain; both peak and Panagia lie outside our map, and even Ortygia is strictly outside the southern limit, though the name has been squeezed in.

The home and grave of the Mother of God have been recently discovered by the Roman Catholics of Smyrna, aided by visions, prayers and faith; and the attempt has been made in the last ten years to restore the Ephesian myth to its proper place in the veneration of the Catholic Church. The story is interesting, but lies beyond our subject. What concerns us is to observe the strong vitality of local religion in Asia Minor amid all changes of outward form. The religious centre is moved a little to and fro, but always clings to a comparatively narrow circle of ground.

The date and even the order of the successive stages in the history of the Ephesian valley cannot as yet be fully determined--though Professor Benndorf's expected memoir will doubtless throw much light on them. About 1100 B.C. the first Greek colonists, coming from Athens, expelled most of the older population and founded a joint city of Greeks and the native remnant beside the shrine of their own Athena, including in their city also a tract along the skirts of Koressos. Its exact situation has not been determined; but it was probably identical with a district called Smyrna, which lay between Koressos and Pion, partly inside, partly southeast from, the Hellenic Ephesus.

For four centuries this was the situation of Ephesus. There was an Ionian city bearing that name on the slopes of Mount Koressos, and above a mile north was the Temple of the Great Goddess Artemis. The Greek colonists in their new land naturally worshipped the deity who presided over the land. Gradually they came to pay some respect to her than to their own patroness and guardian deity Athena, who had led them across the sea from Athens. The holy village around the Hieron of Artemis can hardly have existed in this period: Ephesus was moved to the southern position and transformed into a Greek city. The population of the city was at first divided into three Tribes, of which Epheseis the first was evidently the Anatolian division, while Euonymoi, containing the Athenian colonists, was only the second.

The sea gradually retreated towards the west during this period; and the Temple of Artemis was now a sanctuary within a large sacred precinct in the plain. But the goddess, though worshipped by the Greeks, was not transformed into a Greek deity. She remained an Anatolian deity in character and in ritual. The Divine nature does not change.

A new era began after 560 B.C., when Ephesus was conquered by Croesus. The city was now attached to the Temple of Artemis; and the population was moved back from the higher ground and dwelt once more beside the Temple. Smyrna, the deserted site of the Ionian Ephesus, was now behind the city (as Hipponax says).

The change marked the entire triumph of the Asiatic or Anatolian element over the Greek in the Ephesian population. The Anatolian element had always been strong in the population of the Greek city; the Ephesian Goddess was henceforth the national deity of the city, the patroness of the family and municipal life. Thus, the change of situation about 550 B.C. accompanied a change in spirit and character.

Ephesus was not, however, reduced entirely to the pure Anatolian village system. It was not a mere union of villages with the Temple as the only centre; it was a city with a certain organisation and a certain form of municipal government. Power was apportioned to the different sections of the population by the usual Greek device of a division into Tribes: each Tribe had one vote, and a more numerous body in one Tribe had no more power than a small number of citizens in another. It had its own acropolis, probably the hill of Ayassoluk, overhanging the Temple on the northeast. It struck its own coins in silver and electrum (the sure proof of administrative independence as a city); but they were entirely hieratic in character and types, and for nearly three centuries after 560 it must be ranked rather as an Anatolian town than as a Greek city.

It was, indeed, forced, after 479, to join the union of Greek States which was called the Delian Confederacy; but it seceded at the earliest opportunity; and the goddess was always inclined to side with the Persians against the Greeks, and with oligarchic Sparta against democratic Athens.

With the conquest of Asia by Alexander the Great, after 335, the Greek spirit began to strengthen itself in Ephesus and in general throughout the country. This is first perceptible in the coinage. The bee, the sacred insect and the symbol of the Great Goddess, had hitherto always been the principal type on Ephesian coins. Now about 295 B.C. a purely Greek type, the head of the Greek Artemis, the Virgin "Queen and Huntress chaste and fair," was substituted for the bee on the silver coins, while the less honourable copper coinage retained the old hieratic types.

The importance of this change of type arises from the character of the Great Goddess. She is the expression of a religious belief, which regarded the life of God as embodying and representing the life of nature, and proceeding according to the analogy of the natural world, so that in the drama of Divine life there is a God-Father, a Goddess-Mother, and a Son or a Daughter (the Maiden Kora or other various ideas), born again and again in the annual cycle (or sometimes in longer cycles) of existence. The mutual relations of those beings were often pictured in the Divine drama according to the analogy of some kind of earthly life. In the Ephesian ceremonial the life of the bee was the model: the Great Goddess was the queen-bee, the mother of her people, and her image was in outline not unlike the bee, with a grotesque mixture of the human form: her priestesses were called Melissai (working-bees), and a body of priests attached to the Temple was called Essenes (the drones). The life-history of the bee, about which the Greek naturalists held erroneous views (taking the queen-bee as male, and king of the hive), was correctly understood in the primitive Ephesian cultus; and it is highly probable that the employment for human use of the bee and of various domesticated animals was either originated or carried to remarkable perfection in ancient Asia Minor; while it is certain that the whole doctrine and rules of tending those animals had a religious character and were in close relation to the worship of the Divine power in its various and varying local embodiments.

The reverse of the coins tells the same tale as the obverse. The Anatolian coin shows the palm-tree under which the goddess was born among the southern mountains at Ortygia, and her sacred animal, the stag, cut in half in truly barbaric style. The Hellenic coin shows the bow and quiver of the huntress-maiden, and acknowledges the Anatolian goddess by the small figure of a bee: even in its most completely Hellenised form Ephesus must still do homage to the native goddess.

On the other hand Greek religion was strongly anthropomorphic, and the Hellenic spirit, as it developed and attained fuller consciousness of its own nature, rejected more and more decisively the animal forms and animal analogies in which the Anatolian religion delighted.

Where Greece adopted an Anatolian cult, it tried to free itself from animal associations, and to transform the Divine impersonation after the purely human beautiful Hellenic idea. Thus to substitute the head of the huntress Virgin Artemis for the bee on the coins was to transform an Anatolian conception into a Greek figure, and to blazon the triumph of the Greek spirit over the Oriental.

There followed once more a change in the situation of Ephesus, accompanying the change in spirit that was being wrought in the aims and outlook of the city. Ephesus was moved away from the neighbourhood of the Temple to a situation not far removed from that of the old Greek city. The change, naturally, was strenuously resisted by the priests and the large section of the people that was under their domination. But the will of King Lysimachus, the master of the northwest regions of Asia Minor, who carried on the Hellenising tradition of Alexander, was too strong; and he cleverly overcame the unwillingness of the Anatolian party in the town. The Ephesus of 560-287 BC was in a low-lying situation, surrounded on three sides by higher ground, and in time of rain a great amount of water poured down through the town. Lysimachus took advantage of a heavy rain, and stopped the channels which carried off the water into the gulf, or the river: the town was flooded, and the people were glad to leave it.

The new situation was admirably strong and convenient; and the Hellenic Ephesus of this new foundation lasted for more than a thousand years. Its shape was like a bent bow, the two ends being Pion on the east and the Hill of Astyages on the west; while the sea washed up into the space between, forming an inner harbour, whose quays bordered by stately colonnades and public buildings can still be traced amid the ruins. The outer harbour was part of the land-locked gulf.

A great street ran from the inner harbour right up to the base of Pion. The visitor to Ephesus, after landing at the harbour, would traverse this long straight street, edged by porticoes, with a series of magnificent buildings on either hand, until he reached the left front of the Great Theatre and the beginning of the steep ascent of Pion. The street, as it has been disclosed by the Austrian excavations, is the result of a late reconstruction and bears the name of the Emperor Arcadius, A.D. 395-408; but the reconstruction was only partial, and there can be little doubt that the general plan of the city in this quarter dates from the foundation about 287 B.C., and that this great street is the one which is mentioned in the Bezan text of Acts 19:28. A riot was roused by a speech of Demetrius, delivered probably in a building belonging to a guild of some of the associated trades. After the passions of the mob and their apprehension of financial disaster were inflamed, they rushed forth "into the street," and ran along it shouting and invoking the goddess, until at last they found themselves in front of the Great Theatre. That vast empty building offered a convenient place for a hasty assembly. Even this excited mob still retained some idea of method in conducting business. It was quite in the old Greek style that they should at once constitute themselves into a meeting of the Ephesian People, and proceed to discuss business and pass resolutions. Many a meeting convened in an equally irregular way, simply through a strong common feeling without any formal notice had been held in the great Greek cities, and passed important resolutions. But this meeting was not conducted by persons used to business and possessing authority with the crowd. It was a mere pandemonium, in which for more than an hour the mob howled like Dervishes, shouting their prayers and invocations. Then the Secretary addressed the assembly, and pointed out that such an irregular meeting was not permitted by the Imperial government, which would regard this as a mere riot and punish it with the severity which it always showed to illegal assumption of power.

The death of Lysimachus in 281 B.C. interrupted and impeded for a moment the development of the new city, which he had planned on a great scale. But the position was favourable; and it soon became one of the greatest cities of Asia. Miletus had once been the great seaport of the west coast of Asia Minor; and the main route for the trade between the interior and the countries of the West came down the Meander Valley to Miletus, at the southern entrance to a great gulf extending fully twenty miles into the land. But Miletus had suffered greatly when the Ionian revolt was crushed by the Persians about 500 B.C.; and Ephesus then gained an advantage through Persian favour. Moreover, Ephesus was really a nearer harbour than Miletus even for trade coming down the Meander Valley. Finally, the river Meander was rapidly silting up its gulf, and the harbour of Miletus was probably requiring attention to keep the entrance open; both the gulf of Miletus, then so large, and the harbour have in modern times entirely disappeared, owing to the action of the Meander. Thus Ephesus was heir to much of the trade and prosperity which had belonged to Miletus; though it was destined in its turn, from a similar cause, to see its harbour ruined, and its trade and importance inherited by its rival Smyrna.

Lysimachus had called the new city Arsinoe after his wife, thus breaking definitely with the old tradition as to name and the old Ephesian religious connection; and he indicated the break by making the bust of Arsinoe the principal type on the city coins. The tradition, however, was too strong; and another change of name soon occurred, probably at his death in 281 B.C. The coins of the city began once more to bear the old name of Ephesus. But the Greek huntress virgin still had the place of honour on the silver coins, while the bee was the principal type on the copper coins. The spirit prevalent in the city expresses itself always on the coins.

Another change took place about 196. Ephesus was captured by Antiochus the Great; and the Asiatic spirit again became dominant through the influence of the Syrian monarch. The bee regained its place as the characteristic type on the silver coinage. A period of greater freedom under the Pergamenian influence, 189-133, was marked by an increase in prosperity, and by a great variety in the classes and types of Ephesian coinage.

Ephesus formed part of the Roman Province of Asia, which was organised in 133 B.C. The Roman possession of the city was temporarily interrupted by the invasion of King Mithridates in 88 B.C. It was from Ephesus that he issued orders for the great massacre, in which 80,000 Romans (according to Appian, 150,000 according to Plutarch) were put to death in the Province of Asia. The Ephesians did not spare even the Roman suppliants at the altar of the goddess, disregarding the right of asylum which had hitherto been universally respected, even by invaders. But Sulla soon reconquered Asia; and Ephesus remained undisturbed in Roman possession for many centuries, though sacked by the Goths in A.D. 263.

In the Roman Province of Asia, Pergamum, the old capital of the Kings, continued to be the titular capital; but Ephesus, as the chief harbour of Asia looking towards the west, was far more important than an ordinary city of the Province. It was the gate of the Province, both on the sea-way to Rome, and also on the great central highway leading from Syria by Corinth and Brundisium to Rome. The Roman governors naturally fell into the habit of entering the Province by way of Ephesus, for there was, one might almost say, no other way at first; and this custom soon became a binding rule, with uninterrupted precedents to guarantee it. After the harbour of Ephesus had grown more difficult of access in the second century, and other harbours (probably Smyrna in particular) began to contest its right to be the official port of entrance, the Emperor Caracalla confirmed the custom of "First Landing" at Ephesus by an Imperial rescript.

The drawing expresses the Ephesian pride in this right. It shows a Roman war-vessel, propelled by oars, not sails, lightly built, active and independent of winds. The legend "First Landing" marks it as the ship that conveys the Proconsul to his landing-place in Ephesus. The coin was struck under Philip, A.D. 244-8; but the right was of great antiquity.

The type of a ship occurs in another form with a different meaning on Ephesian coins. A ship under sail is a merchant vessel; and indicates the maritime trade that frequented the harbour of Ephesus. Even if no other evidence were known, this type would furnish sufficient proof that Ephesus possessed a harbour. The same type occurs on coins of Smyrna, but not of any other of the Seven Cities; because none of the others had harbours.

Not only was Ephesus the greatest trading city of the Province Asia, and also of all Asia north of Taurus (as Strabo says); it derived further a certain religious authority in the whole Province from the

Great Goddess Artemis. The Ephesian Artemis was recognised, even in the first century after Christ, as in some sense a deity of the whole Province Asia. This belief was probably a creation of the Roman period and the Roman unity; and it deserves fuller notice as an instructive instance of the effect produced by a Roman idea working itself out in Greek forms.

The Roman administrative idea "Province" was expressed by the Greek word "Nation": in Strabo "the Nation Asia" corresponds to the Latin Asia Provincia. This Greek rendering shows a truly creative instinct: in place of a mere external unity produced by conquest and compulsion it substitutes an internal and organic unity springing from national feeling. But the "Nation" must necessarily have a national religion: without the common bond of religion no real national unity was possible or conceivable to the Greek and the Anatolian mind. As the bond the Imperial policy set up the State religion, the worship of the Majesty of Rome and of the reigning Emperor as the incarnate God in human form on earth (praesens divus) and of the deceased Emperors who had returned to Heaven--after the fashion described in chapter 10. But while the Province loyally accepted this religion, it was not satisfied with it. There was a craving after a native Asian deity, a more real Divine ideal: the Imperial religion was after all a sham religion, and no amount of shows and festivals and pretended religious form could give it religious reality or satisfy the deep-seated religious cravings of the Asian mind. A deity who had been a power from of old in the land was wanted, and not a deity who was invented for the purpose and the occasion.

In the circumstances of the country, and in conformity with the ideas of the time, such a deity could be found only in the tutelary divinity of some great, leading city; and practically only two cities were of national Asian standing, Pergamum and Ephesus. As we have seen in chapter 10, the Pergamenian gods, Dionysos the Leader (Kathegemon) and Asklepios the Saviour (Soter), were being pushed towards that position, and the towns of Asia were encouraged to adopt the worship of these two deities alongside of their own native gods. But the Ephesian goddess had a stronger influence than the deities of Pergamum, for every city of Asia was brought into trading and financial relations with Ephesus, and thus learned to appreciate the power of the goddess. Every city became familiarised with transactions in which the gods of the two parties were named, the Ephesian Artemis and the god or goddess of the city to which the other contracting party belonged. In this way Artemis of Ephesus was in A.D. 55 the deity "whom all Asia and the civilised world worshipped." A commentary on these words of Acts 19:27 is furnished by an inscription of Akmonia in Phrygia, dated 85 A.D., recording the terms of a will, in which the testator invokes as overseers and witnesses a series of deities, the Divine Emperors and the gods of his country, Zeus and Asklepios the Saviour and Artemis of Ephesus: here Zeus is the native Acmonian god, and Asklepios and Artemis are the two provincial gods belonging to the two capitals, the official and the virtual.

While Ephesus was ranked in the estimation of the world by her goddess Artemis, the Imperial worship was not neglected. A shrine and a great altar of Augustus was placed in the sacred precinct of the goddess in the earlier years of his reign: it is taken as a type on coins of the Commune where the two sacred stags mark the close connection between the Imperial and the Ephesian religion even at that early time (see chapter 10).

This was a purely municipal, not a Provincial, cult of Augustus; and in the competition among the cities of Asia in A.D. 26 for the honour of the temple to Tiberius (chapter 19) Ephesus was passed over by the Senate on the ground that it was devoted to the worship of Artemis. But Provincial temples of the Imperial religion were built in Ephesus, one under Claudius or Nero, one under Hadrian, and a third under Severus; and the city boasted that it was Temple-Warden or Neokoros of three Emperors.

Sometimes it styles itself "four times Neokoros"; but the fourth Temple-Wardenship seems to be of Artemis, not of a fourth Emperor; though the fact that the title (which ordinarily was restricted to Imperial temples) was allowed in respect of the temple of Artemis shows that a very close relation was formed between the Imperial religion and the worship of Artemis as a goddess of the whole Province. A coin shows the four temples, containing the statues of Artemis and three Emperors, and marks the closeness of the connection between the cults.

Two subjects still claim some notice, the changes in the relation of sea and land, and the changes in the constitution of the city.

The stages of the former cannot be precisely dated; but the Gulf of Ephesus was gradually filled up as the centuries passed by, and navigation was after a time rendered difficult by shallows and changes of depth, caused by the silting action of the Cayster. The entrance to the gulf grew narrower; and a channel was not easily kept safe for ships. Engineering operations, intended to improve the water-way, were carried out by the Pergamenian kings of the second century B.C. and by the Romans in the first century after Christ; these show the time when the evil was becoming serious. When the ship in which St. Paul travelled from Troas to Jerusalem in A.D. 57 sailed past Ephesus without entering the harbour, this may probably be taken as a sign that ships were beginning to avoid Ephesus unless it was necessary to take or discharge cargo and passengers.

The state of the coast during the second century after Christ is shown by the following incident.

Apollonius of Tyana, defending himself before Domitian, spoke of Ephesus as having now outgrown the site on which it had been placed and extended to the sea. This furnishes a conclusive proof both that the sea no longer reached up to Ephesus when the speech was composed, and that it was not so distant from the city as the modern seashore, for it is impossible to suppose that the city ever reached to the present coastline. The words probably imply that the seashore was near the lower (i.e. western) end of the Hermaion, and that Ephesus extended into the valley of the stream which flows from Ortygia to join the Cayster now, but at that time fell into the sea. It remains uncertain whether Philostratus composed the speech about 210 or found it in his authorities. The difference however is not serious. There is no reason to think that the words are as old as Apollonius' supposed trial about A.D. 90. They represent the ideas that were floating in the Asian world, A.D. 100-200; and even a century would not produce much difference in the coast line.

But even in the second and third centuries after Christ Ephesus was still a great trading city, and therefore must have still had a harbour open, though not easy of access. It is certain that only energetic engineering work kept an open channel. The last kilometre of the modern river course is straight, in contrast with the winding course immediately above; the channel is embanked with a carefully built wall, in order to increase the scour of the water; and this part of the course is evidently the result of a great and well-designed scheme for improving the bed of the river. Probably, this was a new channel, cut specially in order to avoid the shallows of the entrance to the gulf.

The ultimate result, however, is certain. Ephesus ceased to be accessible for shipping, and the city harbour became an inland marsh. It is probable that this result had been accomplished before the time of Justinian, 527-563 A.D.; he chose Ayassoluk for the site of his great Church of St. John Theologos, and this site implies that all thought of maritime relations had ceased.

The constitution of Ephesus sought to maintain by a division into Tribes an equipoise between the diverse elements which were united in the city. Apparently there were originally three, Epheseis, including the native population, Euonymoi, the Athenian colonists, and Bembinaioi (Bembineis), possibly the colonists of other Greek regions (taking name from Bembina, a village of Argolis, beside Nemea). Two more Tribes, Teioi and Karenaioi, were introduced to accommodate new bodies of settlers from the Ionian city Teos and, presumably, from Mysia (where the town Karene was situated). Ephorus, who wrote in the middle of the fourth century, describes these as the five Ephesian Tribes.

A sixth Tribe was introduced at some later time; but the date of its formation is uncertain. It is mentioned under the name Sebaste, i.e. Augustan, a name given to it in honour of Augustus; but the Tribe was not first instituted then, for, had that been so, its divisions (Chiliastyes) would have naturally been called by names characteristic of the period; but they bear names which point to an earlier origin. It would therefore appear that the new name Sebaste was given to one of the existing Tribes; and the latest formed Tribe was chosen for the purpose. As to the origin of the sixth Tribe, nothing is known except that it was later than about 340 B.C., and older than the time of Augustus. The only two occasions on which the formation of a new Tribe seems reasonably probable were the refoundation by Lysimachus about 287 B.C., and the remodelling of the constitution by Antiochus II, 261-246 B.C. Lysimachus introduced bodies of new citizens from the Ionian cities of Lebedos and Colophon; but he did not form a new Tribe to hold them. He classed the Lebedians as a special division (Chiliastys) of the Tribe Epheseis, which he evidently instituted under the name Lebedioi; and if a complete list of the Chiliastyes were preserved, we might find another called Colophonioi. Apparently Lysimachus was anxious to avoid a too marked break with the past, and left the old Tribes unchanged in names and number. It remains that the sixth Tribe must have been formed by Antiochus II. Now it has been shown in chapter 12 that Antiochus placed in Ephesus a body of Jews as citizens, and it is expressly recorded that he settled the constitution on a lasting basis, which remained unchanged at least until 15 B.C. It has also been shown in that chapter that a body of Jewish citizens could be introduced into a Hellenic city only by placing them in a special Tribe. The old five Tribes had their own long-established religious rites, which could not be avoided by any member, and were impossible for Jews. A new Tribe was required whose bond of unity should not be of a kind to exclude the Jews. Antiochus formed a sixth Tribe and placed all his new citizens in it. The original name of this Tribe is unknown; but it was probably such as to give an appearance of Hellenic character (as the Jewish Tribe in Alexandria was called Macedones). The only known Chiliastyes of this Tribe were Labandeos (which seems Carian, and may mark a body of Carian colonists) and Sieus (from the name of an aquatic plant like parsley, that grew in the marshes near Ephesus): the latter seems intended to give a native appearance to this latest and most foreign of classes in the State.

It is not necessary to suppose that the new Tribe consisted exclusively of Jews. It would be sufficient to make two provisions: first, one of the Chiliastyes of the new Tribe must have been reserved for the Jews; secondly, the bond of unity in the whole Tribe must not be a pagan ritual. It must be observed that, while it was hardly possible for the king to tamper with the religion of any of the old Tribes, the character of the new one was entirely within his control.

Chapter 18: The Letter to the Church in Ephesus

These things saith he that holdeth the seven stars in his right hand, he that walketh in the midst of the seven golden lamps.

I know thy works, and thy toil and patience, and that thou canst not bear evil men, and didst try them which call themselves apostles, and they are not, and didst find them false; and thou hast patience and didst bear for my name's sake, and has not grown weary. But I have this against thee, that thou didst leave thy first love. Remember therefore from whence thou art fallen, and repent, and do the first works; or else I come to thee, and will move thy candlestick out of its place, except thou repent. But this thou hast, that thou hatest the works of the Nicolaitans, which I also hate.

He that hath an ear, let him hear what the Spirit saith to the Churches.

To him that overcometh, to him will I give to eat of the tree of life, which is in the Paradise of God.

The message to the Church in Ephesus comes from Him "that holdest the seven stars in His right hand, that walketh in the midst of the seven golden lamps." If we review the openings of the other six letters, none could so appropriately be used to the Church in Ephesus as this description. The only exordium which could for a moment be compared in suitability with it is the opening of the Sardian letter, "he that hath the Seven Spirits of God and the Seven Stars." The second part in that case is almost identical with part of the Ephesian exordium, but the first part is different.

The similarity between the Ephesian and Sardian letters is not confined to the opening address, but can be traced throughout. If Ephesus was the practical centre and leading city of Asia at that time, though not the official capital of the Province, Sardis was the ancient capital of Lydia, and the historical centre of the Asian cities; the tone and spirit of the history of the two Churches had been to a certain degree analogous; and therefore a resemblance in the letters was natural. The Author of the letters assumes much the same character in addressing these two cities, emphasising in both cases his relation with all the Seven Churches. The capital of a country stands for the whole, and he who addresses the practical capital may well lay stress upon his relation to all the other cities of the country. But the similarities and differences between these two letters can be discussed more satisfactorily when we take up the Sardian letter and have both before us.

Ephesus, as in practical importance the leading city of the Province Asia, might be said in a sense to be the centre, to be in the midst of the Seven Churches; and the Divine figure that addresses her appropriately holds in His hand the Seven Stars, which "are the Seven Churches." The leading city can stand for the whole Province, as the Province can stand for the whole Church; and that was so customary and usual as to need no explanation or justification. To the Christians, Ephesus and Asia were almost convertible terms; Ephesus stood for Asia, Asia was Ephesus. Hence in the list of Equivalent names compiled by some later scribe, the explanation is formally given, No. 40, "Asia" means the city Ephesus.

As to the holding of the seven stars, Mr. Anderson Scott, in his admirable little edition, published in the Century Bible, remarks that "in the image before the eye of the Seer the seven stars probably appear as a chain of glittering jewels hanging from the hand of Christ." This image suits excellently the description which we have given already of the Seven Churches as situated on the circling road that goes forth from Ephesus, traverses them all in succession and returns to its point of origin in the representative city of the Province. The analogy from pagan art quoted in chapter 19 shows readily this figure would be understood by the Asian readers.

After the initial address, the letter begins, according to the usual plan, with the statement that the Author has full knowledge of the character and fortunes of the Church. He knows what the Ephesians have done.

The past history of the Ephesian Church had been one of labour and achievement, enduring and energetic. Above all it had been distinguished by its insight into the true character of those who came to it with the appearance of Apostles. It lay on the great highway of the world, visited by many Christian travellers, some coming to it for its own sake, others merely on their way to a more distant destination. Especially, those who were travelling to and from Rome for the most part passed through Ephesus:

hence it was already, or shortly afterwards became, known as the highway of the martyrs, "the passage-way of those who are slain unto God," as Ignatius called it a few years later, i.e., the place through which must pass those who were on their way to Rome to amuse the urban population by their death in the amphitheatre. Occasionally, it is true, they were conducted to Rome by a different road. Ignatius, for example, did not pass through Ephesus, but was taken along the overland route, for some reason unknown to us. The reason did not lie in the season of the year, for he was at Smyrna on 7th August, and probably reached Rome on 17th October, an open time for navigation. But Ignatius knew, though he himself was led by another route, that the ordinary path of death for Eastern martyrs was by land to Ephesus and thence by sea to Rome.

Among the travellers there came to Ephesus, or passed through it, many who claimed to be teachers; but the Ephesian Church tested them all; and, when they were false, unerringly detected them and unhesitatingly rejected them.

The recital of the past history and the services of the Church occupies a much greater proportion of the Ephesian letter than of any other of the Seven. The writer dwells upon this topic with emphatic appreciation. After describing the special kind of work in which the Ephesians had been most active and useful, he returns again to praise their career of patience and steadfastness, and describes their motive-- "for my name's sake"--which enhances their merit. The best counsel, the full and sufficient standard of excellence for the Ephesians, is to do as they did of old. Others may have to improve; but Ephesians are urged not to fall short of their ancient standard of action.

The best commentary on this is found in the letter of Ignatius to the Ephesians, with its profound and frank admiration, which might seem almost to be exaggerated were it not justified by the language of St. John. The Syrian bishop wrote as one who felt that he was honoured in associating with the envoys from the Ephesian Church and in being "permitted by letter to bear it company, and to rejoice with it." Ignatius shows clearly in his letter the reasons for his admiration. The characteristics which he praises in the Ephesian Church are the same as those which St. John mentions. And yet they are so expressed as to exclude the idea that he remembered the words of this letter and either consciously or unconsciously used them: "I ought to be trained for the contest by you in faith, in admonition, in endurance, in long suffering," sect. 3: "for ye all live according to truth and no heresy hath a home among you; nay, ye do not so much as listen to any one if he speak of ought else save concerning Jesus Christ in truth," sect. 6: "as indeed ye are not deceived," sect. 8: "I have learned that certain persons passed through you from Syria, bringing evil doctrine; whom ye suffered not to sow seed in you, for ye stopped your ears," sect. 9: "you were ever of one mind with the Apostles in the power of Jesus Christ," sect. 11.

The ideas are the same; but they are scattered about through Ignatius' letter, and not concentrated in one place. Moreover the words are almost entirely different. The only important words common to those passages of Ignatius and the letter which we are studying are "endurance," which almost forced itself on any writer, and "Apostles"; but Ignatius speaks of the true Apostles, St. John of the false. The idea of testing, which is prominent in St. John, is never explicitly mentioned by Ignatius, and yet it is implied and presupposed in the passages quoted from sections 6, 8, 9. But he was interested only in the result, the successful championing of truth, whereas St. John was necessarily interested quite as much in the way by which the Ephesians attained the result.

The probability, then, is that Ignatius was not familiar with the Ephesian letter of St. John. He could hardly have kept so remote from the expression of this letter, if it had been clear and fresh in his memory. Hence his testimony may be taken as entirely independent of the Revelation, and as showing that the reputation of Ephesus in the Christian world about the beginning of the second century had not grown weaker or less brilliant in the short interval since St. John wrote.

But, while nothing is required of the Ephesians except that they should continue to show their old character, yet a return to their earlier spirit was urgently necessary. The fault of the Ephesian Church was that it no longer showed the same spirit: the intense enthusiasm which characterised the young Church had grown cooler with advancing age. That was the serious danger that lay before them; and it is the common experience in every reform movement, in every religion that spreads itself by proselytising. The history of Mohammedanism shows it on a large scale. No religion has ever exercised a more rapid and almost magical influence over barbarous races than Islam has often done, elevating them at once to a distinctly higher level of spiritual and intellectual life than they had been capable of even understanding before. But in the case of almost every Mohammedanised race, after the first burst of enthusiastic religion, under the immediate stimulus of the great moral ideas that Mohammed taught, has been exhausted, its subsequent history presents a spectacle of stagnation and retrogression.

The problem in this and in every other such case is how to find any means of exercising a continuous stimulus, which shall maintain the first enthusiasm. Something is needed, and the writer of this letter perhaps was thinking of some such stimulus in the words that follow, containing a threat as to what shall be done to Ephesus if it continues to degenerate, and fails to reinvigorate its former earnest enthusiasm. But a less serious penalty is threatened in this case than in some of the other letters--not destruction, nor rejection, not even the extirpation of the weak or erring portion of the Church, but only "I come in displeasure at thee, and will move thy lamp, the Church, out of its place."

Some commentators regard the threat as equivalent to a decree of destruction, and point to the fact that the site is a desert and the Church extinct as a proof that the threat has been fulfilled. But it seems impossible to accept this view. It is wrong method to disregard the plain meaning, which is not destruction but change; and equally so to appeal to present facts as proving that destruction must have been meant by this figurative expression.

Equally unsatisfactory is another interpretation, that Ephesus shall be degraded from its place of honour, which implies an unconscious assumption that Ephesus already occupied its later position of metropolitan authority in the Asian Church. As yet Ephesus had no principate in the Church, except what it derived from its own character and conduct: while its character continued, its influence must continue; if its character degenerated, its influence must disappear. Ephesus has always remained the titular head of the Asian Church; and the Bishop of Ephesus still bears that dignity, though he no longer resides at Ephesus, but at Magnesia ad Sipylum. For many centuries, however, Smyrna has been in practice a much more important See than Ephesus.

The natural meaning must be taken. The threat is so expressed that it must be understood of a change in local position: "I will move thy Church out of its place."

Surely in this milder denunciation we may see a proof that the evil in Ephesus was curable. The loss of enthusiasm which affected that Church was different in kind from the lukewarmness that affected Laodicea, and should be treated in a different way. The half-heartedness of the Laodiceans was deadly, and those who were so affected were hopeless, and should be irrevocably and inexorably rejected. But the cooling of the first Ephesian enthusiasm was a failing that lies in human nature. The failing can be corrected, the enthusiasm may be revived; and, if the Ephesians cannot revive it among themselves by their own strength, their Church shall be moved out of its place.

The interpretation of Grotius comes near the truth: "I will cause thy population to flee away to another place." We do not know whether the form in which he expresses his interpretation is due to the belief current in the country that the Christian people of Ephesus fled to the mountains and settled in a village four hours distant, called Kirkindje, which their descendants still consider to be the representative of the ancient Ephesus. But if Grotius had that fact in view, his interpretation does not quite hit the mark. The writer of the Seven Letters was not thinking of an arbitrary fact of that kind, which might befall any city, and was in no way characteristic of the real deep-seated nature of one city more than of another. He had his eye fixed on the broad permanent character of Ephesian scenery and surroundings, and his thought moved in accord with the nature of the locality, and expressed itself in a form that applied to Ephesus and to no other of the Seven Churches.

There is one characteristic that belongs to Ephesus, distinctive and unique among the cities of the Seven Churches: it is change. In most ancient sites one is struck by the immutability of nature and the mutability of all human additions to nature. In Ephesus it is the shifting character of the natural conditions on which the city depends for prosperity that strikes every careful observer and every student either of history or of nature. The scenery and the site have varied from century to century. Where there was water there is now land: what was a populated city in one period ceased to be so in another, and has again become the centre of life for the valley: where at one time there was only bare hillside or the gardens of a city some miles distant, at another time there was a vast city crowded with inhabitants, and this has again relapsed into its earlier condition: the harbour in which St. John and St. Paul landed has become a mere marsh, and the theatre where the excited crowd met and shouted to Diana, desolate and ruinous as it is, has been more permanent than the harbour. The relation of sea and land has changed in quite unusual fashion: the broad level valley was once a great inlet of the sea, at the head of which was the oldest Ephesus, beside the Temple of the Goddess, near where the modern village stands. But the sea receded and the land emerged from it. The city followed the sea, and changed from place to place to maintain its importance as the only harbour of the valley.

All those facts were familiar to the Ephesians; they are recorded for us by Strabo, Pliny, and Herodotus, but Ephesian belief and record are the foundation for the statements of those writers. A threat of removing the Church from its place would be inevitably understood by the Ephesians as a denunciation of another change in the site of the city, and must have been so intended by the writer. Ephesus and its Church should be taken up, and moved away to a new spot, where it might begin afresh on a new career with a better spirit. But it would be still Ephesus, as it had always hitherto been amid all changes.

Such was the meaning that the Ephesians must have taken from the letter; but no other of the Seven Cities would have found those words so clear and significant. Others would have wondered what they might mean, as the commentators are still wondering and debating. To the Ephesians the words would seem natural and plain.

But after this threat the letter returns to the dominant note. The Ephesian Church was still, as it had been from the beginning, guarding the way, testing all new teachers, and rejecting with sure judgment the unworthy. In the question which beyond all others seemed to the writer the critical problem of the day the Ephesians agreed with him, and hated the works of the Nicolaitans. In two other letters that party in the early Church is more fully described. In the Ephesian letter the Nicolaitans are only named.

The promise contained in the perorations of the Seven Letters is different in every case, and is evidently adapted in each instance to suit the general tone of the letter and the character and needs of the city. To the Ephesian who overcometh, the promise is that he shall eat of the tree of life, which is in the Garden of God. Life is promised both to Smyrna and to Ephesus; yet how differently is it expressed in the two cases. Smyrna must suffer, and would be faithful unto death, but it shall not be hurt of the second death. Ephesus had been falling from its original high level of enthusiasm; it needed to be quickened and reinvigorated, and none of the promises made to the other Churches would suit its need; but the fruit of the tree of life is the infallible cure, the tree whose very leaves were for the healing of the nations, the tree in which every true Christian acquires a right of participation (22:2, 14). The expression is, of course, symbolical; and its real meaning can hardly be specified. It would be vain to ask what St. John had precisely in his mind; but it might be a more hopeful task to inquire what meaning the Asian readers would take from the phrase. It is a Jewish expression; but the Asian readers would take it in the way in which many Jewish ideas seem to have become efficacious in the Province, viz., in a sort of syncretism of Jewish and native Asian thought.

Every image or idea in this letter finds a parallel or an illustration in Jewish thought and literature. Yet it cannot be said with truth that the letter is exclusively Jewish in tone. There is nothing in it which would seem strange or foreign to the Hellenic or Hellenised people for whom the book was in the first instance written. Even the tree of life carried no un-Hellenic connotation to Ephesian readers. The tree was as significant a symbol of life-giving Divine power to the Asian Greeks as to the Jews, though in a different way. Trees had been worshipped as the home of the Divine nature and power from time immemorial, and were still so worshipped, in Asia Minor as in the ancient world generally. On some sacred tree the prosperity and safety of a family or tribe or city was often believed to depend. When the sacred olive-tree on the Acropolis of Athens put forth a new shoot after the city had been burned by the Persians, the people knew that the safety of the State was assured. The belief was widely entertained that the life of a man was connected with some tree, and returned into that tree when he died. The tree which grew on a grave was often thought to be penetrated with the spirit and life of the buried man; and an old Athenian law punished with death any one that had cut a holm-oak growing in a sepulchral ground, i.e. heroon. Sacred trees are introduced in chapter 6, chapter 21 and chapter 17.

It will probably seem to many persons an unworthy and even irrational procedure to trace any connection between the superstitious veneration of sacred trees and the symbolism of St. John. But it was shown in chapter 13 that although Ignatius abhorred paganism, and though the memory of his pagan days caused a lasting sense of shame in his mind, yet he could compare the life of a Christian congregation to the procession at a pagan festival, and could use symbolism derived from the pagan mysteries to shadow forth the deepest thoughts of Christianity. In all those cases the same process takes place: the religious ideas of the pagans are renovated in a Christian form, ennobled and spiritualised. The tree of life in the Revelation was in the mind of the Ephesians a Christianisation of the sacred tree in the pagan religion and folklore: it was a symbolic expression which was full of meaning to the Asian Christians, because to them the tree had always been the seat of Divine life and the intermediary between Divine and human nature. The problem which was constantly present to the ancient mind in thinking of the relation of man to God appears here: how can the gulf that divides human nature from the Divine nature be bridged over? how can God come into effective relation to man? In the holy tree the Divine life is bringing itself closer to man. He who can eat of the tree of life is feeding on the Divine power and nature, is strengthening himself with the body and the blood of Christ. The idea was full of power to the Asian readers.

But to us the "tree of life" carries in itself little meaning. It seems to us at first little more than a metaphor in this passage, and in Revelation 22 it appears to us to be a mere detail in a rather fanciful and highly poetical allegory. A considerable effort is needed before we can even begin dimly to appreciate the power which this idea had in the minds of Ephesian readers: we have to recreate the thoughts and mind of that time, before we can understand their conception of the "tree of life."

Accordingly, although the "tree of life" is different from any expression that occurs, so far as known, in Greek literature, it contains nothing that would seem strange or exotic to Greeks or Asians. And every other idea in the letter would seem equally natural, and would appeal to equally familiar beliefs and habits of life. While we need not doubt that the writer took the "tree of life" from his own Jewish sphere of thought, yet he certainly avoids in all these letters anything that is distinctly anti-Hellenic in expression. So far as the Seven Letters are concerned, he is in advance of, not in hostility to, the best side of Hellenic thought and education.

Thus ends the letter. It is a distinctly laudatory one, when it is examined phrase by phrase: it shows admiration and full appreciation of a great career and a noble history. Yet it does not leave a pleasant impression of the Ephesian Church; and there is a lack of cordial and sympathetic spirit in it. The writer seems not to have loved the Ephesians as he did the Smyrnaeans and Philadelphians. He respected and esteemed them. He felt that they possessed every great quality except a loving enthusiasm. But when, in order to finish with a word of praise, he seeks for some definite laudable fact in their conduct at the present moment, the one thing which he finds to say is that they hated those whom he hated. Their disapproval and their hatred were correctly apportioned: in sympathy and love they were deficient. A common hatred is a poor and ephemeral ground of unanimity.

The Ephesians stand before us in the pathway of the world, at the door by which the West visited the East, and from which the East looked out upon the West, as a dignified people worthy of their great position, who had lived through a noble history in the past, and were on the whole not unworthy of it in the present, who maintained their high tradition--and yet one thing was lacking, the power of loving and of making themselves loved.

Chapter 19: Smyrna: The City of Life

Smyrna was founded as a Greek colony more than a thousand years before Christ; but that ancient Aeolian Smyrna was soon captured by Ionian Greeks, and made into an Ionian colony. Ionian Smyrna was a great city, whose dominion extended to the east far beyond the valley, and whose armies contended on even terms against the power of Lydia. Battles fought against the Lydians on the banks of the Hermus are mentioned by the Smyrnaean poet Mimnermus in the seventh century. But Lydian power with its centre at Sardis was increasing during that period, and Smyrna gradually gave way before it, until finally the Greek city was captured and destroyed about 600 B.C. by King Alyattes. In one sense Smyrna was now dead; the Greek city had ceased to exist; and it was only in the third century that it was restored to the history of Hellenic enterprise in Asia. There was, however, a State named Smyrna during that long interval, when the Ionian Smyrna was merely a historical memory. It is mentioned in an inscription of 368 B.C. as a place of some consequence; but it was no longer what the Greeks called a city. It was essential to the Greek idea of a city that it should have internal freedom, that it should elect its own magistrates to manage its own affairs, and that its citizens should have the education and the spirit which spring from habitually thinking imperially. This Asiatic Smyrna between about 600 and 290 was, as Strabo says, a loose aggregate of villagers living in various settlements scattered over the plain and the surrounding hills; it possessed no sovereign power or self-governing institutions; and it has left no trace on history. Aristides, however, says that there was a town in that period intermediate in position between the old and the later city.

Smyrna was treated more harshly than Ephesus by the Lydian conquerors: apparently the reason was that it was more typically Greek and more hostile to the Asiatic spirit of the Lydian realm, whereas the native Anatolian element was stronger in Ephesus. The purely Greek Smyrna could not be made to wear Lydian harness, and was destroyed. The half-Asiatic Ephesus was easily changed into a useful Lydian town without the complete sacrifice of autonomy and individuality.

The design was attributed to Alexander the Great of marking the triumph of Hellenism by refounding Greek Smyrna; and later coins of Smyrna show his dream, in which the Smyrnaean goddesses, the two Nemeseis or Fates, appeared to him and suggested to him that plan. But it was left for King Lysimachus, after Antigonus had made a beginning, to carry the design into effect. His refoundation of Smyrna and of Ephesus was a part of a great scheme, the completion of which was prevented by his death. The new Hellenic Smyrna was in a different place from the old Ionian city. The earlier city had been on a steep lofty hill overhanging on the north the extreme eastern recess of the gulf: the new city was on the southeast shore of the gulf about two miles away. The aim in the former was security against sudden attack, but there could never have been beside it a very good harbour. The later city was intended to be a maritime and trading centre, a good harbour and a convenient starting-point for a land-road to the east. The type of a merchant ship, which appears on its coins, as on those of Ephesus, indicates its maritime character.

Its maritime power was maintained by two ports. One was a small land-locked harbour, the narrow entrance of which could be closed by a chain: the other was probably only the adjacent portion of the gulf which served as a mooring-ground. The inner harbour lay in the heart of the modern city, where the bazaars now stand. In that situation, half surrounded by houses and close under the hill of Pagos, it was readily liable to grow shallower and to be ultimately filled up; but the small ancient ships found it so useful that the harbour authorities had to keep it carefully. In 1402 Tamerlane besieged the lower city, which was held by the Knights of Rhodes with their stronghold in a castle commanding the harbour; and he blocked the entrance by a mole in the process of his operations. After the entrance was once closed, the negligent government of the now Turkish city was not likely to try to reopen it; moreover as the size of ships increased, the usefulness of so small a harbour ceased. Thus the natural process of filling up the old harbour went on unchecked; and it has long disappeared, though it was still visible in the middle of the eighteenth century and even later.

To its maritime character was due the close association with Rome which Smyrna formed at an early period. From the time that the great republic began to interfere in the affairs of the East, common interests maintained a firm alliance and "friendship" (according to the Latin term) between Rome and Smyrna. A common danger and a common enemy united them. At first Smyrna was struggling to maintain its freedom against the Seleucid power, and Rome's Eastern policy sprang out of the agreement which its great enemy Hannibal had made with the Seleucid king, Antiochus the Great. At a later time Rome supported Smyrna as a counterpoise to the too great maritime power of Rhodes. As early as 195, when Antiochus was still at the height of his power, Smyrna built a temple and instituted a worship of Rome; this bold step was the pledge of uncompromising adherence to the cause of Rome, while its fortunes were still uncertain. After a century, when a Smyrnaean public assembly heard of the distress in a Roman army during the war against Mithridates, the citizens stripped off their own clothes to send to the shivering soldiers.

The faithfulness of Smyrna to this alliance was a just ground of pride to the city, and was fully acknowledged by her powerful friend. Cicero expressed the Roman feeling that Smyrna was "the city of our most faithful and most ancient allies"; and in 26 A.D. the Smyrnaeans argued before the Senate that the new temple to be dedicated by the Commune of Asia to Tiberius should be built in Smyrna, because of their faithful friendship dating from a time before the East had learned that Rome was the greatest power in the world; and they were preferred to all other cities of the Province.

The view of Smyrna in which its character and situation are best seen is got from the deck of a ship lying out in the gulf before the city. The traveller from the west sails up an arm of the sea, which runs far inland. At the southeastern end he finds Smyrna, with the hills behind it on the south and west, the sea on its north side, and on the east a beautiful little valley, nine miles by four, bounded by more distant mountains. The buildings of the city rise out of the water, cluster in the hollow below the hills, and on the lower skirts of Pagos, "the Hill," or straggle up irregularly towards the summit. There is a wonderful feeling of brightness, light, and activity in the scene: in such a matter only the personal experience can be stated, but such is the impression that the view has always made on the present writer. The approach to Constantinople from the east gives a similar impression; and part of the reason lies in the long land-locked sea-way which leads to the harbour, giving in both cases the appearance of inland cities with all the advantage of a situation on the sea.

The Smyrnaeans were specially proud of the beauty of their city. The frequent legend on their coins, "First of Asia," was contested by Pergamum and Ephesus; all three were first of Asia in one respect or another: Smyrna defined her rank on some coins as "First of Asia in beauty and size." Strabo says its beauty was due to the handsomeness of the streets, the excellence of the paving, and the regular arrangement in rectangular blocks. The picturesque element, which he does not mention, was contributed by the hills and the sea, to which in modern times the groves of cypress trees in the large Turkish cemeteries must be added. Groves of trees in the suburbs are mentioned by Aristides as one of the beauties of the ancient city. On the west the city included a hill which overhangs the sea and runs back southward till it nearly joins the western end of Pagos: in the angle the road to the south issued through the Ephesian Gate. The outer edge of the western hill afforded a strong line of defence, which the wall of Lysimachus took advantage of; and Pagos constituted an ideal acropolis, as well as a striking ornament to crown the beauty of the city.

The citizens were also proud of their distinction every branch of literature; and Apollonius of Tyana is said to have encouraged them in this, and to have advised them to rest their self-esteem more in their own character than in the beauty of their city: "for thought," as he said, "though it is the most beautiful of all cities under the sun, and makes the sea its own, and holds the fountains of Zephyrus, yet it is a greater charm to wear a crown of men than a crown of porticoes and pictures and gold beyond the standard of mankind: for buildings are seen only in their own place, but men are seen everywhere and spoken about everywhere and make their city as vast as the range of countries which they can visit."

The words of Apollonius show that "the crown of Smyrna" was a familiar phrase with the Smyrnaeans; and there can be no doubt that the phrase arose form the appearance of the hill Pagos, with the stately public buildings on its rounded top and the city spreading out down its rounded sloping sides. In fact, the words state plainly that the crown of Smyrna consisted of buildings, and, in the picturesque language of current talk (which always catches salient features), buildings are likened to a crown because they stand on a conspicuous place and in an orderly way. As to the modern appearance only a personal impression can be stated: "with Mount Pagos and its ruined castle rising out of the clustering houses, it looks a queenly city crowned with her diadem of towers'": so Mrs. Ramsay in 1901 described Smyrna as it used to appear from the sea. Until about 1890 the brow of the rounded hill was crowned with a well-preserved garland of walls and battlements; and the appearance of the circling city, the hill sloping back towards the centre, and the frowning walls crowning the edge of the rounded summit, has probably made the same impression on many travellers.

Aelius Aristides, who lived much in Smyrna, can hardly find language strong enough to paint the beauty and the crown of Smyrna. He compares the city, as the ideal city on earth, to the crown of Ariadne shining in the heavenly constellation. He describes it as sitting like a statue with its feet planted on seashore and harbours and groves of trees, its middle parts poised equally above the plain and beneath the summit, and its top in the distance gently rising by hardly perceptible gradations to the acropolis, which offered an outlook over the sea and the town, and stood always a brilliant ornament above the city. Thus Smyrna city was a flower of beauty, such as earth and sun had never showed to mankind. He repeats the comparison to a statue and to a flower in several of his orations. The likeness depends partly on the appearance of the city as sloping up from the sea, partly on the orderly arrangement of the part, partly on the circular head with its crown of buildings, viz., Pagos with its acropolis. The idea of the crown is in his mind, though he varies the phrase: the truth was that Aristides in his highly wrought orations would not use a figure that was in everybody's mouth, and he plays with the idea but rarely uses the word. Several of his highly ornate sentences become clearer when we notice that he is expressing in a series of variations the idea of a crown resting on the summit of the hill.

When Aristides says that, since Smyrna has been restored after the disastrous earthquake, "Spring's gates and Summer's are opened by crowns," the reference to some close connection between Smyrna and the crown is so marked that Reiske suggests that the Crowns were the deities of flowers (like Flora in Latin). We now know that the Crown of Smyrna was the head and bloom of the city's flower. Again he declares that, by the revival of Smyrna, "the crown has been preserved to Ionia."

The comparison of Smyrna to a flower has a close connection with the "crown." The crown or garland was usually a circlet of flowers; and the mention of a crown immediately aroused in the ancient mind the thought of a flower. Crowns were worn chiefly in the worship of the gods. The worshipper was expected to have on his head a garland of the flowers or foliage sacred to the god whose rites he was performing. The guests at an entertainment were often regarded as worshippers of Bacchus and wore the sacred ivy: frequently, also, the entertainment was a feast connecting with the ritual of some other deity, and the crown varied accordingly. Thus the ideas of the flower and of the crown suggest in their turn the idea of the god with whose worship they were connected, i.e., the statue of the god. The tutelary deity of Smyrna was the Mother-goddess, Cybele; and when Aristides pictured Smyrna as a statue sitting with her feet on the sea, and her head rising to heaven and crowned with a circlet of beautiful buildings, he had in mind the patroness and guardian of the city, who was represented enthroned and wearing a crown of battlements and towers. Her image was one of the most frequent types on the coins of the city, and in many alliance-coins she appears for Smyrna. The crown of Smyrna was the mural crown of Smyrna's goddess.

From the same origin arises his repeated allusion to the necklace of Smyrna. If there was a crown on the top of the head, a clearly marked street or any line which encompassed the lower part of the hill may be compared to a necklace. He speaks of the city as drawing to itself its various ornaments of sea and suburbs in a variegated necklace: a figurative expression which recalls the chain of the Seven Stars hanging from the hand of the Divine Author of the Seven Letters (as described in the Ephesian Letter).

But what Aristides chiefly thought of, when he mentions the necklace, was the splendid Street of Gold, which he alludes to several times in a more or less veiled and figurative way. He mentions once the streets that took their names from temples and from gold. Apollonius (as already quoted) alludes in similar figurative style to the gold of Smyrna, and connects it with the crown of Smyrna, which shows that it crossed the sloping hill, and by its conspicuous buildings contributed to that orderly arrangement of edifices which constituted the idea of the crown. Aristides, likewise, refers to this magnificent street when he says that, as you traverse the city from west to east, you go from a temple to a temple and from a hill to a hill. It is suggested in Dr. Hastings' Dictionary of the Bible, iv., p. 554, that this street ran from the Temple of Zeus Akraios to the Temple of the Mother-goddess Cybele Sipylene. The latter was probably on the hill Tepejik on the eastern outskirts of the city: the former has been identified recently by Mr. Fontrier, the chief authority on the topography of Smyrna, with certain remains on the western slope of Pagos. A street connecting those two temples would curve round the lower slopes of the hill (owing to the conformation of the ground), and would by its length and its fine buildings form a conspicuous band which might well be compared in ornate rhetoric to a circlet of jewels round the neck of the statue.

The comparison of Smyrna to a statue appears in the address of Apollonius, and it is evident either that the comparison passed through his influence into Smyrnaean usage and became a current expression, or that the biographer of Apollonius deliberately attributed to the older orator a simile which was commonly used in Smyrna (for Aristides, in all his ornate descriptions of Smyrna, catches up and elaborates the expressions familiar among the citizens). The latter supposition is more probable: the biographer's custom was to select prominent and recognised characteristics of a great city like Smyrna, and show that they were all due to wise counsel given by the divinely inspired Apollonius.

Thus Apollonius is described as recommending to the citizens a certain strenuous activity of spirit as the true path to honour and success for their city: "competitive unanimity" is his phrase. Aristides mentions as characteristic of Smyrna "the grace which extends over every part like a rainbow, and strains the city like a lyre into tenseness harmonious with itself and with its beautiful surroundings, and the brightness which pervades every part and reaches up to heaven, like the glitter of the bronze armour in Homer." In these words Aristides is playing on a common idea in Greek philosophy, which is applied by Apollonius to Smyrna. The application is distinctly an older idea taken up by Aristides; and the probability is that this again was the recognised character of Smyrna, which Philostratus in his usual way derives from the wise counsel given by his hero.

The prevalent wind, now called Imbat, i.e. Landward, sets up the long gulf from the western sea; and blows with wonderful regularity through the hot weather, rising almost every day as the sun grows warm, blowing sometimes with considerable strength in the early afternoon, and dying down towards sunset. This westerly breeze, Zephyrus, was in ancient times, and is still, reckoned by the inhabitants as one of the great advantages of their city. It breathes a pleasant coolness through the city in the heat of summer; and people luxuriate in its refreshing breath and never tire of lauding its delightful effect. In ancient times they boasted in the words of Apollonius (already quoted) that they possessed the fountains of Zephyr, and could therefore reckon with certainty on continuous westerly breezes. As Aristides says, "the winds blow through every part of the town, and make it fresh like a grove of trees." The inhabitants never realised that the Zephyr brings with it some disadvantages. It comes laden with moisture, and it prevents free passage of the drainage from the city to the open gulf.

According to Strabo, the one defect in the situation of Smyrna was that the lowest parts of the city were difficult to drain. The level has risen in modern times through the accumulation of soil; but in ancient times there was little difference between the level of sea and land until the rise of the hills was reached. The difficulty of drainage, however was not due solely to the lowness of the level. It was aggravated by the winds. The prevalent wind blowing eastwards up the gulf heaps up the water on the shore, and prevents the discharge from finding its way out to sea. Hence in modern time there is often a malodour on the quay when the west wind is blowing fresh.

But the people of Smyrna did not mention this or any other defect of their city in talking with others. Municipal rivalry and local pride were keen and strong in ancient times. The narrower Greek conception of patriotism which restricted it to the limits of the city made those feelings far more powerful in ancient times; and Rome tried in vain to put Imperial in the place of local patriotism: she could plant the seeds of a wider feeling and raise it to a certain height, but the growth was not so strong and deep-rooted as the municipal pride.

Smyrna boasted that it was the city of Homer, who had been born and brought up beside the sacred river Meles. Homer is one of the most frequent types on coins of the city; and there was a temple called Homereion in the city. The same name was applied to a small bronze coin, which showed the poet sitting, holding a volumen on his knees, and supporting his chin on his right hand.

According to the allusions of Aristides, the Meles was a stream close to the city, between it and the open plain, having an extremely short course, so that its mouth was close to its source; it flowed with an equable stream, unvarying in summer and winter; its channel was more or less artificial; and its water was not cold in winter (when Aristides bathed in it by order of the god Asklepios, and found it pleasantly warm). These characteristics suit only the splendid fountains of Diana's Bath, Khalka-Bunar, on the east outskirts of the modern city, and the stream that flows thence to the sea with an even current and volume. The source is at so low a level that an artificial channel has always been needed to carry off the water. In modern time the locality has been entirely altered; the water is dammed up to supply part of the city; the surplus runs off through a straight cutting to the sea, and all the picturesqueness of the scene has been lost with the disappearance of the trees and the natural surroundings.

This identification is confirmed by the representation of the god Meles, given on a coin of Smyrna. He appears in the ordinary form, which Greek art appropriated to the idea of a river-god, except that he has not a cornucopia resting on his bent left arm. The cornucopia symbolised the fertilising power of the river, which supplies the water that the dry soil of Asia everywhere needs: the river turns an arid desert into a garden. But the Meles, flowing down a little way from the source to the sea, has no opportunity for diffusing fertility, and the cornucopia would be unsuitable to it. It was a stream to give pleasure and health by its fountains, and was worshipped as a healing power; but its water rises at so low a level that it was not used by the agriculturist.

The patron-goddess of Smyrna was a local variety of Cybele, known as the Sipylene Mother. Like the Artemis of Ephesus, her oldest home was in the mountains on the north of the valley, famous in myth and history as Sipylos, where Niobe dwelt and Tantalus reigned; and she came down to the plain with her worshippers, and took up her abode "Before-the-City." She became a more moralised conception in the Ionian Greek city; and Nemesis was the aspect which she bore to the Greek mind. In Smyrna alone, of all the Greek cities, Nemesis was regarded not as a single figure, but as a pair. The twin figures Nemesis often appear as a type on coins of the city: they stand as a rule on the ground, one holding a bridle, the other a cubit-rule with a wheel at her feet, the wheel becomes a chariot drawn by griffins, on which the twin goddesses are borne.

Aristides describes the plain of Smyrna as won from the sea, but not in the same way as some plains (e.g., those of Ephesus and Miletus) were won, viz., by silting up. Probably geologists would confirm his statement that the sea once extended much farther to the East. But when he wrote the change had not taken place in recent time; and little change has taken place between the first century and the twentieth. But in two respects there has been change. The coast in front of the city has advanced, the city has encroached a good deal on the sea, and the inner harbour has been entirely filled up. But in the southeastern corner of the gulf, near the mouth of the Meles, the sea has encroached on the land. The steady action of the west wind through many months of every year drives the sea on that corner and washes away the coast slowly but steadily. But the rivulets which flow into the eastern end of the gulf are all mountain streamlets, which carry little silt, but wash down gravel and pebbles into the plain, and are dry or almost dry in the hot season. The Meles alone flows with a full and unvarying current, but its course is very short.

Under the Roman government Smyrna enjoyed the eventless existence of a city which suffered few disasters and had an almost unbroken career of prosperity. From the sixth century onwards it was the only important harbour for inland caravan trade on the west coast of Asia Minor; and its importance in comparison with other cities of the coast necessarily increased as time passed. In the centuries that followed the lot of every city in Asia Minor was an unhappy one; and Smyrna suffered with the rest. But it was the last to suffer from the eastern raids; and it was generally the ally of western powers in that time, as once it had been the ally of Rome. The circumstances of sea and land gave it lasting vitality. Frequent earthquakes have devastated it, but only seemed to give it the opportunity of restoring itself more beautifully than before. No conquest and no disaster could permanently injure it. It occupied the one indispensable situation; it was the doorkeeper of a world.

The "alliances" of Smyrna were very numerous; and she was the only city which had formed that kind of engagement for mutual recognition of religious rites and privileges with all the rest of the Seven Cities. The Amazon Smyrna, the mythical foundress of the ancient Aeolic city, armed with the Amazons' weapon, the double-axe, wearing the short tunic and high boots of the huntress and warrior, holds out her right hand to greet the peaceful figure of Thyatira, who is dressed in the long tunic and mantle (peplos) of a Greek lady, and rests her raised left hand on a sceptre. Both wear the mural crown, which indicated the genius of a city. Behind the foot of Smyrna appears the prow of a ship.

Its position saved it from conquest till all other cities of the land had long been under Turkish rule; and its commercial relations with the west made it the great stronghold of the European spirit in Asia Minor. The Knights of St. John held it during the fourteenth century. Even after Pagos was captured by the Turks, the castle on the inner harbour was a Christian stronghold till Tamerlane at last took it in 1402. Since then Smyrna has been a Turkish city; but the Christian element has always been strong and at the present time outnumbers the Mohammedan in the proportion of three to one; and the city is called by the Turks Infidel Smyrna, Giaour Ismir.

In the Byzantine ecclesiastical order, Smyrna was at an early time separated from the rest of Asia, and made independent of Ephesus (autokephalos). In the new order which takes its name from Leo VI it appears as a metropolis with six subject bishoprics on the shores of the gulf or in the lower Hermus Valley.

Chapter 20: The Letter to the Church in Smyrna

These things saith the first and the last, which was dead, and lived:

I know thy tribulation, and thy poverty (but thou art rich), and the blasphemy of them which say they are Jews, and they are not, but are a synagogue of Satan. Fear not the things which thou art about to suffer: behold, the devil is about to cast some of you into prison, that ye may be tried; and ye shall have tribulation ten days. Be thou faithful unto death, and I will give thee the crown of life.

He that hath an ear, let him hear what the Spirit saith to the churches.

He that overcometh shall not be hurt of the second death.

The letter to the Smyrnaeans forms in many ways a marked contrast to the Ephesian letter; it is constructed exactly on the same plain, but the topics are of a very different kind. Of all the seven letters this is expressed in the most continuous and unbroken tone of laudation. It is instinct with life and joy. The writer is in thorough sympathy with the Church which he is addressing; he does not feel towards it merely that rather cold admiration which he expresses for the noble history of the Ephesian Church, a history which, alas! belonged only to the past: he is filled with warm affection. The joy that brightens the letter is caused not by ease and comfort and pleasures, but by the triumph over hardship and persecution, by superiority to circumstances; and the life that invigorates and warms it is that strong vitality which overcomes death and rises victorious from apparent dissolution.

Another marked difference between the two letters is this. While the Ephesian letter appeals throughout to the past history of the Church in Ephesus, and attempts to rouse a fresh enthusiasm among the congregation by the memory of their previous glory as Christians, the Smyrnaean letter is to a remarkable degree penetrated with local feeling and urban patriotism, which must be pointed out in the details, one by one.

The Smyrnaean Church is addressed by "the first and the last, which was dead and lived."

The meaning of this opening address is obscured by the unfortunate mistranslation, which mars both the Authorised and the Revised Versions, "was dead and lived again." The insertion of this word again is unjustified and unjustifiable: there is nothing in the Greek corresponding to it, and the quotations from Matthew 9:18, John 5:25, Ezekiel 37:3 (which Alford gives in illustration) do not constitute sufficient defence. The analogy of Revelation 13:2ff corroborates the plain sense of this letter. The idea is, not that life begins a second time after a period of death, but that life persists in and through death. The Divine Sender of the letter to Smyrna "was dead and lived," and so likewise Smyrna itself "was dead and lived." If anything should be inserted in the translation to make the meaning quite clear, the word needed is yet, "which was dead and yet lived."

Again, the phrase "was dead" also is not an exact equivalent of the Greek words: it would be nearer the true force of the Greek to render "became dead" or "became a corpse."

All Smyrnaean readers would at once appreciate the striking analogy to the early history of their own city which lies in that form of address. Strabo, as usual, furnishes the best commentary. He relates that the Lydians destroyed the ancient city of Smyrna, and that for four hundred years there was no "city," but merely a state composed of villages scattered over the plain and the hillsides around. Like Him who addresses it, Smyrna literally "became dead and yet lived." A practical corroboration of these last words is found in an inscription belonging to the fourth century B.C., which mentions Smyrna as existing during the period when, as Strabo says, it had been destroyed and had not been refounded. During those four centuries Smyrna had ceased to exist as a Greek city, but it lived on as a village state after the Anatolian system: then the new period began, and it was restored as an autonomous, self-governing Greek city, electing its own magistrates and administering its own affairs according to the laws which it made for itself.

In a sense both Smyrna and Ephesus had changed their character and situation in ancient time; but the salient fact in the one case was simple change of the city's position, in the other apparent destruction and death under which lay hidden a real continuance of life. Strabo emphatically says that Smyrna was obliterated from the roll of cities for four centuries; but other authorities speak of Smyrna as a State existing during that period of annihilation. The words of the ancients literally are that Smyrna was dead and yet lived. The two letters are adapted to the historical facts with delicate discrimination; change is the word in the first letter, life under and amid death is the expression in the second.

The idea of life is, of course, to be understood in its fullest sense when applied to a Christian congregation. It implies the energetic discharge of all the duties and functions of a Church. The contrast between apparent destruction and real vitality is expressed in several forms through this letter. The Church seemed poor, but was rich. It suffered apparent tribulation, but was really triumphant and crowned with the crown of life. Its enemies on the other hand were pretenders; they boasted that they were the true Jews, but they were not; they claimed to be the people of God, but they were only a synagogue of Satan.

After the introductory address, the letter begins with the usual statement: the writer has full knowledge of the past history of the Smyrnaean Church. The history of the Church had been a course of suffering, and not, as the Ephesian history had been, of achievement and distinction. The Smyrnaean Church had had a more trying and difficult career than any other of the Asian Churches. It had been exposed to constant persecution. It was poor in all that is ordinarily reckoned as wealth; but it was rich in the estimation of those who can judge of the realities of life. There is here the same contrast between appearance and reality as in the opening address: apparent poverty and real wealth, apparent death and real life.

The humble condition and the sufferings of the Smyrnaean Church are in this letter pointedly connected with the action of the Jews, and especially with the calumnies which they had circulated in the city and among the magistrates and the Roman officials. The precise facts cannot be discovered, but the general situation is unmistakable; the Smyrnaean Jews were for some reason more strongly and bitterly hostile to the Christians than the Jews of Asia generally. But the Asian Jews are little more than a name to us. From general considerations we can form some opinion about their position in the cities, as is shown in chapter 12; but in respect of details we know nothing. Accordingly we cannot even speculate as to the reason for the exceptionally strong anti-Christian feeling among the Smyrnaean Jews. We must simply accept the fact; but we may certainly conclude from it that the national feeling among them was unusually strong.

In an inscription of the second century "the quondam Jews" are mentioned as contributing 10,000 denarii to some public purpose connected with the embellishment of the city. Bockh understood this enigmatic phrase to mean persons who had forsworn their faith and placed themselves on the same level as the ordinary pagan Smyrnaeans; but this is certainly wrong. Mommsen's view must, so far as we can judge, be accepted, that "the quondam Jews" were simply the body of the Jews of Smyrna, called "quondam" because they were no longer recognised as a separate nation by the Roman law (as they had been before A.D. 70). The reference proves that they maintained in practice so late as 130-37 their separate standing in the city as a distinct people, apart from the rest of the citizens, although legally they were no longer anything but one section of the general population. Many Jews possessed the rights of citizenship in some at least of the Ionian cities, such as Smyrna. The quondam Jews who made that contribution to embellish Smyrna were probably for the most part citizens.

We may also probably infer from the strong hatred felt by the Jews, that at first many of the Christians of Smyrna had been converted from Judaism. It was the Jewish Christians, and not the pagan converts, whom the national Jews hated so violently. Except in so far as the converts had been proselytes of the synagogue, the Jews were not likely to care very much whether Pagans were converted to Christianity: their violent hatred was roused by the renegade Jews (as they thought) like St. Paul, who tried to place the unclean Pagans on a level with themselves.

The action of the Jews in the martyrdom of Polycarp must be regarded (as a succession of writers have remarked) as corroborating the evidence of this letter. In that case the eagerness of the Jews to expedite the execution of the Christian leader actually overpowered their objection to profane the Sabbath day, and they came into the gay assemblage in the Stadium, bringing faggots to make the fire in which Polycarp should be consumed. It must, however, be observed that they are not said to have been present at the sports in the Stadium. The games were over, as usual, at about the fifth hour, 11 AM. Thereafter the rather irregular trial of Polycarp was held; and about 2 PM the execution took place, and the most bitter opponents of the Christians had ample time to hear the news, assemble to hear the sentence, and to help in carrying it into effect. Undoubtedly, many who would abhor to appear as spectators of the games on a Sabbath would feel justified in putting to death an enemy of their faith on that day.

Severe trials still awaited the Church in Smyrna: "The devil is about to cast some of you into prison"...The expression must be understood as symbolical; and it would not be permissible to take "prison" as implying that imprisonment was the severest punishment which had as yet been, or was likely to be, inflicted on Christians. The inference has even been drawn from this passage that death was still hardly known as a penalty for the crime of Christianity, and was not even thought of as a possibility in the immediate future. In fact, such a sense for the term "prison" would be an anachronism, introducing a purely modern idea. Imprisonment was not recognised by the law as a punishment for crime in the Greek or the Roman procedure. The State would not burden itself with the custody of criminals, except as a preliminary stage to their trial, or in the interval between trial and execution. Fine, exile, and death constituted the usual range of penalties; and in many cases, where a crime would in modern times be punished by imprisonment, it was visited with death in Roman law.

The "prison" into which the devil would cast some of the Smyrnaean Christians must be understood as a brief epitome of all the sufferings that lay before them; the first act, viz., their apprehension and imprisonment, is to be taken as implying all the usual course of trial and punishment through which passed the martyrs described in the later parts of the book. Prison was thought of by the writer of the letter as the prelude to execution, and was understood in that sense by his readers.

That this is so is proved by the promise that follows, "Be thou faithful unto death, and I will give thee the crown of life": Endure all that falls to the lot of the true and steadfast Christians, beginning with arrest and imprisonment, ending with execution: that death will not be the end, but only the entrance to the true life, the birthday of martyrdom. The martyr "was dead and lived."

The importance of this idea in the letter is proved by the conclusion, where it recurs in a slightly varied form: "he that overcometh shall not be hurt of the second death." It is this triumph over death that constitutes the guiding thought of the whole letter, just as change was the guiding thought of the Ephesian letter. He that persists to the end, he that is steadfast and overcomes, shall triumph over death: apparent death affects him; but not the complete and permanent death. Here, again, the final promise is seen to be peculiarly appropriate to the character and needs of the persons addressed.

The mention of the crown would carry a special meaning to the Smyrnaean readers, and would rouse in their hearts many old associations. The "crown of Smyrna" had been before their eyes and minds from childhood (as was shown in chapter 19). The promise now is that a new crown shall be given to Smyrna. She shall wear no longer a mere crown of buildings and towers, nor even the crown of good citizens which Apollonius advised her to put on, but a crown of life. The earthly Smyrna wore a mural crown like that of her patron goddess: the true Smyrna shall wear a crown suited for the servants of the one living God.

Another expression which must be taken in a figurative or symbolic sense is, "thou shalt have tribulation ten days." The "ten days" means simply a period which can be measured, i.e., which comes to an end. The persecution will rage for a time, but it will not be permanent. The Church will live through it and survive it, and has therefore no reason to be afraid of it.

The expression "be faithful," again, would inevitably remind Smyrnaean readers of the history of their city, which had been the faithful friend and ally of Rome for centuries. It cannot be a mere accident that the only one of the Seven Churches, with which the epithet faithful is associated in the letters, is the Church of that city which had established its historic claim to the epithet in three centuries of loyalty, the city which had been faithful to Rome in danger and difficulty, the city whose citizens had stripped off their own garments to send to the Roman soldiers when suffering from cold and the hardships of a winter campaign. The honour in which Smyrna was always held by the Romans was proclaimed to be a return pro singulari fide (Livy, xxxviii, 39); to Cicero it was "the most faithful of our allies"; and its services were rewarded in A.D. 26 by the permission granted to it, in preference even to Ephesus and Sardis, to dedicate the second Asian temple to the reigning Emperor Tiberius and his family.

The same reflection occurs here as in the case of Ephesus. Some may think that such an explanation of the reason why this special form of words in the exordium of this letter was chosen, and why the epithet "faithful" is applied to the Church, is fanciful and even unworthy. It is evident, however, that the study which is here presented has been made from a different point of view. It is not in accordance with right method to form a priori theories of what is right or wrong, dignified or undignified, possible or impossible, in the interpretation of St. John's words. The only true method is to take the words, and ask what they mean, and what must the readers, for whom they were in the first place written, have understood from them. Now considering how exactly those words, "was dead and lived," applied to ancient Smyrna, it seems certain that the reference must inevitably have been appreciated by the Smyrnaeans; and if so, it cannot have been an accidental coincidence. The writer deliberately chose those words to appeal to local sentiment and patriotism. The same remark applies to his choice of "faithful" as the appropriate epithet for the Smyrnaean Church. Not merely had the Church been faithful; the whole city regarded faithfulness as the chief glory of Smyrna; and the topic must have been familiar to all inhabitants and a commonplace in patriotic speeches.

It is evident that the writer of the Seven Letters did not discourage such feelings of attachment to one's native city, but encouraged local patriotism and used it as a basis on which to build up a strenuous Christian life. The practical effect of such teaching as this is that a Christian could be a patriot, proud of and interested in the glory and the history of his own city.

This gives a different impression of the writer's character from what might be gathered from later parts of the Apocalypse; but it is not good method to take parts of a book and determine the author's character from them alone. Rather, the Seven Letters are a truer index to the writer's character than any other part of the Apocalypse, because in these letters he is in closer contact with reality than in any other part of the book.

Accordingly, we must accept the plain evidence of this letter and infer (as in the Ephesian letter already) that to the writer of the letter the life of the Church in Smyrna was not disconnected from the life of the city; and this must be regarded as a general principle to be applied in other cases. The Church was to him the heart and soul of the city, and its members were the true citizens. Just as the so-called Jews in Smyrna were not the true Jews, but a mere synagogue of Satan, so the Pagans were not the true citizens, but mere servants of the devil. The true Jews and the true citizens were the Christians alone. To them belonged the heritage of the city's past history: its faithfulness, its persistence, its unconquerable and indestructible vitality, all were theirs. To them also belonged the whole ancient heritage of the Jews, the promises and the favour of God.

In the letter to Smyrna then we see an influence of which no trace was visible in the Ephesian letter. The stock topics of patriotic orators, the glories of the city, are plainly observable in the letter; and the writer had certainly at some time mixed in the city life, and become familiar with current talk and the commonplaces of Smyrnaean municipal patriotism. Patriotism still was almost entirely municipal, though the Roman Empire was gradually implanting in the minds of ordinary men a wider ideal, extending to a race and an empire, and not confined to a mere city. Greece had vainly tried to make the Hellenic idea strong in the common mind; philosophers had freed themselves from the narrowness of municipal patriotism; but it was left to Rome to make the wider idea effective among men.

In the Ephesian letter, on the other hand, it was the eternal features and the natural surroundings of the city that the writer referred to. The Smyrnaean letter is not without similar reference. The writer did not confine his attention to those ephemeral characteristics which have just been mentioned, or (to speak more accurately) he regarded those characteristics as merely the effect produced by eternal causes. He had thought himself into harmony with the natural influences which had made Smyrna what it was, and which would continue to mould its history; and form this lofty standpoint he could look forward into the future, and foretell what must happen to Smyrna and to the Church (which to him was the one reality in Smyrna). He foresaw permanence, stability, reality surpassing the outward appearance, life maintaining itself strong and unmoved amid trial and apparent death. In Ephesus he saw the one great characteristic, the changing, evanescent, uncertain relations of sea and land and river; and interpreted with prophetic instinct the inevitable future. In Smyrna he saw nothing of that kind. The city must live, and the Church must live in it. Sea and plain and hills were here unchanging in their combined effect, making the seat of a great city. The city must endure much, but only for a definite, limited period; as a city it would suffer from invaders, who would surely try to capture it; and the Church not only would suffer along with the city, but would also suffer from the busy trading community, in which the element hostile to God would always be strong.

And history has justified the prophetic vision of the writer. Smyrna, the recipient of the most laudatory of all the Seven Letters, is the greatest of all the cities of Anatolia. At the head of its gulf, which stretches far up into the land, it is at present the one important seaport, and will remain always the greatest seaport, of the whole country. But the same situation which gives it eternal importance, has caused it to suffer much tribulation. It has been the crown of victory for many victors. It has tempted the cupidity of every invader, and has endured the greed and cruelty of many conquerors; but it has arisen, brilliant and strong, from every disaster. No city of the East Mediterranean lands gives the same impression of brightness and life, as one looks at it from the water, and beholds it spread out on the gently sloping ground between the sea and the hill, and clothing the sides of the graceful hill, which was crowned with the walls and towers of the medieval castle, until they were pulled down a few years ago. The difference in the beauty of the city caused thereby shows how much of the total effect was due to that "crown of Smyrna."

That hill seems at the first view to be only a rounded hillock of 450 feet in elevation. But, when you examine it more closely, you find that it is not merely an isolated conical hill, as it seems from the sea to be. It is really only a part of the vast plateau that lies behind it, and pushes it forward, like a fist, towards the sea. It is far stronger than at first it appeared, for it is really a corner of the main mass of the Asiatic continent, and is supported from behind by its immeasurable strength. Strength surpassing appearance, brightness, life: those are the characteristics of the letter and of the city.

In this letter no one can fail to recognise the tone of affection and entire approval. Whereas the writer urged the people of Ephesus to be as they once were, he counsels the Smyrnaeans to continue as they are now. Ephesus has to recover what it has lost, but Smyrna has lost nothing. The persecution and poverty which had been the lot of its Church from the beginning, and which would still continue for a period, kept it pure. There was nothing in it to tempt the unworthy or the half-hearted; whereas the dignity and high standing of the Ephesian Church had inevitably attracted many not entirely worthy members. The writer looks confidently forward to the continuance of the same steadfastness in Smyrna. He does not even hint at the possibility of partial failure; he does not say, "If thou be faithful, I will give thee the crown"; he merely exhorts them to be faithful as they have been.

Chapter 21: Pergamum: The Royal City: The City of Authority

Pergamum was, undoubtedly, an ancient place, whose foundation reaches back into the beginnings of town life in Asia. The situation is marked out by nature for a great fortified town, but is too large for a mere village. If we could fix the date of its foundation, we should know also the period when society has become so far developed and organised as to seek for defence against foreign invasion, and for offensive power, by combination on a great scale and the formation of a large centre of population. Beyond all other sites in Asia Minor it gives the traveller the impression of a royal city, the home of authority: the rocky hill on which it stands is so huge, and dominates the broad plain of the Caicus so proudly and boldly. The modern town is below the hill, where the earliest village was.

It is difficult to analyse such impressions, and to define the various causes whose combination produces them; but the relation of the vast hill to the great plain is certainly the chief cause. It would be impossible for any stronghold, however large and bold, to produce such an impression, if it stood in a small valley like those of Ephesus and Smyrna, for if the valley and the city were dominated by the still greater mass of the enclosing mountains. The rock rules over and as it were plants its foot upon a great valley; and its summit looks over the southern mountains which bound the valley, until the distant lofty peaks south of the Gulf of Smyrna, and especially the beautiful twin peaks now called the Two Brothers, close in the outlook. Far beneath lies the sea, quite fifteen miles away, and beyond it the foreign soil of Lesbos: the view of other lands, the presence of hostile powers, the need of constant care and watchfulness, all the duties of kingship are forced on the attention of him who sits enthroned on that huge rock. There is here nothing to suggest evanescence, mutability, and uncertainty, as at Sardis or Ephesus; the inevitable impression is of permanence, strength, sure authority and great size. Something of the personal and subjective element must be mixed up with such impressions; but in none of the Seven Cities does the impression seem more universal and unavoidable than in Pergamum.

The history and the coinage of Pergamum can be traced back into the fifth century; but its superiority and headship in Asia began in 282, when Philetaerus threw off allegiance to King Lysimachus and founded the kingdom of Pergamum, which was transmitted through a succession of kings, named Eumenes or Attalus, until 133. During those 151 years Pergamum was the capital of a realm varying in size from the first kingdom, simply the Caicus Valley (and hardly all of it), to the range of territories summed up in the vague expression "all the land on this side of Taurus." For the first few years the Seleucid dynasty supported Philetaerus in opposition to Lysimachus; but soon the rivalry of Seleucid and Pergamenian kings became the governing political fact. The former steadily lost ground until about 222 B.C., when Antiochus the Great restored the power of his dynasty, reduced Attalus I to the original bounds of Pergamenian authority, and threatened even the existence of his kingdom. Roman aid expelled Antiochus in 190, and enlarged the Pergamenian kingdom to its widest extent.

In 133 Attalus III bequeathed the whole kingdom to the Romans, who formed it into the Province of Asia. Pergamum was the official capital of the Province for two centuries and a half: so that its history as the seat of supreme authority over a large country lasts about four centuries, and had not yet come to an end when the Seven Letters were written. The impression which the natural features of its position convey was entirely confirmed to the writer of the letters by its history. It was to him the seat where the power of this world, the enemy of the Church and its Author, exercised authority. The authority was exercised in two ways--the two horns of the monster, as we have seen in chapter 9--civil administration through the Proconsul, and the State religion directed by the Commune of Asia.

The first, and for a considerable time the only, Provincial temple of the Imperial cult in Asia was built at Pergamum in honour of Rome and Augustus (29 B.C. probably). A second temple was built there in honour of Trajan, and a third in honour of Severus. Thus Pergamum was the first city to have the distinction of Temple-Warden both once and twice in the State religion; and even its third Wardenship was also a few years earlier than that of Ephesus. The Augustan Temple (chapter 10) is often represented on its coins and on those struck by the Commune. As the oldest temple of the Asian cult it is far more frequently mentioned and figured than any other Asian temple; it appears on coins of many Emperors down to the time of Trajan, and is generally represented open, to show the Emperor crowned by the Province.

The four patron deities of Pergamum are mentioned in an oracle, advising the people to seek safety from a pestilence through the aid of Zeus, Athena, Dionysos, and Asklepios. These represent, doubtless, four different elements in the Pergamenian population. Zeus the Saviour and Athena the Victory-Bearing had given the State is glorious victories over foreign enemies, and especially the Gauls; and the greatest efforts of Pergamenian art were directed to glorify them as representatives of the Hellenic spirit triumphing over barbarism. The great Altar with its long zone of stately reliefs, showing the gods of Hellas destroying the barbarian giants, was dedicated to Zeus Soter.

While the first two of those gods represent the Greek spirit and influence, the last two were more in accordance with the Anatolian spirit, and their worship bulked far more largely in the religious life of the city. Both of them were near the animal type, and if we could penetrate beneath the outward appearance imparted to them in art by the Greek anthropomorphic spirit, and reach down to the actual ritual of their Pergamenian cult, we should indubitably find that they were worshipped to a great degree as animal-gods, the God-Serpent and the God-Bull. Where the Pergamenian kings were insisting on their Hellenic character or blazoning in art their victory over barbaric enemies, they introduced Zeus and Athena, but when they were engaged in the practical government of their mixed people, mainly Anatolian, though mixed with Greek, they made most use of Asklepios and Dionysos.

Dionysos the Leader (Kathegemon) was the god of the royal family; and the kings claimed to be descended from him, and to be in succession his embodiment and envisagement on earth, just as the Seleucid sovereigns of Syria were the incarnation of Apollo. This cult owed its importance in Pergamum to the kings; and its diffusion through Asia must be attributed to them; but the worship, having once been established, persisted through the Imperial period, for religious institutions were rarely lost so long as paganism lasted. The worship was practised in Imperial times by a religious society, bearing the name Ox-herds (Boukoloi), at the head of which was the Archi-Boukolos; it was accompanied by mysterious rites, and the mystic name of the god seems to have been the Bull.

The anthropomorphic spirit of Greek religion retained very few traces of the bull character in the Hellenic conception of Dionysos; but Asklepios was more closely associated with the serpent. The Hellenic religious spirit represented the god as a dignified human figure, very similar in type to Zeus, supporting his right hand on a staff round which a serpent is twined. His serpent nature clings to him, though only as an attribute and adjunct, in the fully Hellenised form. In the Anatolian ritual the god was the Asklepian serpent, rather than the human Asklepios. Thus the Emperor Caracalla, during his visit to Pergamum, is represented as adoring the Pergamenian deity, a serpent wreathed round the sacred tree. Between the God-Serpent and the God-Emperor stands the little figure of Telesphorus, the Consummator, a peculiarly Pergamenian conception closely connected with Asklepios.

Asklepios the Saviour was introduced from Epidauros in a comparatively recent period, perhaps the fifth century. He appears on coins from the middle of the second century B.C. and became more and more the representative god of Pergamum. On alliance coins he regularly stands for his city.

As Asklepios was imported to Pergamum for Epidaurus in Argolis, it may be asked why his character in ritual was so strongly Anatolian and so little Hellenic. The reason is that he belonged to the old Pelagian stratum in religion, which persisted most strongly in such remote and rural parts of the Peloponnesus; and he had participated little in the progressive Hellenisation of the old Greek gods; now the Pelagian religion was closely kindred in character to the Anatolian.

On the royal coinage Athena and other Hellenic gods are almost the only divine types; but on the cistophori, which were intended to be the common coinage in circulation through the whole Pergamenian kingdom after 200 B.C., neither kings nor specifically Hellenic gods appear, but only symbols taken from the cults of Dionysos and Asklepios. On the obverse is the cista mystica of Dionysos within a wreath of his sacred plant the ivy: the lid of the box is pushed open by a serpent which hangs out with half its length. The relation of the God-Bull to the God-Serpent in the Anatolian ritual is well known: "the bull is father of the serpent, and the serpent of the bull": such was a formula of the Phrygian Mysteries. On the reverse are two Asklepian serpents with their lower parts intertwined and heads erect: between them is a bowcase containing a strung bow.

The monogram of the first three letters of the name Pergamum is the only indication on these coins of Pergamenian origin and domination. It was clearly the intention of the kings in this coinage to avoid all appearance of domination over Asia, and to represent the unity of their realm as a voluntary association in the common religion of the two deities whose ritual is symbolised in barbaric Anatolian forms on the cistophori, without the slightest admixture of Greek anthropomorphism, and whose worship we have already traced in several cities of the Pergamenian realm. The cistophori were struck at first in Pergamum, but soon in most of the great cities of the Pergamenian realm. Only those struck in Pergamum bore the Pergamenian monogram. The others bore the name or symbols of their own place of coinage. These coins are a true historical monument. They express a phase of administration, the Pergamenian ideal of constructive statesmanship, which is attested by no historian and hardly by any other monument.

The cistophori show clearly the point of view from which the symbolism of the Apocalypse is to be interpreted. They reveal a strong tendency in the Asian mind to express its ideas and ideals, alike political and religious, through symbols and types; and they prove that the converted pagan readers for whom the Apocalypse was originally written were predisposed through their education and the whole spirit of contemporary society to regard visual forms, beasts, human figures, composite monsters, objects of nature, or articles of human manufacture, when mentioned in a work of this class, as symbols indicative of religious ideas. This predisposition to look at such things with a view to a meaning that lay underneath them was not confined to the strictly Oriental races; and the symbolism of the Apocalypse ought not to be regarded as all necessarily Jewish in origin. Much of it is plainly Jewish; but, as has been pointed out in chapters 11 and 12, a strong alloy of Judaism had been mingled in the composition of society in the Asian cities, and many Judaic ideas must have become familiar to the ordinary pagans, numbers of whom had been attracted within the circle of hearers in the synagogues, while purely pagan syncretism of Jewish and pagan forms was familiar in various kinds of ritual or magic.

Except for archaeological and antiquarian details, which are numerous, little more is known about Pergamum. Its importance and authority in the Roman administration of the Province Asia are abundantly proved by the evidence which has been quoted above; and yet they are not directly attested by any ancient authority except the Apocalypse, and have to a great extent escaped notice. In the latest study of the Province Asia, a large volume containing an admirable summary of the chief results of modern investigation, published in the summer of 1904 by Monsieur V. Chapot, Pergamum is treated as a place quite secondary to Ephesus and Smyrna in the Roman administration while Ephesus is regarded as in every sense the Roman capital. Consideration of the fact that Pergamum was honoured with the first, the second, and the third Neokorate before any other city of Asia shows beyond question its official primacy in the Province. The Imperial religion "was the keystone of the Imperial policy"; the official capital of the Province was necessarily the centre of the Imperial ritual; and conversely the city where the Imperial religion had its centre must have been officially regarded as the capital of the Province. In many Provinces there was only one seat of the Imperial religion; but in Asia the spirit of municipal pride and rivalry was so strong that it would have endangered the hold of the State cultus on the other great cities, if they had been forced to look to any one city as the sole head of the religion. Roman policy showed its usual adaptability by turning municipal pride to its purpose and making it act in an Imperial channel, so that the object of competition among all the great cities was to attain higher rank in the State religion.

Pergamum, then, as being first promoted to all three stages in the Imperial worship must have been the official capital and titular seat of Roman authority; but there were several capitals (metropoleis), three, and seven, and more than seven.

The name of the city lives in literary language through the word "parchment" (Pergamena), applied to an improved preparation of hide adapted to purposes of writing, which had been used in Ionia from a very early period.

The Jewish community in Pergamum is mentioned in Josephus, Ant. Jud, xiv, 10, 22.

Chapter 22: The Letter to the Church in Pergamum

These things saith he that hath the sharp-pointed two-edged sword.

I know where thou dwellest, where Satan's throne is; and thou holdest fast my name, and didst not deny my faith, even in the days of Antipas my witness, my faithful one, who was killed among you where Satan dwelleth. But I have a few things against thee, because thou hast there some that hold the teaching of Balaam, who taught Balak to cast a stumbling-block before the children of Israel, to make them eat things sacrificed to idols and commit fornication. After that fashion hast thou too some that hold the teaching of the Nicolaitans. Repent therefore; or else I come upon thee quickly, and I will make war against them with the sword of my mouth.

He that hath an ear let him hear what the Spirit saith to the Churches.

To him that overcometh will I give of the hidden manna; and I will give him a white stone, and upon the stone a new name written, which no man knoweth but he that receiveth it.

In this letter, the intimate connection between the Church and the city, and the appropriateness, in view of the rank and position of the city, of the opening address to the Church are even more obvious than in the two previous letters. "These things saith he that hath the sharp two-edged sword." The writer is uttering the words of Him who wears the symbol of absolute authority, and is invested with the power of life and death. This is the aspect in which he addresses himself to the official capital of the Province, the seat of authority in the ancient kingdom and in the Roman administration. To no other of the Seven Cities could this exordium have been used appropriately. To Pergamum it is entirely suitable. He that hath the absolute and universal authority speaks to the Church situated in the city where official authority dwells.

The distinguishing characteristic of this letter is the oft-recurring reference to the dignity of Pergamum as the seat of Roman official authority; and we have to follow out this reference in one detail after another. The author of the letter speaks as invested with an authority similar and yet immeasurably superior to that of the Imperial government. The sword which he bears is the sharp-pointed, double-edged, cut-and-thrust sword used in the Roman armies, not the Oriental scimitar, or the mere cutting sword employed by many nations, and especially by the Greek soldiers. The name by which it is here called denoted a barbarian and non-Greek sword (originally a Thracian term), and therefore was suitable for the weapon borne by the Romans, who were a "barbarian" race, in contrast with the Greeks. The Romans did not themselves refuse the epithet "barbarian": e.g., the Roman adaptations of Greek plays are said by the Roman poets even to be "translations in a barbarian tongue." Hence St. Paul in Romans 1:14, when he speaks of himself as indebted both to Greeks and to barbarians, means practically (though not quite exclusively) Greeks and Romans.

In Roman estimation the sword was the symbol of the highest order of official authority, with which the Proconsul of Asia was invested. The "right of the sword," just gladii, was roughly equivalent to what we call the power of life and death (though, of course, the two expressions are not exactly commensurate); and governors of Provinces were divided into a higher and a lower class, according as they were or were not invested with this power. When the Divine Author addresses Pergamum in this character, His intention is patent, and would be caught immediately by all Asian readers of the Apocalypse. He wields that power of life and death, which people imagine to be vested in the Proconsul of the Province.

The writer knows well the history of the Church in Pergamum. Its fortunes had been mainly determined by the rank and character of the city as the seat of government and authority; and He who knows its history expresses the fulness of His knowledge in the striking words, "I know where thou dwellest, where Satan's throne is." In these remarkable words is compressed a world of meaning. "Satan" is a term here employed in a figurative sense to denote the power or influence that withstands the Church and all who belong to it. The usage is similar to that seen in 1 Thessalonians 2:18: it has elsewhere been pointed out that in that passage "Satan" probably implies the clever device whereby, without any formal decree of expulsion or banishment (which would have been difficult to enforce or to make permanent), the Apostle was prevented from returning to Thessalonica. Similarly, in the present case, "Satan" is the official authority and power which stands in opposition to the Church.

But the situation has now developed greatly. When St. Paul was writing that letter to the Thessalonians, the civil power that hindered him was the authority of the city magistrates. The Imperial administration had not at that time declared itself in opposition to the new teaching, and was in practice so conducted as to give free scope to this or almost any other philosophic or moral or religious movement. But before the Seven Letters were written, the Imperial government had already ranged itself definitely in opposition to the Church of Christ. The procedure against the Christians was fixed and stereotyped. Their loyalty was now tested by the one criterion recognised alike by public opinion and by government policy, viz., their willingness to perform the ritual of the State religion, and make offering to the Imperial God, the Divine Emperor. Those who refused to comply with this requirement were forthwith condemned to death as traitors and enemies of the State.

In this State religion of the Empire, the worship of the Divine Emperors, organised on a regular system in Asia as in all other Provinces, Satan found his home and exercised his power in opposition to God and His Church. Pergamum, as being still the administrative capital of the Province, was also the chief seat of the State religion. Here was built the first Asian Temple of the divine Augustus, which for more than forty years was the one centre of the Imperial religion for the whole Province. A second Asian Temple had afterwards been built at Smyrna, and a third at Ephesus; but they were secondary to the original Augustan Temple at Pergamum.

In this Pergamenian Temple, then, Satan was enthroned. The authority over the minds of its Asian subjects, possessed by the State, and arrayed against the Church, was mainly concentrated in the Temple. The history of the Church in Pergamum had been determined by its close proximity to the seat of State opposition, "where Satan's throne is."

Such, beyond all doubt, was the chief determining fact in prompting this remarkable expression. But it is probable that other thoughts in a secondary degree influenced the language here. The breadth of meaning in these letters is so great, that one suggestion is rarely sufficient; the language was prompted by the whole complex situation. In many cases we cannot hope to do more than describe some one side of the situation, which happens to be known to us; but here we can see that the form of the expression was clearly determined in some degree by the historical associations and the natural features of the city. Pergamum had for centuries been the royal city, first of the Attalid kings, and afterwards of the viceroy or Proconsul who represented the Emperor in the Province. History marked it out as the royal city, and not less clearly has nature done so. No city of the whole of Asia Minor--so far as I have seen, and there are few of any importance which I have not seen--possesses the same imposing and dominating aspect. It is the one city of the land which forced from me the exclamation "A royal city!" I came to it after seeing the others, and that was the impression which it produced. There is something unique and overpowering in its effect, planted as it is on its magnificent hill, standing out boldly in the level plain, and dominating the valley and the mountains on the south. Other cities of the land have splendid hills which made them into powerful fortresses in ancient time; but in them the hill is as a rule the acropolis, and the city lies beneath and around or before it. But here the hill was the city proper, and the great buildings, chiefly Roman, which lie below the city, were external ornaments, lending additional beauty and stateliness to it.

In this case, again, the natural features of the city give a fuller meaning to the words of the letter.

Some confusion is caused by the peculiar relation between Ephesus and Pergamum. Each of the two was in a sense the metropolis of Asia. It is impossible, in the dearth of information, to define the limits of their circles of influence; and it was, in all probability, hardly possible to do so very exactly at the time when the Seven Letters were written. Pergamum was the historical capital, originally the one metropolis of Asia, and still the official capital. But Pergamum was badly situated for commerce and communication; it did not lie on any of the great natural lines of trade between Rome and the East (though it was situated on the Imperial Post-road to the East, in the form in which that route was organised by Augustus and lasted throughout the first century); and therefore it could not permanently maintain its premier rank in the Province. The sea-ends of the two great roads across Asia Minor were at Ephesus and Smyrna; one or other of those two cities must inevitably become the capital of the Roman Province; and the circumstances of the time were more in favour of Ephesus. Smyrna, indeed, offered the better harbour, more accessible for ships, at the head of a gulf extending far up into the land, bringing sea-borne trade nearer the heart of the country; it had permanent vitality as the chief city of Asia; and the future was with it. But Ephesus commanded the most important land route; and this gave it a temporary advantage, though the changing nature of its situation denied it permanent possession of the honour.

The Christian Church and its leaders had from the first seized on Ephesus as the centre of the Asian congregations, whether through a certain unerring instinct for the true value of natural facts, or because they were driven on in that direction by circumstances--but are not these merely two different expressions and aspects of one fact? Pergamum, however, and even Smyrna, had also a certain claim to the primacy of Asia; and it is interesting to observe how all those varied claims and characteristics are mirrored and expressed in these letters. To the superficial eye Pergamum was, apparently, even yet the capital; but already in the time of St. Paul, A.D. 56, the Ephesians had claimed primacy in Asia for their goddess (Acts 19:27), and at a later period the Imperial policy was induced to grant official Roman recognition and to make the worship of the goddess part of the State religion of the Province. Considering the close connection in ancient times between religion, political organisation, and the sentiment of patriotism, we must conclude that this wider acceptance of Ephesian religion over the whole of Asia, beginning from non-official action, and finally made official and Imperial, marked and implied the rise of Ephesus to the primacy of the Province; but, at the time when the Seven Letters were written, the popular recognition of the goddess in the Asian cities had not been confirmed by Imperial act.

As being close to the centre of the enemy, Pergamum had been most exposed to danger from State persecution. Here, for the firs time in the Seven Letters, this topic comes up. The suffering which had fallen to the lot of Smyrna proceeded chiefly from fellow-citizens, and, above all, from the Jews; but the persecution that fell to the lot of Pergamum is clearly distinguished from that kind of suffering. In Pergamum it took the form of suffering for the Name, when Christians were tried in the proconsular court, and confronted with the alternative of conforming to the State religion or receiving immediate sentence of death. Naturally, that kind of persecution originated from Pergamum, and had there its centre; but many martyrs were tried and condemned there who were not Pergamenians. Prisoners were carried from all parts of the Province to Pergamum for trial and sentence before the authority who possessed the right of the sword, jus gladii, the power of life and death, viz., the Roman Proconsul of Asia.

Two errors must here be guarded against. "Antipas, my witness, who was killed among you," is the only sufferer mentioned. But it would be utterly erroneous to infer (as some have done) that Antipas had been the only Christian executed as yet in Pergamum or in the Province. His name is mentioned and preserved only as the first in the already long series: the subsequent chapters of the Revelation, which tell of the woman drunk with the blood of the saints, show what were the real facts. That one name should stand as representative of the whole list is entirely in the style of the Apocalypse.

In the second place, it would be equally erroneous to argue that persecution was still only partial and local, not universal, and that only members of the Church of Pergamum had as yet suffered death. It is not even certain that Antipas was a member of that congregation: the words are not inconsistent with the possibility that Antipas was brought up for trial from some other city, and "killed among the Pergamenians." A wide-spread persecution had already occurred, and the processes of law had been fully developed in it. The Apocalypse places us in view of a procedure developed far beyond that which Tacitus describes as ruling in the reign of Nero; and such a formed and stereotyped procedure was elaborated only through the practice and precedents established during later persecution.

The honourable history and the steadfast loyalty of the Pergamenian Church, however, had been tarnished by the error of a minority of the congregation, which had been convinced by the teaching of the Nicolaitans. This school of thought and conduct played an important part in the Church of the first century. Ephesus had tried and rejected it; the Smyrnaean congregation, despised and ill-treated by their fellow-citizens, had apparently not been much affected by it; in Pergamum a minority of the Church had adopted its principles; in Thyatira the majority were attracted by it, and it there found its chief seat, so far as Asia was concerned. Probably the controversy with regard to the Nicolaitan views was fought out and determined in Asia more decisively than in any other Province, though the same questions must have presented themselves and demanded an answer in every Province and city where the Graeco-Roman civilisation was established. The character of this movement, obscure and almost unknown to us, because the questions which it raised were determined at so early a date, will be most conveniently treated under Thyatira; but it is necessary here to point out that it was evidently an attempt to effect a reasonable compromise with the established usages of Graeco-Roman society and to retain as many as possible of those usages in the Christian system of life. It affected most of all the cultured and well-to-do classes in the Church, those who had most temptation to retain all that they could of the established social order and customs of the Graeco-Roman world, and who by their more elaborate education had been trained to take a somewhat artificial view of life and to reconcile contradictory principles in practical conduct through subtle philosophical reasoning.

The historian who looks back over the past will find it impossible to condemn the Nicolaitan principles in so strong and even bigoted fashion as St. John condemned them. But the Apostle, while writing the Seven Letters, was not concerned to investigate all sides of the case, and to estimate with careful precision exactly how much could be reasonably said on behalf of the Nicolaitans. He saw that they had gone wrong on the essential and critical alternative; and he cared for nothing more. To him, in the absorbing interest of practical life, no nice weighing of comparative right was possible; he divided all Christians into two categories, those who were right and those who were wrong. Those who were wrong he hated with his whole heart and soul; and he almost loved the Ephesians, as we have seen, because they also hated the Nicolaitans. The Nicolaitans were to him almost worse than the open and declared enemies of Christ on the pagan side; and he would probably have entirely denied them the name of Christians.

But the historian must regard the Nicolaitans with intense interest, and must regret deeply that we know so little about them, and that only from their enemies. And yet at the same time he must feel that nothing could have saved the infant Church from melting away into one of those vague and ineffective schools of philosophic ethics except the stern and strict rule that is laid down here by St. John. An easy-going Christianity could never have survived; it could not have conquered and trained the world; only the most convinced, resolute, almost bigoted adherence to the most uncompromising interpretation of its own principles could have given the Christians the courage and self-reliance that were needed. For them to hesitate or to doubt was to be lost.

Especially, it is highly probable that the Nicolaitans either already had, or soon would have, reached the conclusion that they might justifiably comply with the current test of loyalty, and burn a little incense in honour of the Emperor. The Church was not disloyal; even its most fanatical defenders claimed to be loyal; then why should its members make any difficulty about proving their loyalty by burning a few grains of incense? A little incense was nothing. An excellent and convincing argument can readily be worked out; and then--the whole ritual of the State religion would have followed as a matter of course; Christ and Augustus would have been enthroned side by side as they were in the compromise attempted by the Emperor Alexander Severus more than a century later; and everything that was vital in Christianity would have been lost. St. John, like St. Paul in 1 Corinthians, saw the real issue that lay before the Church--either it must conquer and destroy the Imperial idolatry, or it must compromise and in so doing be itself destroyed. Both St. Paul and St. John answered with the most hearty, unwavering, uncompromising decisiveness. Not the faintest shadow of acquiescence in idolatry must be permitted to the Christian. On this the Nicolaitans, with all good intention, went wrong; and to St. John the error was unpardonable. He compares the Nicolaitans to the Israelites who were led astray into pleasure and vice by the subtle plan of Balaam. No words of condemnation are too strong for him to use. Their teaching was earthly, sensual, devilish. In their philosophical refinements of argumentation he saw only "the deep things of Satan."

It is clear also that the Nicolaitans rather pitied and contemned the humbler intelligence and humbler position of the opposite section in the Church; and hence we shall find that both in the Thyatiran and in the Pergamenian letter St. John exalts the dignity, authority and power that shall fall to the lot of the victorious Christian. Christ can and will give His true followers far more than the Nicolaitans promise. No power or rank in the world equals the lofty position that Christ will bestow; the Imperial dignity and the name of Augustus cannot be compared with the dignity and name of the glorified Christ which He will give to His own.

Further light is, as usual, thrown on the opening address of the letter by the promise at the end: "To him that overcometh will I give of the hidden manna, and I will give him a white stone, and upon the stone a new name written, which no one knoweth but he that receiveth it."

The "white stone" was, doubtless, a tessera, and ought, strictly speaking, to be called by that name, but the word is not English and therefore is unsuitable. There is no English word which gives an adequate rendering, for the thing is not used among us, and therefore we have no name for it. It was a little cube or rectangular block of stone, ivory, or other substance, with words or symbols engraved on one or more faces. Such tesserae were used for a great variety of purposes. Here it is a sort of coupon or ticket bearing the name, but it is not to be given up: it is to remain secret, not to be shown to others, but to be kept as the private possession of the owner.

An explanation of the white pebble or tessera with the New Name has been sought in many different objects used in ancient times, or ideas current among ancient peoples, Greek, Roman, and Jewish. Some scholars quote the analogy of the tessera given to proved and successful gladiators inscribed with the letters SP, which they regard as a new title spectatus, i.e., tried and proved; but this analogy, though tempting in some ways, will not bear closer examination. The letters SP on the gladiatorial tesserae are considered by Mommsen to stand, not for spectatus, but for spectavit. Various theories are proposed about the meaning; but no theory makes out that a new name was given to the proved gladiator with the tessera: he was simply allowed to retire into private life after a proved and successful career, instead of being compelled to risk his reputation and life when his powers were failing. The analogy fails in the most essential points.

Moreover, it is necessary that any suggestion as to the origin of the sayings in the Seven Letters should be taken from a phase of life familiar to the society to which they were addressed. But gladiatorial exhibitions and professional gladiators (to whom alone the tesserae were given) were an exotic in the Eastern Provinces: they were not much to the taste of the Hellenes, but were an importation from Rome. The influence of Roman fashions over the Provinces was, indeed, strong enough to make gladiatorial exhibitions a feature in many of the greater festivals in Asia; but it does not appear that they ever became really popular there, or that gladiatorial metaphors and allusions to the life of professional gladiators ever passed into current speech. None of the gladiatorial tesserae which are known as yet have been found in the Province Asia. There is therefore no reason to think that the Asian readers would have caught the allusion to such tesserae even if St. John had intended it (which is altogether unlikely).

Still more unsatisfactory are the comparisons suggested between this white stone and the voting ballot used by jurors or political voters, the tessera that served as an entrance-ticket to distributions, banquets, or other public occasions, and so on through all the various purposes served by such tesserae or stones. All are unsatisfactory and elusive; they do not make the reader feel that he has gained a clear and definite impression of the white pebble.

Yet, while none of these analogies is complete or satisfactory in itself, perhaps none is entirely wrong. The truth is that the white pebble with the New Name was not an exact reproduction of any custom or thing in the social usage of the time. It was a new conception, devised for this new purpose; but it was only a working up into a new form of familiar things and customs, and it was therefore completely intelligible to every reader in the Asian Churches. It had analogies with many things, though it was not an exact reproduction of any of them. Probably the fact is that the pebble is simply an instrument to bear the Name, and all the stress of the passage is laid on the Name which is thus communicated. The reason why the pebble is mentioned lies in a different direction from any of the suggestions quoted above.

Two facts, however, are to be noticed with regard to this "white pebble." In the first place, it is lasting and imperishable. Hence, such a translation as "ticket" or "coupon" would--apart from the modern associations--be unsuitable. A "ticket" is for a temporary purpose; this pebble is eternal. According to the ancient view a close relation existed between permanent validity and record on some lasting imperishable material. The mere expression in writing of any idea or word or right or title gave it a new kind of existence and an added effectiveness, placed it in short on a higher plane in the universe. But this new existence was, of course, dependent on the permanence of the writing, i.e., on the lasting nature of the material. Horace plays with the popular idea, when he declares that his lyric poetry is a monumentum aere perennius: laws, the permanent foundation of peace and order in a city, were written on bronze; but poetry will outlast even bronze. The New Name, then, must be written, not simply left as a sound in the air; and it must be written, not on the parchment made in the city but on an imperishable material like this pebble.

In the second place the colour is important. It was white, the fortunate colour. Suitability of the material to the subject in writing seems to have been considered to some degree in ancient time. Dr. Wunsch, one of the leading authorities, lays great stress on the fact that curses and imprecations were usually written on lead, as proving that lead was the deadly and ill-omened metal in Greece; and since many imprecations were found at Tel-Sanda-hannah in the southwest of Palestine engraved on limestone tablets, there is some temptation to regard limestone as selected for a similar reason, and to contrast its dark, ill-omened hue with the "white stone" engraved with the New Name in this case. Some doubt however is cast on this theory of material by the fact that a private letter, of a kind which would not be written on a material recognised as deadly and ill-omened, has recently been found incised on a leaden tablet: it is published as the oldest Greek letter in the Austrian Jahreshefte, 1904, p. 94.

Equally difficult is the allusion to the New Name. We take it as clear and certain that the "new name" is the name which shall be given to the conquering Christian; and the words are connected with the already established custom of taking a new name at baptism.

The name acquired in popular belief a close connexion with the personality, both of a human being and of a god. The true name of a god was kept secret in certain kinds of ancient religion, lest the foreigner and the enemy, by knowing the name, should be able to gain an influence over the god. The name guaranteed, and even gave, existence, reality, life: a new name implied the entrance on a new life.

This old superstition takes a peculiar form among the modern Jews of Palestine. It is their custom to change a person's name in the case of a dangerous illness, as is mentioned by Mr. Macalister in the Quarterly Statement of the Palestine Exploration Fund, April, 1904, p. 153. The new name, which is retained ever afterwards, if the patient survives, frequently has reference to life, or is that of some Old Testament saint whose life was specially long.

Accordingly the New Name that is given to the victorious Christian marks his entrance on a new and higher stage of existence; he has become a new person. Yet this alone would make an inadequate and unsatisfying explanation. We miss the element of authority and power, which is imperatively demanded to suit the case of Pergamum. To furnish this element the New Name must be the name of God. Here, again, we find ourselves brought close to the sphere of popular religion, superstition and magic. Knowledge of the compelling names of God, the names of God which influence nature and the mysterious forces of the universe, was one of the chief sources of the power which both the Mysteries and the magic ritual claimed to give their votaries. The person that had been initiated into the Mysteries learned not merely the landmarks to guide him along the road to the home of the Blessed--the white poplar and the other signs by the way--he learned also the names of God which would open the gates and bars before him, and frighten away hostile spirits or transform them into friends. Mr. Anderson Scott gives an excellent note on this passage, which may be supplemented from Dieterich's

Mithrasliturgie, pp. 32-39. He who knows the right name of a demon or divine being can become lord over all the power that the demonic being possesses, just as he who knows the name of a man was considered to possess some power over the man, because the name partakes of reality and not merely marks a man's personality, but is almost identified with it.

Probably no incompatibility between these two aspects of the New Name, as the name of God and as the name of the Individual Christian, was felt by the ancient readers of this letter. The name that was written on the white stone was at once the name of the victorious Christian and the name of God. These two points of view approximated towards one another, and passed into one another. Personal names frequently were derived from, or even identical with, a Divine name. The ordinary thought of primitive Greek and of Anatolian religion--that the heroised dead had merely returned to the Divine Mother who bore them, and become once more identified with and merged in the divine nature--also helped to obliterate the difference which we in modern times feel between the two points of view. Here and in the Philadelphian letter the name of God is also the name of the victorious Christian, written on him in the latter case, given him on a white tessera in the Pergamenian letter. Pergamum and Philadelphia are the two Churches which are praised because they "held fast my name," and "did not deny it"; and they are rewarded with the New Name, at once the Name of God and their own, an eternal possession, known to the bearers only, the symbol and instrument of wider power; they shall not merely be "Christians," the people of Christ; they shall be the people of His new personality as He is hereafter revealed in glory, bearing that New Name of His glorious revelation.

The allusion to the "hidden manna" is one of the few touches in the Seven Letters derived purely and exclusively from the realm of Jewish belief and superstition. It is not even taken from the Old Testament; but is a witness that some current Jewish superstitions acquired a footing in the early Christian Church. According to a Jewish tale the manna laid up "before the Testimony" in the Ark was hidden in a cave of Mount Sinai, and would be revealed when Messiah came. That superstition is here used as a symbol to indicate the heavenly food that should impart strength to the Christian. It is, however, quite probable that there is some special suitability in this symbol, due to popular, mixed Jewish and pagan, belief current in Asia, which we have failed to catch.

As to the spirit in which popular beliefs are here used, Mr. Anderson Scott in the note just quoted has said all that there is to say. The same form of expression, which is so frequent elsewhere in the Seven Letters, occurs here. A contrast is intended between the ordinary popular custom and the better form in which that custom is offered to the true Christian: to the victorious Christian shall be given the possession of a far more powerful and efficacious name than any which he could learn about in the various kinds of popular ritual, a name which will mark the transformation of his whole nature and his recreation in a new character.

The promises and the principles of Christianity had to be made intelligible to minds habituated to think in the customary forms of ancient popular thought; and they are therefore expressed in the Apocalypse according to the popular forms, but these forms must be understood as merely figurative, as mere attempts, necessarily imperfect, to reach and teach the popular mind. The words and thoughts in the Seven Letters, when taken singly and separately, are to a remarkable extent such as a pagan mystic of the first or second century might have used; and we shall probably find that some champion will hereafter appear to prove that the Seven Letters took their origin from no mere Christian, but from a pagan mystic circle tinged with semi-Gnostic developments of Christianity. The same view has already been advocated by influential scholars with regard to the epitaph of the Phrygian bishop, Avircius Marcellus--with equal unreason in both cases (unless perhaps the Seven Letters present a more startlingly pagan resemblance in some parts than the bishop's epitaph). Those who advocate such theories fail to catch the spirit which lies in the Christian document as a whole. The whole, in literature, is far more than the sum of the separate parts: there is the soul, the life, the spirit that gives vitality and unity to the parts. To miss that character in such a document is to miss what makes it Christian. To miss that, is to miss everything. All those mystic rites and popular cults were far from being mere imposture or delusion; they had many elements of truth and beauty; they were all trying to reach the same result as Christianity, to satisfy the wants of the popular mind, to guide it right in its groping after God. They all used many of the same facts and rites, insisted on many similar customs and methods, employed often the same words and symbols as Christianity used; and yet the result is so utterly different in character and spirit that one would have been inclined to say that not even a single paragraph or sentence of any Christian document could have been mistaken for a product of one of those Mystic circles of devotees, had it not been for the treatment that the testament of Avircius Marcellus has recently received from some high authorities--discussed point by point, detail after detail, without regard to the spirit of the whole, and thus proved to be non-Christian by ignoring all that is Christian in it.

There is, however, a certain obscurity, which must evidently be intentional, in this passage; more is meant than lies on the surface. Now the earlier part of the letter is characterised by an unmistakable and yet carefully veiled opposition to the State religion and to the government which had provoked that opposition; and this quality in the letter guides us to the proper understanding of the conclusion, which is one of the most remarkable passages in the Seven Letters. The readers of this letter, who possessed the key to its comprehension, hidden from the common world, could not fail to be struck with the analogy between this New Name and the Imperial title Augustus. That also had been a new name, deliberately devised by the Senate to designate the founder, and to mark the foundation of the new Empire: it was an old sacred word, used previously only in the language of the priests, and never applied to any human being: hence Ovid says: "Sancta vocant augusta patres" (Fast., 1., 609). That old word was appropriated in 27 B.C. to the man who had been the saviour of Rome, and whom already the popular belief had begun to regard as an incarnation of the divine nature in human form, sent down to earth to end the period of war and introduce the age of peace. This sacred, divine name marked out the man to whom it was applied as one apart from the world, standing on a higher level, possessor of superhuman power in virtue of this new name and transmitting that power through the name to his descendants.

The analogy was striking; and the points of difference were only to the advantage of the Christian. His new name was secret, but all the more efficacious on that account. The readers for whom this letter was written--the Christians of Pergamum, of all Asia, of the whole world--would catch with certainty the hidden meaning. All those Christians, when they were victorious, were to be placed in the same position as, or rather higher than, Augustus, having a New Name, the Name of God, their own secret possession, which no man would know and therefore no man could tamper with by acquiring control through knowledge. As Augustus had been set above the Roman world by his new name, so they would be set above the world by theirs.

This is the answer which the Church made to the persecuting Emperor, who beyond all his predecessors prided himself on his divine nature and his divine name. To insult, proscription, a shameful death, it returns a triumphant defiance: the Emperor is powerless: the supreme power and authority remain with the victorious Christian, who defeats the Emperor by virtue of the death which the Emperor inflicts. Here for the first time in the Seven Letters the absolute and inexorable opposition between the Church and the Imperial government is clearly expressed. It is not merely that the State persecutes the Church. The Church proscribes and sets itself above the Augustan government and the Augusti themselves. And this is done in the letter to the Church of that city where the Imperial government with the Imperial religion had placed its capital and its throne.

The taking of a new name, and the meaning attached to this in the usage of the time, was orally illustrated by the late Dr. Hort, from the case of Aelius Aristides, the famous orator of Hadrianoi and Smyrna, as I am informed by a correspondent, though the lecture in which the illustration was stated seems never to have been published. The facts are known from various passages of Aristides, chiefly in the Lalia (Hymn) to Aesculapius and in the Sacred Discourses.

The case of Aristides, who was born probably in A.D. 117, may be taken as applicable to the period of the Apocalypse. Aristides had a new name, which was given him by the God, appearing to him in the form of Aesculapius. That deity was his chief protector and adviser and helper, though the mother of the God also regarded him as her protege and favourite. Aesculapius cured him of his disease, guided him in his life by ordering him to devote himself to oratory, revealed himself to his favoured servant, and gave him the name Theodorus. There is much probability that the name was given in a vision, though the circumstances are not quite clear.

The evidence lies chiefly in a remarkable passage at the end of Aristides' Hymn to Aesculapius, which Reiske declares himself unable to understand, though he suggests that it refers to some prophecy vouchsafed to Aristides by Aesculapius in a dream. Words which Reiske could not understand must be very obscure; and hence the passage has attracted little attention.

It is rather bold to suggest an explanation where that excellent scholar says "non intelligo"; but the words of Aristides seem to illustrate the passage before us so well, that an interpretation may be offered. The words and the situation are as follows. Aristides has just related how through the orders and aid of Aesculapius he had appeared in Rome and given a successful display of oratory before the two Emperors, the ladies of the Imperial family and the whole Imperial court, just as Ulysses had been enabled by Athena to display his eloquence in the ball of Alcinous before the Phaeacian audience. He proceeds in the following very enigmatic words: "And not only had these things been done in this way, but also the Symbol or Synthema was with me encouraging me, whilst you showed in act that there were many reasons why you brought me before the public, viz., that I might be conspicuous in oratory, and that the most perfect (the highest circles and the educated class) might hear with their own ears the better counsels (i.e. the teaching of a true philosophy and morality)."

The nature of the Synthema which Aristides received from the god he does not explain. The obscurity in which he leaves it is obviously intentional. It was a secret between the god and himself; he, and he alone, had been initiated by the god into this ministry, and it was not to be published for every one to know. Only they should understand who might be initiated into the same mystery: the word and the sign would be enough for them: others who were outside should remain ignorant.

But Aristides adds one word which gives a hint as to the purpose and effect of the Synthema: the

Synthema was something that addressed him in an earnest, rousing way, a practical sign and proof that the god for various reasons brought him before the assembled world in order that he should gain distinction as an orator and that the noblest should hear with their own ears good counsel on good subjects. The Synthema then was a symbol always present with him and speaking direct to him; it as a pledge of success from the god who gave it, and thus filled him with god-given confidence. Hence it served for a call to action as an orator; for it recalled the orders and assurances and promises which the god had given him in the past, and was a pledge that there still subsisted between the god and his votary that same bond of connection and mutual confidence.

Aristides does not expressly say that the Synthema was connected with the new name that was bestowed on him by the god; but there can hardly be any doubt that the name and the sign stood in some close relation to one another, and were given him at the same time, probably (as Reiske thought) in a dream. In that dream or vision the god had commissioned him to the profession of oratory, had promised him constant aid, had guaranteed him brilliant success, and as a proof and pledge of the promised aid had bestowed on him a new name, Theodorus, "the gift of god," and a sign. So much seems practically certain. Only one thing has to be added, which seems to spring directly from these facts: the Sign must have been the form in which the new name was communicated. Perhaps in writing, perhaps in some other way, Aristides had always with him the proof of the god's presence and aid. The name was the power of the god, at once encouraging him to effort and guaranteeing success.

In a sense not unlike this, the term Synthemata was used to indicate the signs or words of a symbolic code which two persons arranged with one another in order that their letters might convey more meaning to the intended recipient than to any chance reader who was not aware of the secret.

It is to be observed that, though Aristides regarded Aesculapius as his special protector and guide in life, the name which was given him was not Asclepiodoros, but Theodoros. Aesculapius, who gave him the name, was merely the form in which the ultimate divine power envisaged itself to Aristides; it was "the god," and not Aesculapius, whose name he bore.

Orators of that period seem commonly to have regarded themselves as sent by divine mission, and as charged with a message of divine truth. So Dion Chrysostom several times claims divine mission; and in one of his speeches at Tarsus he explains that all that happens to us in an unexpected, unintended, self-originated way, ought to be regarded by us a sent to us by the god, and therefore, as he has appeared in that way before the Tarsian audience, they should regard him as speaking with authority as the divine messenger. The speech was delivered probably in the third period of Dion's career, which began when he received news of the death of Domitian, and thus his case illustrates strictly contemporary belief about those travelling orators and teachers, who in many ways show so close analogy to the Christian Apostles and travelling preachers.

Chapter 23: Thyatira: Weakness Made Strong

Thyatira was situated in the mouth of a long vale which extends north and south connecting the Hermus and Caicos Valleys. Down the vale a stream flows south to join the Lycus (near whose left bank Thyatira was situated), one of the chief tributaries of the Hermus, while its northern end is divided by only a ridge of small elevation from the Caicos Valley. The valleys of the two rivers, Hermus and Caicos, stretch east and west, opening down from the edge of the great central plateau of Anatolia towards the Aegean Sea. Nature has marked out this road, a very easy path, for the tide of communication which in all civilised times must have been large between the one valley and the other. The railway traverses its whole length now: in ancient times one of the chief routes of Asia Minor traversed it.

Not merely did all communication and trade between those two great and rich valleys pass up and down the vale; but also, in certain periods and in certain conditions of the general economy of Asia Minor and the Aegean lands, a main artery of the Anatolian system of communication made use of it. The land-road connecting Constantinople with Smyrna and the southwestern regions of Asia Minor goes that way, and has been at some periods an important route. The Imperial Post-road took that course in Roman times. Above all, when Pergamum was the capital of Asia under the kings, that was the most important road in the whole country; and its importance as the one great route from Pergamum to the southeast (including all the vast regions of the central Anatolian plateau, Syria and the East generally) was proportionate to the importance which the official capital of the Province retained under the Roman administration.

In the middle of that vale, with a very slight rising ground to serve for a citadel or acropolis, Thyatira was built by Seleucus I, the founder of the Seleucid dynasty, whose vast realm, extending from the Hermus Valley to the Himalayas, was everywhere bounded loosely according to the varying strength of rival powers. The boundary at this northwestern extremity was determined at that period by the power of Lysimachus, who ruled parts of Thrace, Mysia and the coastlands as far south as Ephesus. For defence against him, a colony of Macedonian soldiers was planted at Thyatira between 300 and 282 B.C. The situation chosen implies that the Caicos Valley belonged at that moment to Lysimachus. Now Philetaerus governed Pergamum and guarded the treasure of Lysimachus for many years, and during that time the whole Caicos Valley would naturally go along with Pergamum, while the Hermus Valley belonged to the Seleucid realm.

In 282 Philetaerus revolted and founded the Pergamenian kingdom. At first he was encouraged by Seleucus in order to weaken Lysimachus; but soon this bond of a common enmity was dissolved at the death of the enemy, and then Thyatira was a useful garrison to hold the road, first in the interest of the Seleucid kings and afterwards on the Pergamenian side. So long as the kings of Pergamum were masters of Thyatira they were safe from Seleucid attack; but if the Syrian kings possessed that key to the gate of the Caicos Valley, Pergamum was narrowed in its dominion and weakened in its defences. Thus, the relation between the two cities was necessarily a very close one. The condition of Thyatira was the best measure of the power of Pergamum.

This historical sketch is necessary, in order to show the character of Thyatira and the place which it holds in history. It came into existence to be a garrison-city; and its importance to the two rival dynasties who alternately ruled it lay in its military strength. But no city has been given by nature less of the look or strength of a fortress than Thyatira. It lies in an open, smiling vale, bordered by gently sloping hills, of moderate elevation, but sufficient to overshadow the vale. It possesses no proper acropolis, and the whole impression which the situation gives is of weakness, subjection and dependence. The most careless and casual observer could never take Thyatira for a ruling city, or the capital of an Empire. It is essentially a handmaid city, built to serve an Empire by obstructing for a little the path of its enemies and so giving time for the concentration of its military strength.

The natural weakness of the position imposed all the more firmly on the kingdom whose frontier it guarded the necessity of attending to its military strength by careful fortification and by maintaining in it a trained and devoted garrison. The military spirit of the soldier-citizens had to be encouraged to the utmost. This tendency towards militarism must inevitably characterise Thyatira in all times of uncertainty and of possible warfare: the function of the city was to make a weak position strong, supply a defect, and guard against an ever-threatening danger.

The religion of an ancient city always summed up its character in brief. The Thyatiran religion is obscure, and our chief authority lies in the coins of the city. A hero Tyrimnos represents the Thyatiran conception of the city's function in the world. He goes forth on horseback with the battle-axe over his shoulder, the fit representative of a military colony, to conquer, and to dash his enemies in pieces. How far he may have a Macedonian origin, as brought with them by the first Macedonian soldiers who were settled there, remains doubtful; but his aspect in art is entirely that of a common Anatolian heroic figure.

This hero Tyrimnos is closely related in nature to the tutelary god of Thyatira, whose full titles are recorded in inscriptions: he was styled Propolis because he had his temple in front of the city, Propator as the divine ancestor (doubtless both of the city as a whole and specially of some leading family or families), Helios the sun-god, Pythian Tyrimnaean Apollo, a strange mixture of Hellenic and Anatolian names. This god is never named on the coins, so far as published; but he often appears as a type on them, a standing figure, wearing only a cloak (chlamys) fastened with a brooch round his neck, carrying a battle axe over one shoulder, and holding forth in his right hand a laurel-branch, which symbolises his purifying power. This elaborate and highly composite impersonation of the Divine nature, with so many names and such diversity of character, seems to have been produced by a syncretism of different religious ideas in the evolution of the city.

Thyatira was certainly inhabited before the time of Seleucus. The site is so favourable that it must become a centre of population from the beginning of history in the valley. But it was made a city by Seleucus with a great accession of population. Previously it had been a mere Anatolian village round a central temple. The foundation of the garrison city was not without effect on the religion of the locality. It was inevitable that the newcomers should worship the god whose power in the country had been proved by the experience of generations; but they brought with them also their own religious ideas, and these ideas necessarily affected their conception of the nature of this god whom they found at home in the land and whose power they respected and trusted. Tyrimnos, whatever his origin may have been, was the heroic embodiment of the spirit of the garrison city; and the Anatolian god of the locality took into himself some of the nature of the hero, as Helios Tyrimnaios Pythios Apollo, a conception at once Anatolian, military, and Hellenic. The god united in himself the character of all sections of the population, so that all might find in him their own nature and the satisfaction of their own religious cravings.

He stands for his city in alliance-coins with Pergamum; and frequently a female figure, wearing a turreted crown (the accepted representation of the genius of any fortified city), holds him forth on her extended right hand, thus intimating that Thyatira was devoted to the service of this god. The Emperor Elagabalus, in the dress of a Roman general, is shown with his right hand in that of Apollo Tyrimnaios, supporting between them an urn, over which is the name "Pythia." The urn is the regular symbol of those gymnastic and other competitive sports in which the Hellenic cities delighted; and the name inscribed above shows that the Thyatiran games were modelled upon the Pythian games of Greece. Between the Emperor and the god is an altar flaming with the sacrifice. The coin was, indubitably, struck in gratitude for some favour granted by the Emperor in connection with those games in Thyatira. What the favour was can be determined with great probability.

The union of the Emperor and the god in supporting these games is the symbolic fashion of intimating, in a way adapted for the surface of a coin, that the Emperor and the god were united in the honour of the festival, that is to say, the festival was no longer celebrated in honour of the god alone, but included both Emperor and god. In other words Elagabalus sanctioned the addition of the honourable title Augustan to the old Tyrimnaean festival. During the third century the feast and the games regularly bear the double title, an example of the closer relation between the Imperial and the popular religion in Asia under the later Empire.

Seleucus I, the founder of Thyatira, is mentioned by Josephus as having shown special favour to the Jews and made them citizens in the cities which he founded in Asia. The probability that he settled a body of Jews in Thyatira must therefore be admitted, for he knew well that soldiers alone could not make a city (see chapter 11). Beyond this it is not possible to go with certainty; but some slight indications are known of the presence of Jews in Thyatira. Lydia the Thyatiran in Philippi was "God-fearing," i.e., she had come within the circle of influence of the Synagogue. Professor E. Schurer in a very interesting paper has suggested the possibility that the sanctuary of Sambethe the Oriental (Chaldean, or Hebrew, or Persian) Sibyl in the Chaldean's precinct before the city of Thyatira might have been formed under Hebrew influence: according to this suggestion the sanctuary would have arisen in an attempted syncretism of Jewish and pagan religious ideas. But this remains as yet a mere tantalising possibility.

The history of Thyatira is a blank. Its fate in the many centuries of fighting between Mohammedans (Arabs first, then Turks) and Christians must have been a sad one. It is one of those cities whose situation exposes them to destruction by every conqueror, and yet compels their restoration after every siege and sack. It lies right in the track of invasion: it blocks the way and must be captured by an invader; it guards the passage to a rich district, and hence it must be defended to the last, and so provoke the barbarity of the assailant: but it could never be made a really strong fortress in ancient warfare, so as to resist successfully. Yet the successful assailant must in his turn refortify the city, if he wants to hold the country. He must make it the guardian of his gate; he must make it a garrison city. Its situation defines its history; but the history has not been recorded.

The same local conditions which ensured for Thyatira so unfortunate a fate in unsettled times favoured its prosperity in a period of profound peace. The garrison city could never be a large one, for a multitude of inhabitants devoted to the arts of peace would seriously detract from its military strength. But in the long peace of the Roman Empire Thyatira ceased to be a mere military city, though the historical memory and the military character of the municipal religion still persisted. The city grew large and wealthy. It was a centre of communication. Vast numbers passed through it. It commanded a rich and fertile vale. Many of the conditions of a great trading city were united there.

This period of great prosperity and increase was only beginning when the Seven Letters were written. Thyatira was still a small city, retaining strong memories of its military origin, and yet with fortifications decayed and dismantled in the long freedom from terror of attack, which had lasted since 189 B.C. Yet the Roman peace had at first brought no prosperity, only oppression and extortion. When the Empire at last was inaugurated, prosperity returned to Asia (see chapter 10); and Thyatira soon began to take advantage of its favourable situation for trade, though it was not till the second century after Christ that the full effect became manifest.

The coinage of Thyatira is a good index of the character of the city. As a military colony, in its earlier stage of existence, it struck various classes of coins, including cistophori. This coinage came to an end before 150 B.C.; for the military importance of Thyatira lay in its position as a frontier city; and that ceased after 189 B.C. It was not until the last years of the reign of Claudius, 50-4 A.D., that it began again to issue coins. They gradually became more numerous; and in the latter part of the second century, and in the third century, the coinage of Thyatira was on a great scale, indicating prosperity and wealth in the city.

It is therefore not surprising that more trade-guilds are known in Thyatira than in any other Asian city. The inscriptions, though not specially numerous, mention the following: wool-workers, linen-workers, makers of outer garments, dyers, leather-workers, tanners, potters, bakers, slave-dealers and bronze-smiths. The dealers in garments and the salve-dealers would have a good market in a road-centre. Garments were sold ready made, being all loose and free; and from the mention of dealers in outer garments we may infer the existence of special trades and guilds for other classes of garments. The woman of Thyatira, a seller of purple, named Lydia, who was so hospitable to St. Paul and his company at Philippi (Acts 16:14), belonged doubtless to one of those guilds: she sold not simply purple cloth but purple garments, and had emigrated to push the trade in Thyatiran manufactures in the Macedonian city. The purple in which she dealt cannot be regarded as made with the usual dye, for that was obtained from a shell-fish found chiefly on the Phoenician and the Spartan coasts. The colour in which Lydia dealt must have been a product of the Thyatiran region; and Monsieur Clerc, in his work on the city, suggests what is at once seen plainly to be true, that the well-known Turkey-red was the colour which is meant. This bright red is obtained from madder-root, which grows abundantly in those regions. It is well known that the ancient names of colours were used with great laxity and freedom; and the name purple, being established and fashionable, was used for several colours which to us seem essentially diverse from one another.

The divine smith, Hephaestus, dressed as a workman, is here seated at an anvil (represented only by a small pillar), holding in his left hand a pair of forceps, and giving the finishing blow with his hammer to a helmet, for which the goddess of war, Pallas Athene, is holding out her hand. Considering that a guild of bronze-smiths is mentioned at Thyatira, we cannot doubt that this coin commemorates the peculiar importance for the welfare of Thyatira of the bronze-workers' handicraft; and we must infer that bronze work was carried to a high state of perfection in the city.

Chapter 24: The Letter to the Church in Thyatira

These things saith the Son of God, who hath his eyes like a flame of fire, and his feet are like bright bronze:

I know thy works, and thy love and faith and ministry and patience, and that thy last works are more than the first. But I have this against thee, that thou sufferest the woman of thine, Jezebel, which calleth herself a prophetess; and she teacheth and seduceth my servants to commit fornication, and to eat things sacrificed to idols. And I gave her time that she should repent; and she willeth not to repent of her fornication. Behold, I set her on a banqueting couch, and them that commit adultery with her, to enjoy great tribulation, except they repent of her works. And I will kill her children with death; and all the churches shall know that I am he which searcheth the reins and hearts: and I will give unto each one of you according to your works. But to you I say, to the rest that are in Thyatira, as many as have not this teaching, which know not the deep things of Satan, as they say; I lay upon you no other burden. Howbeit that which ye have, hold fast till I come.

And he that overcometh, and he that keepeth my works unto the end, to him will I give authority over the nations: and he shall rule them with a rod of iron, as the vessels of the potter are broken to shivers; as I also have received of my Father: and I will give him the morning star.

He that hath an ear, let him hear what the Spirit saith to the churches.

This is in many respects the most obscure, as it is certainly the longest, and probably in a historical view the most instructive of all the Seven Letters. Its obscurity is doubtless caused in a considerable degree by the fact that the history of Thyatira, and the character and circumstances of the city in the first century after Christ, are almost entirely unknown to us. Hence those allusions to the past history and the present situation of affairs in the city, which we have found the most instructive and illuminative parts of the letters to Ephesus, Smyrna, and Pergamum, are in the case of Thyatira the most obscure. We have some idea of what were the proper topics for an orator to enlarge on when he wished to please the people of Ephesus or Pergamum. We know how a rhetorician like Aelius Aristides tickled the ears of the Smyrnaeans. We know what events in the past history of those cities, as well as of Sardis, had sunk into the heart of the inhabitants, and were remembered by all with ever fresh joy or sorrow. Even in the case of the secondary cities, Laodicea and Philadelphia, we learn something from various ancient authorities about the leading facts of their history and present circumstances, the sources of their wealth, the staple of their trade, the disasters that had befallen them. But about Thyatira we know extremely little. Historians and ancient writers generally rarely allude to it, and the numerous inscriptions which have been discovered and published throw little or no light (so far as we can at present detect) upon the letter which we are now studying.

There is a considerable resemblance between the Thyatiran and Pergamenian letters. Those were the only two of the Seven Cities which had been strongly affected by the Nicolaitan teaching, and both letters are dominated by the strenuous hatred of the writer for that heresy. Moreover, those two cities lay a little apart from the rest, away in the north. They were the two Mysian cities of the Seven. Pergamum was always called a Mysian city. Thyatira was sometimes called "the last, i.e. the most southerly, city of Mysia"; and it stood in the closest relations with Pergamum, when the latter was the capital of the Attalid kings; although, in the proverbial uncertainty of the Mysian frontier, most people considered it a city of Lydia. It may therefore be presumed that the two had a certain local character in common.

Accordingly, there may be traced a common type both in the preliminary addresses and in the promises at the end of those two letters. The strength of authority, the sword as the symbol of the power of life and death, the tessera inscribed with the secret name of might--such are the topics that give character to the Pergamenian exordium and conclusion. The Thyatiran letter proceeds from "the Son of God, who hath His eyes like a flame of fire and His feet like unto brighter bronze" (the very hard alloyed metal, used for weapons, and under proper treatment assuming a brilliant polished gleam approximating to gold); to the victorious Christian of Thyatira is promised "authority over the nations, and he shall rule them with a rod of iron as the vessels of the potter are broken to shivers"; the terror and, as one might almost say, the cruelty of this promise is mitigated by the conclusion, "and I will give him the morning star." The spirit of the address and the promise is throughout of dazzlingly impressive might, the irresistible strength of a great monarch and a vast well-ordered army.

The words which are used in this Thyatiran address have an appropriateness, which we can only guess at. The term "chalkolibanos," which may be rather vaguely rendered "bright bronze," never occurs except in the Apocalypse. Its exact sense was doubtless known to the guild of the bronze-workers in Thyatira; but only the name of this city guild has been preserved, without any information as to the industry which they practised. This is one of the details on which better local knowledge would almost certainly throw light.

It may be regarded as probable, though no other authority ever mentions this obscure term, that chalkolibanos was made in Thyatira; but all that can be stated with certainty is that the city was a trading and manufacturing centre, that we know of an exceptionally large and varied series of trade-guilds in it, and that among them occurred the bronze-smiths and modellers in bronze (either as two separate guilds or as one). The word chalkolibanos occurs also in 1:15, but (as has been pointed out in chapter 13) the description of "one like unto a son of man," 1:12ff, was obviously composed with a view to the Seven Letters, so as to exhibit there, united in one personality, the various characteristics which were to be thereafter mentioned separately in the letters. Accordingly the chalkolibanos may probably have suggested itself in the first place for the purposes of the Thyatiran letter; so that its use in 1:15 may be secondary, merely to prepare for the letter.

The omission of the "sword" as the symbol of might also shows characteristic accuracy in the choice of details. The sword was the symbol of higher official authority according to the Roman usage. It shows, therefore, a marked appropriateness that the writer should use the term "sword" in reference to Pergamum, the official capital and seat of the Roman Proconsul, but avoid it in the case of Thyatira. On the other hand the "rod of iron" is expressive of might that is not thought of as associated with formal authority, but merely arises from innate strength. Thyatira could not properly bear the sword, but only the iron bar.

The original character of Thyatira had been military. It was a colony of Macedonian soldiers, planted to guard the long pass leading north and south between the Hermus Valley and the Caicus Valley, between Sardis and Pergamum. Its tutelary deity was Tyrimnos, originally apparently a hero, but merged in the divine nature as Apollo Tyrimnaios. The hero is represented often as a horse-man with a double-edge battle-axe on his shoulder, an appropriate deity for a military colony. The glitter and brilliance and smashing power of a great army, or a military colony, or the Divine Author of the Thyatiran letter, are embodied in him.

In short, just as in the case of Pergamum, so here again, the promise sets the true and victorious Christian in the place and dignity of the Roman Emperor. Rome was the only power on earth that exercised authority over the nations, and ruled them with a rod of iron, and smashed them like potsherds: to the Roman State that description is startlingly applicable. Accordingly the promise here designates the victor as heir to a greater, more terrible, more irresistible strength than even the power of the mighty Empire with all its legions. The opposition was more precisely and antithetically expressed in the case of Pergamum, at least to the readers who were within the circle of ancient ideas and education; though probably the modern mind is likely to recognise the antithesis between the Church and the Empire more readily and clearly in the Thyatiran letter, since we at the distance of nearly 2,000 years can more readily call up in imagination the military strength of the Empire and its armies. But in the first century the minds of men were filled and awed by the thought of the Emperor as the central figure of the whole earth, concentrating on himself the loyal religious feelings of all nations, and holding in his hands that complete authority, indefinable because too wide for definition, which the autocrat of the civilised world exercised by the simple expression of his will; and that is the idea to which the Pergamenian letter appealed.

It could not escape the attention of an Asian reader at that time that this irresistible power and strength were promised to the city which was at that time the smallest and feeblest, and in general estimation the least distinguished and famous, of all the Seven Cities, except perhaps Philadelphia, which might vie with Thyatira for the last place on the list.

The local surroundings of Thyatira accentuate this comparatively humble character of its fortunes. It lies in the middle of a long valley between parallel ridges of hills of no great elevation, which rise with gentle slope from the valley. Thus there is the most marked contrast between the situation of Thyatira--now "sleeping safe in the bosom of the plain" under the peace of the Roman rule, though (if any enemies had existed) easily open to attack from every side, dominated by even those low and gentle ranges of hills on east and west, beautiful with a gentle, smiling, luxuriant softness and grace--and the proud and lofty acropolis of Sardis, or the huge hill of Pergamum, or the mountain-walls of Ephesus and the castled hill of Smyrna, each with its harbour, or the long sloping hillside on which Philadelphia rises high above its plain, or the plateau of Laodicea, not lofty, yet springing sharp and bold from the plain of the Lycus, crowned with a long line of strong walls and so situated on the protruding apex of a triangular extent of hilly ground that it seems to stand up in the middle of the plain.

Military skill, such as the Pergamenian kings had at their command, could of course so fortify Thyatira as to make it strong enough to hold the passage up the long valley. The importance of the city to the kings lay in the fact that it guarded the road from the Hermus Valley and the East generally to Pergamum. Its function in the world at first had been to serve as attendant and guard to the governing royal city. Now, under the long peace of the Imperial rule, it had become a town of trade and peaceful industry, profiting by its command of a fertile plain and still more by its situation on a great road; and beyond all doubt the military character of its foundation by the kings, as a garrison of Macedonian soldiers to block the road to their capital from the south, was now only a historical memory.

Thus Thyatira of all the Seven Cities seemed in every way the least fitted by nature and by history to rule over the nations; and it could not fail to be observed by the Asian readers as a notable thing, that the Church of this weakest and least famous of the cities should be promised such a future of strength and universal power. Beyond all doubt the writer of the Seven Letters, who knew the cities so well, must have been conscious of this, and must have relied on it for the effect which he aimed at.

As we go through the Seven Letters point by point, each detail confirms our impression of the unhesitating and sublime confidence in the victory of the Church which prompts and enlivens them. The Emperor, the Roman State with its patriotism, its religion, and its armies, the brutal populace of the cities, the Jews, and every other enemy of the Church, all are raging and persecuting and slaying to the utmost of their power. But their power is naught. The real Church stands outside of their reach, immeasurably above them, secure and triumphant, "eternal in the heavens," while the individual Christians work out their victory in their own life and above all by their death; so that the more successfully the enemy kills them off, the more absolute is his defeat, and the more complete and immediate is their victory. The weakest and least honoured among those Christian martyrs, as he gains his victory by death, is invested with that authority over the nations, which the proud Empire believed that its officials and governors wielded, and rules with a power more supreme than that of Rome herself.

The conclusion of the promise, "I will give him the morning star," seems to have been added with the calculated intention of expressing the other side of the Christian character. The honour promised was evidently too exclusively terrible. But the addition must be in keeping with the rest of the promise. The brightness, gleam and glitter, as of "an army with banners," which rules through the opening address and the concluding promise, is expressed in a milder spirit, without the terrible character, though the brilliance remains or is even increased, in the image of "the morning star."

Having observed the close relation between the Pergamenian and the Thyatiran letter, we shall recognise a similar analogy between the Ephesian and the Sardian, and again between the Smyrnaean and the Philadelphian letters. Those six letters constitute three pairs; and each pair must be studied not only in its separate parts, but also in the mutual relation of the two parts. Only the Laodicean letter stands alone, just as Laodicea stood apart from the other six, the representative of the distant and very different Phrygian land.

As usual, the letter proper begins with the statement that the writer is well acquainted with the history and fortunes of the Thyatiran Church. The brief first statement is entirely laudatory. "I know thy works, and thy love and faith and ministry and patience, and that thy last works are more than the first." Whereas Ephesus had fallen away from its original spirit and enthusiasm, Thyatira had grown more energetic as time elapsed.

But after this complimentary opening, the letter denounces the state of the Thyatiran Church in the most outspoken and unreserved way. It had permitted and encouraged the Nicolaitan doctrine, and harboured the principal exponent of that teaching in the Province.

We observe here, first of all, that the Nicolaitan doctrine had not caused any falling off in the good deeds of the Church. On the contrary, it was probably the emulation between the two parties or sections of the Church, and the desire of the Nicolaitans to show that they were quite as fervent in the faith as the simpler Christians whose opinions they desired to correct, that caused the improvement in the "works" of the Thyatiran Church. We recognise that it was quite possible for Nicolaitans to continue to cherish "love and faith and ministry and patience," and to improve in the active performance of the practical work of a congregation (among which public charities and subscriptions were doubtless an important part). Public subscriptions for patriotic and religious purposes were common in the Graeco-Roman world; the two classes were almost equivalent in ancient feeling; all patriotic purposes took a religious form, and though only the religious purpose is as a rule mentioned in the inscriptions in which such contributions are recorded, the real motive in most cases was patriotic, and the custom of making such subscriptions was undoubtedly kept up by the Christian Church generally (see Acts 11:29, 24:17; 1 Cor 16:1, 2; 2 Cor 9:1-5). The Thyatiran Nicolaitans, true to their cherished principle of assimilating the Church usage as far as possible to the character of existing society, would naturally encourage and maintain the custom. It makes this letter more credible in other points, that in this one it cordially admits and praises the generosity of the whole Thyatiran Church, including the Nicolaitans.

It seems therefore to be beyond all doubt that, as a rule, the Nicolaitans of Thyatira, with the prophetess as their leader, were still active and unwearied members of the Church, "full of good works," and respected by the whole congregation for their general character and way of life. The sentiment entertained with regard to them by the congregation is attested by the letter: "Thou sufferest the woman Jezebel, which calleth herself a prophetess, and she teacheth." It is evident that the lady who is here so rudely referred to was generally accepted in Thyatira as a regular teacher, and as a prophetess and leader in the Church. There was no serious, general, active opposition to her; and therein lay the fault of the whole congregation; she had firmly established herself in the approval of the congregation; and, as we have seen, she was so respected because by her liberal and zealous and energetic life she had deserved the public esteem. She was evidently an active and managing lady after the style of Lydia, the Thyatiran merchant and head of a household at Philippi; and it is an interesting coincidence that the only two women of Thyatira mentioned in the New Testament are so like one another in character. The question might even suggest itself whether they may not be the same person, since Lydia seems to disappear from Philippian history (so far as we are informed of it) soon after St. Paul's visit to the city. But this question must undoubtedly be answered in the negative, for it is utterly improbable that the hostess of St. Paul would ever be spoken about so mercilessly and savagely as this poor prophetess is here. The prophetess furnishes just one more example of the great influence exerted by women in the primitive Church.

The extremely bitter and almost virulent tone in which the prophetess is spoken of seems, therefore, not to be due to her personal character, but to be caused entirely by the principles which she set forth in a too persuasive and successful way: she was exercising an unhealthy influence, and her many excellent qualities made her the more dangerous, because they increased the authority of her words. At the present day, when we love milder manners and are full of allowance for difference of opinion and conduct in others, the harshness with which disapproval is here expressed must seem inharmonious and repellent. But the writer was influenced by other ways of thinking and different principles of action; and we should not estimate either him or the prophetess by twentieth century standards.

It may be added that I have read more than once Professor E. Schurer's paper on the Thyatiran Jezebel--at first with admiration and interest, but with growing dissatisfaction during subsequent thought, until in a final closer study of the whole Seven Letters it seems to me to be entirely mistaken in its whole line of interpretation. He finds in "Jezebel" a prophetess and priestess of the temple of a Chaldean Sibyl in Thyatira, where a mixture of pagan rites with Jewish ideas was practised.

It is unnecessary here to dilate on the importance of the order of prophets in the primitive Church; but we should be glad to know more about this Thyatiran prophetess, a person of broad views and reasonable mind, who played a prominent pat in a great religious movement, and perished defeated and decried. She ranks with the Montanist prophetesses of the second century, or the Cappadocian prophetess about whom Firmilian wrote to Cyprian in the third century; one of those leading women who seem to have emphasised too strongly one side of a case, quite reasonable in itself, through failure to see the other side sufficiently. They all suffer the hard fate of being known only through the mouth of bitter enemies, whose disapproval of their opinions was expressed in the harsh, opprobrious, half-figurative language of ancient moral condemnation. Thus for the most part they are stigmatised as persons of the worst character and the vilest life.

We take a much more favourable view of the character of the lady of Thyatira than the commentators usually do. Thus Mr. Anderson Scott speaks of her teaching as "encouragement to licentiousness," and of the "libertinism which was taught and practised in Thyatira"; and she is generally regarded as entirely false, abandoned and immoral in her life and her teaching. This usual view is founded mainly on the misinterpretation of 2:22, which will be explained in the sequel. It seems to us to miss completely the real character and the serious nature of the question which was being agitated at the time, and which probably was finally determined and set at rest by the decision stated in the Seven Letters and in the oral teaching of the author. In this and various other so-called "heresies" the right side was not so clear and self-evident as it is commonly represented in the usual popularly accepted histories of the Church and commentaries on the ancient authorities. The prophetess was not all evil--that idea is absolutely contradictory of the already quoted words of the letter, 2:19--and the opposite party had no monopoly of the good in practical life.

The strong language of 2:20, 21 is due in part to the common symbolism found in the Old Testament and elsewhere, describing the lapses of Israel into idolatry as adultery and gross immorality. But in greater measure it is due to the fact that the idolatrous ritual of paganism was always in practice associated with immoral customs of various kinds; that, although a few persons of higher mind and nobler nature might perhaps recognise that the immorality was not an essential part of the pagan ritual, but was due to degeneracy and degradation, it was impossible to dissociate the one from the other; and that the universal opinion of pagan society accepted as natural and justifiable and right--if not carried to ruinous extremes--such a way of life, with such relations between the sexes, as Christianity and Judaism have always stigmatised as vicious, degrading, and essentially wrong. The principles of the Nicolaitans seemed to St. John certain to lead to an acquiescence in this commonly accepted standard of pagan society, and he held that the Nicolaitan prophetess was responsible for all that followed from her teaching. That he was right no one can doubt who studies the history of Greek and Roman and West Asiatic paganism as a practical force in human life. That there were lofty qualities and some high ideals in those pagan religions the present writer has always recognised and maintained in the most emphatic terms; but, in human nature, the inevitable tendency of paganism was towards a low standard of moral life, as has been set forth more fully in an account of the Religion of Greece and Asia Minor in Hastings' Dictionary of the Bible, vol. v., pp. 109-155.

A third reason also determined the author to employ the strong language which occurs in 2:20. Evidently the decision of the Apostolic Council, though relating to a different question, dictated the form which the author of the letter has employed. That decision was evidently present in his memory as authoritative on an allied question; and he alludes to it in an easily understood way, which he evidently expected his readers to appreciate. He turns in verse 24 to address the section of the Thyatiran Church which had not accepted the Nicolaitan teaching, and tells them that he lays no other burden upon them. The burden which has been already imposed on all Christians by the Council is sufficient, "These necessary things, that ye abstain from things sacrificed to idols . . . and from fornication" (Acts 15:28). The expression, "no other burden," implies that the necessary minimum burden is already before the writer's mind, and that he assumes it to be also before the readers' mind; he assumes that the readers have already caught the allusion in 2:20, "She teacheth and seduceth my servants to commit fornication and to eat things sacrificed to idols," i.e., she teaches them to violate the fundamental rule of the Apostolic Council. But, as he implies, while this minimum burden must be borne and cannot be avoided by any sophistry and skilful religious casuistry--which the Nicolaitans regarded as high transcendental conception of the things of God, but which is really "the cryptic lore and deep lies of the devil"--he imposes on them no further burden. This is sufficient, but it is inevitable: there is no more to be said. The Nicolaitans explain this away, and thereby condemn themselves.

The following sentences are the one main source of all the little we can gather about the Nicolaitan principles. The allusions in the Pergamenian letter, obscure in themselves, become more intelligible when read in connection with the words here. The obscurity is due to our ignorance of what was familiar to the original Asian readers. They were living through these questions, and caught every allusion and hint that the writer of the letter makes.

The questions which are here treated belong to an early period in the history of the Church. They are connected with the general conduct of pagan converts in the Church. How much should be required of them? What burdens should be imposed on them? The principles that should regulate their conduct are here regarded, of course, from the point of view of their relation to the general society of the cities in which they lived. They had for the most part been members, and some of them leading members, of that society before their conversion. We may here leave out of sight the Christianised Jews in the Asian congregations, who had in a way been outside of ordinary pagan society from the beginning; for, though they were a part, and possibly even an influential part, of the Church, yet the Seven Letters were not intended specially for them, and hardly touch the questions that most intimately concerned them. These letters are addressed to pagan converts, and set forth in a figurative way the principles that they should follow in their relations with ordinary society and the Roman State.

On the other hand, the relation of the pagan converts to Judaism is hardly alluded to in the Seven Letters. That question was now past and done with; the final answer had been given; there was no need for further instructions about it. In practice, of course, the relation between Jewish Christians and pagan converts continued to exist in the congregations; but the general principles were now admitted, and were of such a kind as to place an almost impassable barrier between the national Jews and the Church. To the writer of the Seven Letters, the Jews were the sham Jews, "the synagogue of Satan," according to a twice repeated expression: God had turned away from them, and had preferred the pagan converts, who now were the true seed of Abraham: the sham Jews would have to recognise the facts, accept the situation, and humble themselves before the Gentile Christians: "Behold, I give of the Synagogue of Satan, of them which say they are Jews and they are not, but speak falsely; behold I will make them to come and worship before thy feet, and to know that I have loved thee." Thus the situation in the Church was developed now far beyond what it had been in the time of St. Paul: and his settlement of the Jewish question had been accepted completely by the Church, and is stated as emphatically and aggressively here by this Jewish writer as by Paul himself.

It is unnecessary here to repeat the elaborate discussion of this subject which is given in the Expositor, present series, vol. ii., pp. 429-444; vol. iii., pp. 93-110. There some of the many difficulties are described which presented themselves every day to the converts from paganism. It was accepted on all hands that they were to continue to live in the world, and were not to seek to withdraw entirely out of it (1 Cor 5:10). There were certain accepted customs, rules of politeness and courtesy, ways of living and acting, which were recommended by their gracious, refined, elegant character, and other ways which without any special gracefulness were recommended simply because they were the ordinary methods of behaviour. If we live in a long-established and cultivated society, we must do many things, not because we specially approve of them, or derive pleasure or advantage of any kind from them, but simply from consideration for the feelings of others, who expect us to do as the rest of society does. There are even some things which we hardly quite approve; and yet we do not feel that we ought to condemn them openly, or withdraw in a marked way from social gatherings where they are practised. Such extremely strict carrying out of our own principles would quickly become harsh, rude, and misanthropic; and would justly expose any one who was often guilty of it to the charge of self-conceit and spiritual pride.

How much might one accept; and what must one condemn? Such questions as these were daily presenting themselves to the Christians in the Graeco-Roman cities; and they were then almost invariably complicated by the additional difficulty that all established usages, social customs, rules of polite conduct, forms of graceful courtesy, were (with rare exceptions) implicated in and coloured by idolatrous associations. Grace before meat, thanksgiving after food, were in the strictest sense slight acts of acknowledgment of the kindness and the rights of pagan divinities. Such ceremonies had often become mere forms, and those who complied with those customs were often hardly conscious of the religious character of the action. How far was the Christian bound to take notice of their idolatrous character and to avoid acting in accordance with them, or even to express open disapproval of them? So far as we can gather, the rule laid down by St. Paul, and the practice of the Church, was that only in quite exceptional, rare cases should open disapproval of the customs of society be expressed; in many cases, where the idolatrous connection was not obvious, but only veiled or remote, the Christian might (and perhaps even ought to) comply with the usual forms, unless his attention was expressly called by any one of the guests to the idolatrous connection; in that case the rude remark was equivalent to a challenge to deny or affirm boldly his religion, and the Christian must affirm his religion, and refuse compliance. Also, where the idolatrous character of the act was patent and generally recognised, the Christian must refuse compliance. Hence there was a general tendency among the Christians to avoid situations, offices, and paths of life, in which the performance of idolatrous ceremonial was necessary; and on this account they were generally stigmatised as morose, hostile to existing society, and deficient in active patriotism, if not actually disloyal.

Besides these slighter cases, there were many of a much more serious character. The Roman soldier, marching under the colours of his regiment, was marching under the standard of idolatry, for the standards (signa) were all divine, and worship was paid to them by the soldiers as a duty of the service, and all contained one or more idolatrous symbols or representations; moreover he was frequently required, standing in his place in the ranks, to take part in idolatrous acts of worship. The soldier could not retire and take to some other way of life, for he was bound to the service through a long term of years. Here, again, the rule and practice of the Church seems to have been that in ordinary circumstances the converted soldier should remain passive, and as far as possible silent, during the ceremony at which he was compulsorily present, but should not actively protest. A similar practice was encouraged by the Church in other departments of life and work. But in every case, and in every profession, the Christian, who in ordinary circumstances might remain passive and unprotesting, was liable to be pointedly challenged as to whether he would willingly perform this act of worship of the deity whom he considered false. In case of such a challenge, there was only one course open. The Christian could not comply with a demand which was expressly made a test of his faith.

But apart from those many doubtful cases where the right line of conduct was difficult to determine and might vary according to circumstances, there was a large number of cases in which the decision of the early leaders of the Church was absolute and unvarying. In whatsoever society, or company, or meeting, or ceremonial, the condition of presence and membership lay in the performance of pagan ritual as an express and declared act of religion, the Christian must have no part or lot, and could not accept membership or even be present. Here the Nicolaitans took the opposite view, and could defend their opinion by many excellent, thoroughly reasonable and highly philosophic arguments. To illustrate this class of cases, we may take an example of a meeting which was permissible, and of one which was not, according to the opinion of those early leaders of the Church. A meeting of the citizens of a city for political purposes was always inaugurated by pagan ritual, and according to the strict original theory the citizens in this political assembly were all united in the worship of the patron national deity in whose honour the opening ceremonies were performed; but the ritual had long become a mere form, and nobody was in practice conscious that the condition of presence in the assembly lay in the loyal service of the national deity. The political condition was the only one that was practically remembered: every member of a city tribe had a right to be present and vote. The Christian citizen might attend and vote in such a meeting, ignoring and passing in silence the opening religious ceremony.

But, on the other hand, there were numerous societies for a vast variety of purposes, the condition of membership in which was professedly and explicitly the willingness to engage in the worship of a pagan deity, because the society met in the worship of that deity, the name of the society was often a religious name, and the place of meeting was dedicated to the deity, and thus was constituted a temple for his worship. The Epistles of Paul, Peter, Jude, and the Seven Letters, all touch on this topic, and all are agreed: the true Christian cannot be a member of such clubs or societies. The Nicolaitans taught that Christians ought to remain members; and doubtless added that they would exercise a good influence on the societies by continuing in them.

This very simple and practical explanation will, doubtless, seem to many scholars to be too slight for the serious treatment that the subject receives in the two letters which we are studying. Such scholars regard grave matters of dogma as being the proper subject for treatment in the early Christian document; they will probably ridicule the suggestion that the question, whether a Christian should join a club or not, demanded the serious notice of an apostle, and declare that this was the sort of question on which the Church kept an open mind, and left great liberty to individuals to act as they thought right (just as they did in regard to military service, magistracies, and other important matters); and they will require that Nicolaitanism should be regarded from a graver dogmatic point of view. The present writer must confess that those graver subjects of dogma seem to him to have been much over-estimated; it was not dogma that moved the world, but life. Frequently, when rival parties and rival nations fought with one another as to which of two opposed dogmas was the truth, they had been arrayed against one another by more deep-seated and vital causes, and merely inscribed at the last the dogmas on their standards or chose them as watchwords or symbols. We are tired of those elaborate discussions of the fine, wire-drawn, subtle distinctions between sects, and those elaborate discussions of the principles involved in heresies, and we desire to see the real differences in life and conduct receive more attention.

It is not difficult to show how important in practical life was this question as to the right of Christians to be members of social clubs. The clubs were one of the most deep-rooted customs of Graeco-Roman society: some were social, some political, some for mutual benefit, but all took a religious form. New religions usually spread by means of such clubs. The clubs bound their members closely together in virtue of the common sacrificial meal, a scene of enjoyment following on a religious ceremony. They represented in its strongest form the pagan spirit in society; and they were strongest among the middle classes in the great cities, persons who possessed at least some fair amount of money and made some pretension to education, breeding and knowledge of the world. To hold aloof from the clubs was to set oneself down as a mean-spirited, grudging, ill-conditioned person, hostile to existing society, devoid of generous impulse and kindly neighbourly feeling, an enemy of mankind.

The very fact that this subject was treated (as we have seen) so frequently, shows that the question was not easily decided, but long occupied the attention of the Church and its leaders. It was almost purely a social and practical question; and no subject presents such difficulties to the legislator as one which touches the fabric of society and the ordinary conduct of life. In 1 Corinthians (as was pointed out in the Expositor, loc. cit., ii., p. 436) the subject, though not formally brought before St. Paul for decision, was practically involved in a question which was submitted to him; but he did not impose any absolute prohibition; and he tried to place the Corinthians on a higher plane of thought so that they might see clearly all that was involved and judge for themselves rightly.

After this the question must have frequently called for consideration, and a certain body of teaching had been formulated. It is clear that the Pergamenian and Thyatiran letters assume in the readers the knowledge of such teaching as familiar; and 2 Peter 2:1ff refers to the same formulated teaching (Expositor, loc. cit., iii. p. 106ff). This teaching quoted examples from Old Testament history (especially Balaam or Sodom and Gomorrah) as a warning of the result that must inevitably follow from laxity in this matter; it drew scathing pictures of the revelry, licence and intoxication of spirit which characterised the feasts of these pagan religious societies, where from an early hour in the afternoon the members, lounging on the dining-couches, ate and drank and were amused by troops "of singing and of dancing slaves"; it argued that such periodically recurring scenes of excitement must be fatal to all reasonable, moderate, self-restraining spirit. The steadily growing body of formulated moral principles on the subject was set aside by the Nicolaitans, who taught, on the contrary (as is said in 2 Peter, loc. cit.), that men should have confidence in their own character and judgment, and who promised to set them free from a hard law, while they were in reality enticing back to lascivious enjoyment the young converts who had barely "escaped the defilements of the world."

The author of the letters now before us depends for his effect on the knowledge, which he assumes his readers to possess, of such striking pictures as that in 2 Peter of the revels accompanying club-feasts. Such revels were not merely condoned by pagan opinion, but were regarded as a duty, in which graver natures ought occasionally to relax their seriousness, and yield to the impulses of nature, in order to return again with fresh zest to the real work of life. St. John had himself often already set before his readers orally the contrast between that pagan spirit of liberty and animalism, and the true Christian spirit; and had counselled the Thyatiran prophetess to wiser principles.

Thus, this controversy was of the utmost importance in the early Church. It affected and determined, more than any other, the relation of the new religion to the existing forms and character of Graeco-Roman city society. The real meaning of it was this--should the Church accept the existing forms of society and social unions, or declare war against them? And this again implied another question--should Christianity conform to the existing, accepted principles of society, or should it force society to conform to its principles? When the question is thus put in its full and true implication, we see forthwith how entirely wrong the Nicolaitans and their Thyatiran prophetess were; we recognise that the whole future of Christianity was at stake over this question; and we are struck once more with admiration at the unerring insight with which the Apostles gauged every question that presented itself in the complicated life of that period, and the quick sure decision with which they seized and insisted on the essential, and neglected the accidental and secondary aspects of the case. We can now understand why St. John condemns that very worthy, active, and managing, but utterly mistaken lady of Thyatira in such hard and cruel and, one had almost said, unfair language; he saw that she was fumbling about with questions which she was quite incapable of comprehending, full of complacent satisfaction with her superficial views as to the fairness and reasonableness of allowing the poor to profit by those quite praiseworthy associations which did so much good (though they contained some regrettable features which might easily be ignored by a philosophic mind), and misusing her influence, acquired by good works and persuasive speaking, to lead her fellow-Christians astray. If she were successful, Christianity must melt and be absorbed into the Graeco-Roman society, highly cultivated, but over-developed, morbid, unhealthy, "fast" (in modern slang). But she would not be successful. The mind which could see the Church's victory over the destroying Empire consummated in the death of every Christian had no fear of what the lady of Thyatira might do. "I will kill her children (i.e., her disciples and perverts) with death; and all the Churches shall know that I am he which searcheth the reins and hearts." Probably "death" is here to be understood as "incurable disease," according to the universal belief that disease (and especially fever, in which there is no visible affection of any organ) was the weapon of Divine power.

It was a hard and stern discipline, which undoubtedly left out some of the most charming, right and lovable sides of life and human nature; but it may be doubted if any less stern discipline could have availed to teach the world as it then was and bend it to the reign of law. It is a case similar to that of Scotland under the old Calvinistic regime, stern and hard and narrow; but would any milder and more lovable rule ever have been able to tame a stubborn and self-willed race, among whom law had never before been able to establish itself firmly?

And as to the prophetess, she had had long time to think and to learn wisdom; the question had been agitated for a great many years; but she had learned nothing and forgotten nothing, and only clung more closely to the policy of compromising with idolatry. Her end is expressed with a grim irony, which was probably far more full of meaning to the Thyatirans than to modern readers: there are allusions in the passage that escape us. She should have her last great sacrificial meal at one of those associations. "I set her on a dining-couch, and her vile associates with her, and they shall have opportunity to enjoy great--tribulation: unless they repent, for she has shown that she cannot repent."

Probably, part of the effect of this denunciation depends on the ancient custom and usage as regards women. Though women had in many respects a position of considerable freedom in Anatolian cities, as has been pointed out by many writers, yet it may be doubted whether ladies of good standing took part in the club-dinners. We do not know enough on the subject, however, to speak with any confidence; and can only express the belief that the status of ladies in the Lydian cities lent point to this passage. Possibly thus to set her down at the dinner table was equivalent to saying that in her own life she would show the effect of the principles which she taught others to follow, and would sit at the revels like one of the light women. That women were members of religious associations (though not, apparently, in great numbers) is of course well know; but that is only the beginning of the question. What was their position and rule of life? How far did thy take part in the meal and revel that followed the sacrifice? To these questions an answer has yet to be discovered.

It may be regarded as certain that the importance of the trade-guilds in Thyatira made the Nicolaitan doctrine very popular there. The guilds were very numerous in that city, and are often mentioned in great variety in the inscriptions. It was, certainly, hardly possible for a tradesman to maintain his business in Thyatira without belonging to the guild of his trade. The guilds were corporate bodies, taking active measures to protect the common interests, owning property, passing decrees, and exercising considerable powers; they also, undoubtedly, were benefit societies, and in many respects healthy and praiseworthy associations. In no other city are they so conspicuous. It was therefore a serious thing for a Thyatiran to cut himself off from his guild.

To the remnant of the Thyatiran Church--those who, while suffering the prophetess, and not showing clearly that they "hated the works of the Nicolaitans," yet had not actively carried out her teaching in practice--one word was sufficient. It was enough that they should follow the established principle, and act according to the law as stated in the Apostolic Council at Jerusalem. No burden beyond that was laid upon them; but that teaching they must obey, and that burden they must bear, until the coming of the Lord.

NOTE.--A confirmation of the suggestion made above may be found in an inscription just published in Bulletin de Corresp. Hellen., 1904, p. 24. A leading citizen is there recorded to have given a dinner, as part of a religious ceremony, to all the male and female community; and the men dined in one temple and the women in another.

Chapter 25: Sardis: The City of Death

Sardis was one of the great cities of primitive history: in the Greek view it was long the greatest of all cities. At the beginning of record it stands forth prominently as the capital of a powerful empire. Its situation marks it out as a ruling city, according to the methods of early warfare and early kings; it was however more like a robber's stronghold than an abode of civilised men; and in a peaceful and civilised age its position was found inconvenient. In the Roman period it was almost like a city of the past, a relic of the period of barbaric warfare, which lived rather on its ancient prestige than on its suitability to present conditions.

The great plain of the Hermus is bounded on the south by the broad ridge of Mount Tmolus, which reaches from the main mass of the Central Anatolian plateau like an arm extended westwards towards the sea. In front of the mountains stretch a series of alluvial hills, making the transition from the level plain to the loftier ridge behind. On one of those hills stood Sardis. The hills in this neighbourhood are of such a character that under the influences of the atmosphere each assumes the form of a small elongated plateau having very steep sides, terminating towards the north in a sharp point, and on the south joined by a neck to the main mass of Tmolus. One of those small elevated plateaux formed the site of the original Sardis, an almost impregnable fortress already as it came from the hand of nature without any artificial fortification. Only a small city could be perched on the little plateau; but in the primitive time, when Sardis came into existence, cities were small.

It was actually inaccessible except at one point, viz., the neck of land on the south, which still offers the only approach. On all other sides the rock walls were smooth, nearly perpendicular, and absolutely unscalable even without a defender (except in rare conditions described in the sequel). The local myth expressed the facts in a religious form by saying that the ancient Lydian King, Meles, carried a lion, the symbol of Sardis and type of the oldest Lydian coins, round the whole city except at one point. The story is told by Herodotus, i., 84; but he (or a glossator) has given an incorrect explanation, to the effect that Meles thought it unnecessary to carry the lion round the southern side of the city, because there it was precipitous. The exact opposite was the case: the only approach to the old city must have been from the beginning and must always be on the south. The story is a popular explanation of the fact that the south alone was accessible and not precipitous.

This southern approach is far from being easy. It is a tedious and difficult climb at the present day, when the hill-sides are overgrown with thorns, and only a sheep-track exists in place of a path. Even when the summit was inhabited and a carefully made road led up to the southern gates, the approach must have been long and steep by a winding road, which could be defended with perfect ease. The plateau is fully 1,500 feet above the plain, from which its sides rise perpendicularly.

This small city on its lofty plateau was an ideal stronghold for a prince of primitive times. It was large enough for his needs; it could be easily fortified and defended at the only point where fortification or defence was needed. It was like a watch-tower overlooking the whole of the great plain. That primitive capital of the Hermus Valley seems to have been called, not Sardis (which was a plural noun), but Hyde; and it is mentioned by Homer under that name.

In this we part company from the guide whom usually we follow with such implicit confidence, Strabo. He considers that Sardis was founded later than the time of Homer, because it is not named by him. We must, however, consider Sardis as coeval with the beginnings of the Lydian kingdom, about 1,200 B.C. It was the princely capital from the time that there began to be princes in Lydia. nature has made it the overseer of the Hermus Valley; and its foundation marked out its master for the headship first of that valley, and thereafter of the rest of Lydia, whose fate was dependent on the Hermus Valley.

As civilisation and government grew more complex, and commerce and society were organised on a greater scale, the lofty plateau proved too small for the capital of an empire; and a lower city was built on the west and north sides of the original city, and probably also on the east side. The old city was now used as an acropolis, and is so called by Herodotus. The new city was very distinctly separated from the old by the great difference of level and by the long, steep, and difficult approach at the southern end of the old city. Hence the double city was called by the plural noun, Sardeis, like Athenai and various others.

The lower city lay chiefly on the west side, in a glen between the acropolis-hill and the little river Pactolus, which flows northwards out of Mount Tmolus to join the Hermus. The wealth of the Lydian kings, ruling in Sardis, which arose from trade, a fertile territory carefully cultivated, and the commerce of the East, was explained in popular Greek legend as due to the golden sands of the Pactolus. Whether this was a pure fable, or only an exaggeration, must be left uncertain. There was no gold in the Pactolus during the Roman period, nor is there any now; but it is said to be possible that the river, having in earlier time traversed an auriferous area, might have cut for itself a path below the level of the gold-bearing rock, and thus ceased to bring down golden sand. No auriferous rock, however, is now known to exist in the mountains of Tmolus; though, of course, no proper search has been made in recent centuries.

As the capital of the great kingdom of Lydia, Sardis had a history marked by frequent wars. In it the whole policy of a warlike kingdom was focused. To fight against Lydia was to fight against Sardis. The master of Sardis was the master of Lydia. Thus in early centuries Sardis stood forth pre-eminent in the view of the Greek cities as the Oriental enemy on whose action their fate depended. They were most of them involved in war with Sardis, and fell one by one beneath its power. It was the great, the wealthy, the impregnable city, against which none could strive and prevail. In the immemorial contest between Asia and Europe, it represented Asia, and the Greek colonies of the coastlands stood for Europe. Sardis was the one great enemy of the Ionian cities: it learned from them, taught them, and conquered them all in succession. Among an impressionable people like the Greeks, such a reputation lived long; and Sardis was to their mind fully justified in inscribing on its coins the proud title, "Sardis the First Metropolis of Asia, and of Lydia, and of Hellenism." The Hellenism which found its metropolis in Sardis was not the ancient Greek spirit, but the new form which the Greek spirit had taken in its attempt to conquer Asia, profoundly modifying Asia, and itself profoundly modified in the process. Hellenism in this sense was not a racial fact, but a general type of aspiration and aims, implying a certain freedom in development of the individual consciousness and in social and political organisation. The term summed up the character of "the Hellenes in Asia," i.e., the Hellenised population of Asia.

The destruction of the powerful kingdom, and the capture of the impregnable city, by a hitherto hardly known and utterly despised enemy, was announced to the Greek cities soon after the middle of the sixth century B.C. The news came almost without preparation, and was all the more impressive on that account. To the student of the past it seems still to echo through history, as one of the most startling and astonishing reverses of all time. To the Greeks it was unique in character and effect. It was known that the Lydian king had consulted the Delphic Apollo before he entered on the war, and that he had begun operations with full confidence of victory, relying on the promise of the god. The Greek mind loved to dwell on this topic, and elaborated it with creative fancy, so that the truth is almost hidden under the embellishing details in the pages of Herodotus. But all the details have only the effect (as was their intention) of making more clear and impressive the moral lesson. To avoid over-confidence in self, to guard against pride and arrogance, not to despise one's enemy, to bear always in mind the slipperiness and deceitfulness of fortune--such was the greatest part of true wisdom, as the Greeks understood it; and nowhere could the lesson be found written in plainer and larger letters than in the fall of Sardis.

According to the story as thus worked up by Greek imagination, Croesus the king had been vainly warned by the wise Greek, Solon the law-giver, when he visited Sardis, to beware of self-satisfaction and to regard no man as really happy, until the end of life had set him free from the danger of a sudden reverse. In preparing for his last war, Croesus employed all possible precaution; he was thoroughly on his guard against any possible error; and he took the gods themselves as his counsellors and helpers. He had tried and tested all the principal prophetic centres of the Greek world; and the Delphic Oracle alone had passed the test, and won his confidence.

He then asked about the war against Cyrus, which he had in mind; and he heard with delight that, if he crossed the Halys, he would destroy a mighty Empire. He crossed the Halys, and received a crushing defeat. But it was only a first army that had met this disaster. He returned to prepare a greater army for the ensuing year. Cyrus followed him up with disconcerting rapidity; and besieged him in Sardis, before any new levies were ready. The great king, safe in his impregnable fortress, regarded this as an incident annoying in itself, but only the beginning of destruction for the rash enemy. The armies of Lydia were being massed to crush the insolent invader, who should be ground between the perpendicular rocks of the acropolis and the gathering Lydian hosts. Such was the calculation of Croesus, when he retired one evening to rest: he was wakened to find that the enemy was master of the acropolis and that all was lost.

The rock of the acropolis is a coarse and friable conglomerate, which melts away gradually under the influences of the atmosphere. It always preserves an almost perpendicular face, but at times an oblique crack develops in the rock-wall, and permits a bold climber to work his way up. Such a weak point betrayed Sardis.

According to the popular tale this weak point existed from the beginning of history n Sardis, because, when the divine consecration and encompassing of the new fortress had been made at its foundation, this point had been omitted; thus the tale would imply that the weak point was known to the defenders and through mere obstinate folly left unguarded by them. But such a legend is usually a growth after the fact. The crumbling character of the rock on which the upper city of Sardis stood shows what the real facts must have been. In the course of time a weakness had developed at one point. Through want of proper care in surveying and repairing the fortifications, this weakness had remained unobserved and unknown to the defenders; but the assailants, scrutinising every inch of the walls of the great fortress in search of an opportunity, noticed it and availed themselves of it to climb up, one at a time. On such a lofty hill, rising fully 1,500 feet above the plain, whose sides are, and must from their nature always have been, steep and straight and practically perpendicular, a child could guard against an army; even a small stone dropped on the head of the most skilful mountain-climber, would inevitably hurl him down. An attack made by this path could succeed only if the assailants climbed up entirely unobserved; and they could not escape observation unless they made the attempt by night. Hence, even though this be unrecorded, a night attack must have been the way by which Cyrus entered Sardis. He came upon the great city "like a thief in the night."

It is right, however, to add that the account that we have given of the way in which Sardis was captured differs from the current opinion in one point. The usual view is that Cyrus entered Sardis by the isthmus or neck on the south. That was the natural and necessary path in ordinary use; the only road and gateway were there; and inevitably the defence of the city was based on a careful guard and strong fortification at the solitary approach. The enemy was expected to attack there; but the point of the tale is that the ascent was made on a side where no guard was ever stationed, because that side was believed to be inaccessible. The misapprehension is as old as the time of Herodotus (or rather of some old Greek glossator, who has interposed a false explanation in the otherwise clear narrative). The character of the rock shows that this opinion--current already among the Greeks--is founded on a confusion between the one regular approach, where alone attack was expected and guarded against, and the accidental, unobserved, unguarded weak point, which had developed through the disintegration of the rock.

There can be no doubt that the isthmus, as being the solitary regular approach, must always have been the most strongly fortified part. At present the plateau is said not to be accessible at any other point except where the isthmus touches it; but there are several chinks and clefts leading up the north and west faces, and it is probable that by one of them a bold and practised climber could make his way up. These clefts vary in character from century to century as the surface disintegrates; and all of them would always be regarded by the ordinary peaceful and unathletic oriental citizen as inaccessible. But from time to time sometimes one, sometimes another, would offer a chance to a daring mountaineer. By such an approach it must have been that Cyrus captured the city.

History repeated itself. The same thing happened about 320 years later, when Antiochus the Great captured Sardis through the exploit of Lagoras (who had learned surefootedness on the precipitous mountains of his native Crete). Once more the garrison in careless confidence were content to guard the one known approach, and left the rest of the circuit unguarded, under the belief that it could not be scaled.

The Sardian religion was the fullest expression of the character and spirit of the city; but it has not yet been properly understood. The coins show several remarkable scenes of a religious kind, evidently of purely local origin and different from any subjects otherwise known in hieratic mythology; but they remain unexplained and unintelligible. The explanation of them, if it could be discovered, would probably illuminate the peculiar character of the local religion; but in the meantime, although various other deities besides Cybele and Kora-Persephone appear on the coins, and although abundant archaeological details might be described, no unifying idea can be detected, which might show how the Sardians had modified, and put their own individual character into, the general Anatolian religious forms.

The general Anatolian temper of religion is summarised in the following words (taken from the Cities and Bishoprics of Phrygia, i., p. 87): "Its essence lies in the adoration of the life of Nature--that life subject apparently to death, yet never dying but reproducing itself in new forms, different and yet the same. This perpetual self-identity under varying forms, this annihilation of death through the power of self-reproduction, was the object of an enthusiastic worship, characterised by remarkable self-abandonment and immersion in the divine, by a mixture of obscene symbolism and sublime truths, by negation of the moral distinctions and family ties that exist in a more developed society, but do not exist in the free life of Nature. The mystery of self-reproduction, of eternal unity amid temporary diversity, is the key to explain all the repulsive legends and ceremonies that cluster round that worship, and all the manifold manifestations or diverse embodiments of the ultimate single divine life that are carved on the rocks of Asia Minor."

The patron deity of the city was Cybele, two columns of whose temple still protrude from the ground near the banks of the Pactolus. She was a goddess of the regular Anatolian type; and her general character is well known.

But the specialised character of the Sardian goddess Cybele, the qualities and attributes which she gathered from the local conditions and from the ideas and manners of the population, are unknown, and can hardly even be guessed at for lack of evidence. To the Greek mind the Sardian Cybele seemed more like the Maiden Proserpine than the Mother Demeter; and the coins of the city often show scenes from the myth of Proserpine. For example, the reverse of the coin shows the familiar scene of Pluto carrying off Proserpine on his four-horse car.

The strange and uncouth idol, under whose form the goddess was worshipped, often appears on coins; and in alliance-coins Sardis is often symbolised by this grotesque figure, whose half-human appearance is quite of the Anatolian type. Thus an "alliance" or religious agreement between Ephesus, represented by Artemis in her usual idol with her stags at her side, and Sardis, symbolised by the curious veiled image of her own goddess (whom numismatists usually call in Hellenising style Kora or Persephone).

The Sardian goddess was the mother of her people. She dwelt with nature, in the mountains of Tmolus and in the low ground by the sacred lake of Koloe, on the north side of the Hermus. Here by the lake was the principal necropolis of Sardis, at a distance of six or eight miles from the city, across a broad river--a remarkable fact, which points to some ancient historical relation between Sardis and Koloe (implying perhaps that the people of Koloe had been moved to found the original city of Sardis). Here the people of the goddess returned at death to lie close to the wild sedge-encircled home of the mother who bore them.

The lion, as type of the oldest, Lydian coins, was certainly adopted, because it was the favourite animal and the symbol of the Sardian goddess. The Anatolian goddess, when envisaged in the form of Cybele, was regularly associated with a pair of lions or a single lion.

Healing power was everywhere attributed to the local embodiment of the divine idea, but in Sardis it was with exceptional emphasis magnified into the power of restoring life to the dead. It was, doubtless, associated specially with certain hot springs, situated about two miles from Sardis in the front hills of Tmolus, which are still much used and famous for their curative effect. As the hot springs are the plain manifestation of the divine subterranean power, the god of the underworld plays a considerable part in the religious legend of the district. He appeared to claim and carry off as his bride the patron-goddess of the city, in the form of Kora-Persephone, as she was gathering the golden flower, the flower of Zeus, in the meadows near the springs; the games celebrated in her honour were called Chrysanthia; and it may be confidently inferred that crowns of the flower called by that name were worn by her worshipers. The name of "Zeus's flower" also is mentioned on the coins.

Zeus Lydios is often named on Sardian coins, embodying the claim of the city to stand for the whole country of Lydia as its capital. He is represented exactly like the god of Laodicea (chapter 29), a standing figure, wearing a tunic and an over-garment, resting his left hand on the sceptre, and holding forth the eagle on his right hand.

Sardis suffered greatly from an earthquake in A.D. 17, and was treated with special liberality by the Emperor Tiberius: he remitted all its taxation for five years, and gave it a donation of ten million sesterces (about 400,000 pounds). Taken from a coin struck by the grateful city, the veiled genius of Sardis is shown kneeling on one knee in supplication before the Emperor, who is dressed in the toga, the garb of peace, and graciously stretches forth his hand towards her. The coin bears the name of Caesareian Sardis: for the city took the epithet in honour of the Imperial benefactor and retained it on coins for quite a year after his death, and in inscriptions for as long as ten or fifteen years after his death.

The reverse of the same coin shows the Imperial mother, the deified Empress Livia, sitting like a goddess after the fashion of Demeter, holding in her left hand three corn-ears, the gift of the goddess to mankind, and resting her right hand high on the sceptre. This type is a good example of the tendency to fuse the Imperial religion with the local worship, and to regard the Imperial gods as manifestations and incarnations on earth of the divine figure worshipped in the district. Livia here appears in the character of Demeter, a Hellenised form of the Anatolian goddess.

The assumption of the epitaph Caesareia was doubtless connected with the erection of a temple in honour of Tiberius and Livia, as the divine pair in the common form of the mother goddess and her god-son. But there is no reason to think that this was a Provincial temple (which would carry with it for the city the title of Temple-Warden). It was only a Sardian temple, and seems to have been suffered to fall into decay soon after the death of the Imperial god.

It is plain that the greatness of Sardis under the Roman rule was rotted in past history, not in present conditions. The acropolis ceased during that period to be the true city; it was inconvenient and useless; and it was doubtless regarded as a historical and archaeological monument, rather than a really important part of the living city. Apart from the acropolis there is nothing in the situation of Sardis to make it a great centre of society, and it has long ceased to be inhabited. The chief town of the district is now Salikli, about five miles to the east, in a similar position at the foot of Tmolus, but more conveniently situated for travellers and trade.

Thus, when the Seven Letters were written, Sardis was a city of the past, which had no future before it. Its greatness was connected with a barbarous and half-organised state of society, and could not survive permanently in a more civilised age. Sardis must inevitably decay. Only when civilisation was swept out of the Hermus Valley in fire and bloodshed by the destroying Turks, and the age of barbarism was reintroduced, did Sardis again become an advantageous site. The acropolis was restored as a fortress of the kind suited for that long period of uncertainty and war which ended in the complete triumph of Mohammedanism and the practical extermination of the Christian population (save at Philadelphia and Magnesia) throughout the Hermus Valley.

Sardis occupied a high position in the Byzantine hierarchy. It was the capital of the Province Lydia, instituted about A.D. 295, and the Bishop of Sardis was Metropolitan and Archbishop of Lydia, and sixth in order of dignity of all the bishops, whether Asiatic or European, that were subject to the Patriarch of Constantinople.

Chapter 26: The Letter to the Church in Sardis

These things saith he that hath the seven Spirits of God, and the seven stars:

I know thy works, that thou hast a name that thou livest, and thou art dead. Be thou watchful, and stablish the things that remain, which were ready to die: for I have found no works of thine fulfilled before my God. Remember therefore how thou hast received and didst hear; and keep it, and repent. If therefore thou shalt not watch, I will come as a thief, and thou shalt not know what hour I will come upon thee. But thou hast a few names in Sardis which did not defile their garments: and they shall walk with me in white; for they are worthy.

He that overcometh shall thus be arrayed in white garments; and I will in no wise blot his name out of the book of life, and I will confess his name before my Father, and before his angels.

He that hath an ear, let him hear what the Spirit saith to the churches.

The analogy between the Ephesian and Sardian letters is close, and the two have to be studied together. History had moved on similar lines with the two Churches. Both had begun enthusiastically and cooled down. Degeneration was the fact in both; but in Ephesus the degeneration had not yet become so serious as in Sardis. Hence in the Ephesian letters the keynote is merely change, instability and uncertainty; in the Sardian letter the keynote is degradation, false pretension and death.

In those two letters the exordium takes a very similar form. To the Ephesian Church "these things saith he that holdeth the seven stars in his right hand, he that walketh between the seven golden lamps." To the Sardian Church the letter proceeds from him "that hath the seven spirits of God and the seven stars." The sender of both letters stands forth as the centre, the pivot and the director of the Universal Church, and in particular of the entire group of the Asian Churches. Effective power exercised over the whole Church is indicated emphatically in both cases, and especially in the Sardian address. "The Seven Spirits of God" must certainly be taken as a symbolic or allegorical way of expressing the full range of exercise of the Divine power in the Seven Churches, i.e., in the Universal Church as represented here by the Asian Churches. If one may try in inadequate and rough terms to express the meaning, the "Spirit of God" is to be understood as the power of God exerting itself practically in the Church; and, since the Church is always regarded in the Revelation as consisting of Seven parts or local Churches, the power of God is described in its relation to those Seven parts as "the Seven Spirits of God."

This indirect way of expression is liable to become misleading, if it be not carefully interpreted and sympathetically understood. It is forced on the writer by the plan of his work, which does not aim at philosophic exposition, but attempts to shadow forth through sensuous imagery "the deep things of God," in the style of the Jewish literary form which he chose to imitate.

Under the phraseology, "the Seven Spirits of God," the writer of the Revelation conceals a statement of the great problem: "how does the Divine power make itself effective in regard to the world and mankind, when it is entirely different in nature and character from the ordinary world of human experience? How can a thing act on another which is wholly different in nature, and lies on a different plane of existence?" The Divine power has to go forth, as it were, out of itself in order to reach mankind. The writer had evidently been occupying himself with this problem; and, as we see, the book of the Revelation is a vague and dim expression of the whole range of this and the associated problems regarding the relation of God to man. But the book is not to be taken as a solution of the problems. It is the work of a man who has not reached an answer, i.e., who has not yet succeeded in expressing the question in philosophic form, but who is struggling to body forth the problems before himself and his readers in such imagery as may make them more conceivable.

The most serious error in regard to the book of the Revelation consists in regarding it as a statement of the solution. No solution is reached in the book; but the writer's aim is to convey to his readers his own perfect confidence that the Divine nature is effective on human nature and on the world of sense, all-powerful, absolutely victorious in this apparent contest with evil or anti-Christ; that in fact there is not really any contest, for the victory is gained in the inception of the conflict, and the seeming struggle is only the means whereby the Divine power offers to man the opportunity of learning to understand its nature.

The Spirit of God, and still more "the Seven Spirits of God," are therefore not to be understood as a description of the method by which the Divine activity exerts itself in its relation to the Church; for, if looked at so, they are easily perverted and elaborated into a theory of intermediate powers intervening between God and the world, and thus there must arise the whole system of angels (which in human nature, as ideas and custom then tended, inevitably degenerated into a worship of angels, according to Colossians 2:18; just as a few centuries later the respect for the saints and martyrs of the Church degenerated into a worship of them as powers intervening between man and the remote ultimate Divine nature). The "Seven Spirits" form simply an expression suited to reach the comprehension of men at that time, and make them image to themselves the activity of God in relation to the Seven Churches, and to the whole Universal Church. That this is a successful attempt to present the problem to human apprehension cannot be maintained. The book is the first attempt of a writer struggling to express great ideas; but the ideas have not yet been thought out clearly in his mind and he has been led away to imitate a rather crude model fashionable in Jewish circles at the time. He has reached an infinitely higher level, alike in a literary and a religious view, than any other work of that class known to us; but an ineradicable fault clings to the whole class.

The Church of Sardis, then, is addressed by Him who controls and directs the Divine action in the Churches as they exist in the world, and who holds in His hand the Seven Churches, with their history and their destiny. This expression of His power is varied from that which occurs in the address of the Ephesian letter, of course in a way suited to the Sardian Church, though it is not easy for us to comprehend wherein lies the precise suitability. As everywhere throughout this study, we can hardly hope to do more than reach a statement of the difficulties and the problems, though often a clear statement of the question involves the suggestion of a reply (and in so far as it does this it involves personal opinion and hypothesis, and is liable to fall into subjectivity and error).

We observed the peculiar suitability of the Ephesian address to the situation of Ephesus as the centre and practical leader of the whole group of Asian Churches. Hence the final detail in that address-- "He that walketh in the midst of the seven golden lamps"; for (as is shown in chapter 6) the lamps symbolise the Churches on earth, as the seven Stars symbolise the seven Churches, or their spiritual counterparts, in heaven. Instead of this the Sardian address introduces "the Seven Spirits of God." A more explicit and definite expression of the activity of the Divine nature in the Churches on earth evidently recommended itself as suitable in addressing the Sardian Church.

One cannot evade the question, what is the reason why this expression commended itself for the Sardian letter? wherein lies its suitability? To answer the question, it is obviously necessary to look at the prominent point of difference between Sardis and Ephesus (which we have already stated). Ephesus had changed and cooled, but the degeneration had not yet become serious; restoration of its old character and enthusiasm was still possible. As a Church Ephesus might possibly be in the future as great as it had been in the past. But the Church of Sardis was already dead, though it seemed to be living. Its history was past and done with. A revivification of its former self was impossible. There remained only a few in it for whom there was some hope. They might survive, as they had hitherto shown themselves worthy. And they shall survive, for the power which has hitherto sustained them will be with them and keep them to the end. In this scanty remnant saved from the wreck of the formerly great Church of Sardis, the Divine power will show itself all the more conspicuous. Just as in the comparatively humble city of Thyatira the faithful few shall be granted a strength and authority beyond that of the Empire and its armies, so in this small remnant at Sardis the Divine power will be most effective, because they stand most in need of it.

It is not to be imagined that this consideration exhausts the case. There remains much more that is at present beyond our ken. The more we can learn about Sardis, the better we shall understand the letter.

In none of the Seven Letters is the method of the writer, and the reason that guided him in selecting the topics, more clearly displayed than in the letter to the Church in Sardis. The advice which he gives to the Sardians is, in a way, universally suitable to human nature: "Be watchful; be more careful; carry out more completely and thoroughly what you have still to do, for hitherto you have always erred in leaving work half done and incomplete. Try to make that eager attention with which you at the beginning listened to the Gospel, and the enthusiasm with which at first you accepted it, a permanent feature in your conduct. If you are not watchful, you will not be ready at the moment of need; my arrival will find you unprepared, because in an hour that ye think not the Son of Man cometh'; any one can make ready for a fixed hour, but you must be always ready for an unexpected hour."

Advice like that is, in a sense, universal. All persons, every individual man and every body of men, constantly require the advice to be watchful, and to carry through to completion what they once enter upon, for all men tend more or less to slacken in their exertions and to leave half-finished ends of work. In all men there is observable a discrepancy between promise and performance; the first show is almost always superior to the final result.

But why are these precise topics selected for the Sardian letter, and not for any of the others? Why does the reference to the thief in the night suggest itself in this letter and not in any other? It is plain that

Ephesus was suffering from the same tendency to growing slackness as Sardis, and that its first enthusiasm had cooled down almost as lamentably as was the case in the Sardian Church. Yet the advice to Ephesus, though like in many respects, is expressed in very different words.

But in almost every letter similar questions suggest themselves. There were faithful Christians in every one of the Churches; but the word "faithful" is used only of Smyrna. Every Church was brought into the same conflict with the Roman State; but only in the Pergamenian letter is the opposition between the Church and the Empire expressly mentioned, and only in the Thyatiran letter is the superiority in strength and might of the Church over the Empire emphasised.

In the Sardian letter the reason is unusually clear; and to this point our attention must now be especially directed.

No city in the whole Province of Asia had a more splendid history in past ages than Sardis. No city of Asia at that time showed such a melancholy contrast between past splendour and present decay as Sardis. Its history was the exact opposite of the record of Smyrna. Smyrna was dead and yet lived. Sardis lived and yet was dead.

Sardis was the great city of ancient times and of half-historical legend. At the beginning of the Greek memory of history in Lydia, Sardis stood out conspicuous and alone as the capital of the great Oriental Empire with which the Greek cities and colonies were brought in contact. Their relations with it formed the one great question of foreign politics for those early Greek settlers. Everything else was secondary, or was under their own control, but in regard to Sardis they had always to be thinking of foreign wishes, foreign rights, the caprice of a foreign monarch and the convenience of foreign traders, who were too powerful to be disregarded or treated with disrespect.

That ancient and deep impression the Asiatic Greeks, with their tenacious historical memory, never entirely lost. Sardis was always to them the capital where Croesus, richest of kings, had ruled--the city which Solon, wisest of men, had visited, and where he had rightly augured ruin because he had rightly mistrusted material wealth and luxury as necessarily hollow and treacherous--the fortress of many warlike kings, like Gyges, whose power was so great that legend credited him with the possession of the gold ring of supernatural power, or Alyattes, whose vast tomb rose like a mountain above the Hermus Valley beside the sacred lake of the Mother Goddess.

But to those Greeks of the coast colonies, Ephesus and Smyrna and the rest, Sardis was also the city of failure, the city whose history was marked by the ruin of great kings and the downfall of great military strength apparently in mid-career, when it seemed to be at its highest development. It was the city whose history conspicuously and pre-eminently blazoned forth the uncertainty of human fortunes, the weakness of human strength, and the shortness of the step that separates over-confident might from sudden and irreparable disaster. It was the city whose name was almost synonymous with pretensions unjustified, promise unfulfilled, appearance without reality, confidence that heralded ruin. Reputed an impregnable fortress, it had repeatedly fallen short of its reputation, and ruined those who trusted in it. Croesus had fancied he could sit safe in the great fortress, but his enemy advanced straight upon it and carried it by assault before the strength of the Lydian land was collected.

Carelessness and failure to keep proper watch, arising from over-confidence in the apparent strength of the fortress, had been the cause of this disaster, which ruined the dynasty and brought to an end the Lydian Empire and the dominance of Sardis. The walls and gates were all as strong as art and nature combined could make them. The hill on which the upper city stood was steep and lofty. The one approach to the upper city was too carefully fortified to offer any chance to an assailant. But there was one weak point: in one place it was possible for an active enemy to make his way up the perpendicular sides of the lofty hill, if the defenders stood idle and permitted him to climb unhindered.

The sudden ruin of that great Empire and the wealthiest king of all the world was an event of that character which most impressed the Greek mind, emphasising a moral lesson by a great national disaster. A little carelessness was shown; a watchman was wanting at the necessary point, or a sentinel slept at his post for an hour; and the greatest power on the earth was hurled to destruction. The great king trusted to Sardis, and Sardis failed him at the critical moment. Promise was unfulfilled; the appearance of strength proved the mask of weakness; the fortification was incomplete; work which had been begun with great energy was not pushed through to its conclusion with the same determination.

More than three centuries later another case of exactly the same kind occurred. Achaeus and Antiochus the Great were fighting for the command of Lydia and the whole Seleucid Empire. Antiochus besieged his rival in Sardis, and the city again was captured by a surprise of the same nature: a Cretan mercenary led the way, climbing up the hill and stealing unobserved within the fortifications. The lesson of old days had not been learned; experience had been forgotten; men were too slack and careless; and when the moment of need came, Sardis was unprepared.

A State cannot survive which is guarded with such carelessness; a people at once so slack and so confident cannot continue an imperial power. Sardis, as a great and ruling city, was dead. It had sunk to be a second-rate city in a Province. Yet it still retained the name and the historical memory of a capital city. It had great pretensions, which it had vainly tried to establish in A.D. 26 before the tribunal of the

Roman Senate in the contention among the Asian cities recorded by Tacitus, Annals, iv., 55. When in that year the Asian States in the provincial Council (called the Commune of Asia) resolved to erect a temple to Tiberius and Livia his mother and the Senate, as a token of gratitude for the punishment of an oppressive and grasping administrator, eleven cities of the Province contended for the honour of being the seat of the Temple. Nine were quickly set aside, some as too unimportant, Pergamum as already the seat of a Temple to Augustus, Ephesus and Miletus as taken up with the ritual of Artemis and of Apollo; but there was much hesitation between the claims of Smyrna and of Sardis. Envoys of Sardis pleaded the cause of their city before the Senate. They rested their claim on the mythical or historical glory of the city as the capital of the Lydians, who were a sister-race to the Etruscans, and had sent colonists to the Peloponnesus, and as honoured by letters from Roman generals and by a special treaty which Rome had concluded with Sardis in 171-168 B.C.: in conclusion, they boasted of the rivers, the climate, and the rich territory around the city. The case, however, was decided in favour of Smyrna.

No one can doubt that this Sardian letter took its form in part through the memory of that ancient history. It was impossible for the Sardians to miss the allusion, and therefore the writer must have intended it and calculated on it. Phrase after phrase is chosen for the evident purpose of recalling that ancient memory, which was undoubtedly still strong and living among the Sardians, for the Hellenic cities had a retentive historical recollection, and we know that Sardis, in the great pleading in A.D. 26, rested its case on a careful selection of facts from its past history, though omitting the facts on which we have here laid stress, because they were not favourable to its argument. "I know thy works, that thou hast a name that thou livest, and thou art dead. Be thou watchful, and stablish the things that remain, which were ready to die: for I have found no works of thine fulfilled before my God . . . If therefore thou shalt not watch, I will come as a thief, and thou shalt not know what hour I will come upon thee."

It seems therefore undeniable that the writer has selected topics which rise out of and stand in close relation to the past history of Sardis as a city. In view of this evident plan and guiding purpose, are we to understand that he preferred the older historical reference, and left aside the actual fortunes of the Church as secondary, when he was sketching out the order of his letter? Such a supposition is impossible. The writer is in those words drawing a picture of the history and degeneration of the Sardian Church; but he draws it in such a way as to set before his readers the continuity of Sardian history. The story of the Church is a repetition of past experience; the character of the people remains unchanged; their faults are still the same; and their fate must be the same.

If this view be correct--and it seems forced on us unavoidably by the facts of the case--then another inference must inevitably follow: the writer, so far from separating the Church of Sardis from the city of Sardis, emphasises strongly the closeness of the connection between them. The Church of Sardis is not merely in the city of Sardis, it is in a sense the city; and the Christians are the people of the city. There is not in his mind the slightest idea that Christians are to keep out of the world--as might perhaps be suggested from a too exclusive contemplation of some parts of the Revelation; the Church here is addressed, apparently with the set purpose of suggesting that the fortunes of ancient Sardis had been its own fortunes, that it had endured those sieges, committed those faults of carelessness and blind confidence, and sunk into the same decay and death as the city.

That this is intentional and deliberate cannot be questioned for a moment. What this writer said he meant. There is no accident or unintended significance in those carefully chosen and well-weighed words. In regard to this letter the same reflections arise as were already suggested in the case of the other letters, and especially the Smyrnaean and Pergamenian. In his conflict with the Nicolaitans the writer was never betrayed into mere blind opposition to them; he never rejected their views from mere hatred of those who held them; he took the wider view which embraced everything that was right and true in the principles of the Nicolaitans--and there was a good deal that was rightly thought and well said by them--together with a whole world of thought which they had no eyes to see. In the Seven Letters he repeatedly gives marked emphasis to the principle, which the Nicolaitans rightly maintained, that the Christians should be a force in the world, moulding it gradually to a Christian model. Here and everywhere throughout the Letters the writer is found to be reiterating one thought, "See how much better the true eternal Church does everything than any of the false pretenders and opponents can do them."

In regard to one detail after another he points out how far superior is the Christian form to that in which it is tendered by the Imperial State, by the cities, or by false teachers. If Laodicea clothes its citizens with the glossy black woollen garments of its famous industry, he offers white garments to clothe the true Laodiceans. If the State has its mighty military strength and its imperial authority, he points out to the true remnant among the Thyatirans that a more crushing and irresistible might shall be placed in their hands, and offers to the Pergamenian victors a wider authority over worlds seen and unseen. If the Nicolaitans emphasise the intimate relation between the life of the Church and the organisation of the State and the society amid which the Church exists, he states with equal emphasis, but with the proper additions, that the Church is so closely connected with the State and the City that it can be regarded as sharing in a way their life, fortunes and powers.

It is not fanciful to trace here, as in other cases, a connection between the spirit of the advice tendered and the permanent features of nature amid which the city stood and by which it was insensibly moulded. Sardis stood, or rather the upper and the only fortified city stood, on a lofty hill, a spur projecting north from Mount Tmolus and dominating the Hermus Valley. The hill has still, in its dilapidated and diminished extent, an imposing appearance; but it undoubtedly offered a far more splendid show two or three thousand years ago, when the top must have been a high plateau of moderate extent, the sides of which were almost perpendicular walls of rock, except where a narrow isthmus connected the hill with the mountains behind it on the south. Towards the plain on the north, towards the glens on east and west, it presented the most imposing show, a city with walls and towers, temples, houses and palaces, filling the elevated plateau so completely that on all sides it looked as if one could drop a stone 1,500 feet straight into the plain from the outer buildings.

The rock, however, on which Sardis was built was only nominally a rock. In reality, as you go nearer it, you see that it is only mud slightly compacted, and easily dissolved by rain. It is, however, so constituted that it wears away with a very steep, almost perpendicular face; but rain and frost continually diminish it, so that little now remains of the upper plateau on which the city stood; and in one place the top has been worn to an extremely narrow neck with steep descents of the usual kind on both sides, so that the visitor needs a fairly cool head and steady nerve to walk across it. The isthmus connecting the plateau with the mountains of Tmolus on the south has been worn away in a lesser degree.

The crumbling, poor character of the rock must always have been a feature that impressed the thinking mind, and led it to associate the character of the inhabitants with this feature of the situation. Instability, untrustworthiness, inefficiency, deterioration--such is the impression that the rock gives, and such was the character of Sardian history and of the Sardian Church.

But Sardis was not entirely degenerate and unworthy. Even in it there were a few persons who maintained their Christian character and "did not defile their garments." This strong expression shows wherein lay the guilt of Sardis. It was different essentially from the fault of Thyatira, the city which comes next to Sardis in the severity of its condemnation. Thyatira was in many ways distinguished by excellence of conduct, and the corporate life of its Church was vigorous and improving, so that its "last works were more than the first"; but a false theory of life and a false conception of what was right action were leading it astray. Sardis was not Christian enough to entertain a heresy or be led astray by a false system; it had lost all vigour and life, and had sunk back to the ordinary pagan level of conduct, which from the Christian point of view was essentially vicious and immoral in principle.

The Sardian Church fell under the condemnation pronounced by St. Paul (1 Cor 5:10) against those who, having become Christians and learned the principles of morality, relapsed into the vices which were commonly practised in pagan society. These were to be treated far more severely than the pagans, though the pagans lived after the same fashion; for the pagans lived so on principle, knowingly and intentionally, because they held it to be right, whereas the Christians had learned that it was wrong, and yet from weakness of will and character slipped back into the evil. With them the true Christians were not to keep company, but were to put them out of their society and their meetings. With pagans who lived after the same fashion, however, it was allowable to associate (though it lies in the nature of the case, and needs no formal statement, that the association between Christians and pagans could never be so intimate as that of Christians with one another).

A peculiarly kind and loving tone is perceptible in this part of the letter. There is a certain reaction after the abhorrence and disgust with which the weak degeneracy of Sardis has been described; and in this reaction the deserts of the faithful few are painted with a loving touch. They have kept themselves pure and true, and "they shall walk with me in white, for they are worthy." Their reward shall be to continue to the end white and pure, as they have kept themselves in Sardis.

This warm and affectionate tone is marked by the form of the final promise, which begins by simply repeating what has been already said in the letter. In most of the other letters the final promise comes as an addition; but here the love that speaks in the letter has already uttered the promise, and there is nothing left in the conclusion except to say it again, and to add explicitly what is already implied in it, life. "He that overcometh shall thus be arrayed in white garments; and I will in no wise blot his name out of the Book of Life, and I will confess his name before my Father and before his angels." The reward of all victors shall be the reward just promised to the few faithful in Sardis, purity and life--to have their name standing always in the Book, openly acknowledged and emblazoned before God.

In the Smyrnaean letter also the concluding promise is to a certain extent anticipated in the body of the letter, as here; and the tone of that letter is throughout warm and appreciative, beyond the rest of the Seven Letters. Where this letter rises to the tone of love and admiration, it approximates to the character of the Smyrnaean letter, and like it ends with the promise of life.

The "Book of Life" is here evidently understood as an official list (so to say) of the citizens of the heavenly city, the true Jerusalem, the Elect City, peopled by the true Christians of all cities and provinces and nations. As in all Greek and Roman cities of that time there was kept a list of citizens, according to their class or tribe or deme, in which new citizens were entered and from which degraded citizens were expunged, so the writer of this letter figuratively mentions the Book of Life. There is a remnant in Sardis whose names shall never be deleted from the Book, from which most Sardians have been expunged already.

That undoubtedly is the meaning which would be taken from the words here by Asian readers. Mr. Anderson Scott points out that in the Jewish Apocalyptic literature a wider sense is given to the term, and the "Book of Life" is regarded as a record of exploits, a history of the life and works of God's people. That this second sense was in the writer's mind elsewhere is certain; but it is certain that he speaks and thinks of two distinct kinds of books: one is a series of books of record: the other is the Book of Life. This is clear from the words of 20:12: I saw the dead great and small, standing before the Throne; and books were opened: and another book was opened, which is (the Book) of Life: and the dead were judged out of the things which were written in the books, according to their works. With this passage 13:8, 17:8, 20:15 should be compared, and from it they should be interpreted. The wider sense could not be gathered by the Asian readers from this reference, and was assuredly not intended by the writer of the letter.

This is one of many points of difference which strongly mark off the Apocalypse of John from the common Apocalyptic literature of that age and earlier times; and this immense difference ought never to be forgotten (though it is perhaps not always remembered clearly enough) by those scholars who, in studying the great influence exerted by the older literature of this class on our Apocalypse, have seen in it an enlarged Christian edition of an originally Jewish Apocalypse.

White was widely considered among the ancient nations as the colour of innocence and purity. On this account it was appropriate for those who were engaged in the worship of the gods, for purity was prescribed as a condition of engaging in divine service though usually the purity was understood in a merely ceremonial sense. All Roman citizens wore the pure white toga on holidays and at religious ceremonies, whether or not they wore it on ordinary days; in fact, the great majority of them did not ordinarily wear that heavy and cumbrous garment; and hence the city on festivals and holidays is called "candida urbs," the city in white. Especially on the day of a Triumph white was the universal colour--though the soldiers, of course, wore not the toga, the garb of peace, but their full-dress military attire with all their decorations--and there can hardly be any doubt that the idea of walking in a Triumph similar to that celebrated by a victorious Roman general is here present in the mind of the writer when he uses the words, "they shall walk with me in white." A dirty and dark-coloured toga, on the other hand, was the appropriate dress of sorrow and of guilt. Hence it was worn by mourners and by persons accused of crimes.

The Asian readers could know of a Roman Triumph only from literature and report, for in the strictest sense Triumphs could be celebrated only in Rome, and only by an Emperor in person; but, in proportion as the Triumph in the strict old Roman sense became rare, the splendour and pomp which had originally been appropriated to it alone were more widely employed; as, for example, in the procession escorting the presiding magistrate, the Praetor, to the games in the Roman Circus; and there is no doubt that the great provincial festivals and shows, which were celebrated in the chief Asian cities according to Imperial policy as a means of diffusing Roman ideas and ways, were inaugurated with a procession modelled after the stately Roman procession in which the Praetor was escorted in triumph to the circus, as Juvenal describes it:--

> What! had he seen, in his triumphant car,
> Amid the dusty Cirque, conspicuous far,
> The Praetor perched aloft, superbly drest
> In Jove's proud tunic with a trailing vest
> Of Tyrian tapestry, and o'er him spread
> A crown too bulky for a human head:
> Add now the Imperial Eagle, raised on high,
> With golden beak, the mark of majesty,
> Trumpets before, and on the left and right
> A cavalcade of nobles, all in white.

Thus though the Triumph itself could never have been seen by the readers of this letter, they knew it as the most typical celebration of complete and final victory, partly from report and literature, partly from frequently seeing ceremonies in the great Imperial festivals which were modelled after the Triumph. Hence, St. Paul in writing to the Colossians, 2:15, uses a similar metaphor: "he made a show of the principalities and the powers, openly triumphing over them in it," which (as Lightfoot and scholars generally recognise) means that the powers of the world were treated as a general treats his conquered foes, stripped of their honours, and paraded in the Triumph as a show to please the citizens and to glorify the conqueror.

The Triumph was in origin a religious ceremonial. The victorious general who celebrated it played for the moment the part of the Roman god Jupiter; he wore the god's dress and insignia, and resigned them again when he reached the Temple of Jupiter Optimus Maximus on the Capitoline Mount. But it need not be thought strange that St. John and St. Paul should use this pagan ceremonial to express metaphorically the decisive triumph of Christ over all opposing powers in the world, when we have seen that Ignatius describes the life of the true Christian as a long religious procession similar to those which were celebrated in the pagan ritual.

The warm and loving tone in the latter part of the Sardian letter need cause no wonder. There is always something peculiarly admirable and affecting in the contemplation of a pure and high life which maintains unspotted rectitude amid surrounding degradation and vileness. No characters stand out in clearer relief and more striking beauty than the small bands of high-minded Romans who preserved their nobility of spirit and life amid the degeneracy and servility of the early Empire. The same distinction marks this remnant of purity amid the decaying and already dead Church of Sardis. Even the thought of it rouses a warm interest in the modern reader's mind and we understand how it inspires this part of the letter with an unusual warmth of emotion, which contrasts with the coldness that we observed in the Ephesian letter.

Hence also we see how the analogy between these two letters, the Sardian and the Ephesian, ceases towards the end of the letter. The standard of conduct throughout the Ephesian Church had been uniform; the whole Church had acted correctly and admirably in the past; the whole Church was now cooling down and beginning to degenerate. No exception is made; no remnant is described that had not lost heart and enthusiasm. The changeable nature of Ephesus had affected all alike. And therefore the penalty is pronounced, that the Church shall be moved out of its place. It is a conditional penalty; but there is no suggestion that any portion of the Church has escaped or may escape it. The Church as a whole must revivify itself, or suffer the penalty; and Ephesus cannot alter its nature; changeableness is the law of its being. There is no real hope held out that the penalty may be avoided; and the promise at the conclusion is couched in the most general terms; this Church is cooling and degenerating, but to him that overcometh vigour and life shall be given.

On the other hand, the Sardian Church has not been uniform in its conduct, and it shall not all suffer the same fate. The Church as a whole is dead; but a few, who form bright and inspiring exceptions, shall live as citizens of the heavenly city. There is no hint that Sardis shall be spared, or the Church survive it. Its doom is sealed irrevocably; and yet a remnant shall live.

Sardis today is a wilderness of ruins and thorns, pastures and wild-flowers, where the only habitations are a few huts of Yuruk nomads beside the temple of Cybele in the low ground by the Pactolus, and at the distance of a mile two modern houses by the railway station. And yet in a sense a remnant has escaped and still survives, which does not indeed excite the same loving tenderness as makes itself felt in the latter part of this letter, yet assuredly merits our sympathy and interest. In the plain of the Hermus, which Sardis once dominated there are a few scattered villages whose inhabitants, though nominally Mohammedans, are clearly marked off by certain customs from the Turkish population around. Their women (according to the account given us at Sardis) usually bear Christian names, though the men's names are of the ordinary Mohammedan class; they have a kind of priests, who wear black head-dress, not the white turban of the Mohammedan hodjas and imams; the villages hold private assemblies when these "black-heads" (Kara-Bash) pay them visits; they practise strict monogamy, and divorce (which is so easy for true Mohammedans) is not permitted; they drink wine and violate other Mohammedan rules and prohibitions; and it is believed by some persons who have mixed with them that they would become Christians forthwith, if it did not mean death to do so. At the same time they are not at all like the strange people called Takhtaji or Woodmen: the latter are apparently a survival of ancient paganism, pre-Christian in origin.

Chapter 27: Philadelphia: The Missionary City

Philadelphia was the only Pergamenian foundation among the Seven Cities. It derived its name from Attalus II, 159-138 B.C., whose truth and loyalty to his brother Eumenes won him the epithet Philadelphus. The district where it was situated, the valley of the Cogamis, a tributary of the Hermus, came into the possession of the Pergamenian King Eumenes at the treaty of 189. From that time onward the district was in the heart of the Pergamenian realm; and therefore the new city could not have been founded as a military colony to guard a frontier, like Thyatira. Military strength was, of course, never entirely neglected in those foundations of the Greek kings; and especially a city founded, like Philadelphia, on an important road, was charged with the duty of guarding the road. But military strength and defence against invasion were required chiefly near the eastern frontier, far away on the other side of Phrygia, where an enemy should be prevented from entering the realm. Philadelphia was founded more for consolidating and regulating and educating the central regions subject to the Pergamenian kings. The intention of its founder was to make it a centre of the Graeco-Asiatic civilisation and a means of spreading the Greek language and manners in the eastern parts of Lydia and in Phrygia. It was a missionary city from the beginning, founded to promote a certain unity of spirit, customs, and loyalty within the realm, the apostle of Hellenism in an Oriental land. It was a successful teacher. Before A.D. 19 the Lydian tongue had ceased to be spoken in Lydia, and Greek was the only language of the country.

If sufficient information had been preserved about the religion of Thyatira and Philadelphia, it would have been possible to understand and describe the nature of those two Graeco-Asiatic cities and to specify the difference in character between a Seleucid and a Pergamenian foundation. From the religious establishment of each city, it would have been easy to distinguish what elements in each were native Anatolian, what were introduced from Europe, and what were brought in by colonists from Oriental lands, and how these were blended to produce a composite Graeco-Asiatic religion corresponding to the purposes which the new cities were intended to serve. This would be an object-lesson in practical government and religion, for those two cities are types of the fusion of Greek and Asiatic thought and custom, as attempted by the two chief Hellenising kingdoms in the Asiatic continent. But literary sources are silent, and the information furnished by coins and inscriptions is too scanty, sporadic, and superficial to be of much value.

The coins, as a rule, were much more Hellenised than the actual cults. Hellenised ideas about the gods, being more anthropomorphic, were more easily adapted to the small types which coins admitted; and, moreover, they belonged to the higher education, and obtained on that account more than their relative share of notice in such public and official monuments as coins. Philadelphia, also, was a centre for the diffusion of Greek language and letters in a peaceful land by peaceful means.

A subject like that represents Philadelphia in a purely Greek and an entirely non-religious fashion by two men exactly similar in attitude and dress, standing and looking upon the genius of Ephesus as she carries the idol of her own Artemis towards a temple built in the Roman style. The two men are two brothers, and their identity of outward form is symbolical of their unanimity and mutual affection, and makes them a suitable envisagement of the nature of a city, whose name means brotherly love. This coin commemorates an "alliance," or agreement as to common religious and festal arrangements, between the two cities. Apparently the temple is to be understood as Philadelphian; and the Ephesian goddess is being introduced into established Philadelphian ritual in the presence of the twin Hellenised founders of the city.

Thoroughly Graeco-Roman in character, too, is the coin type. Here the front of a temple is represented as open, to show a statue of the sun-god, with head surrounded by rays: he holds out the globe of the sun (or is it the solid earth?) in his right hand, and carries a sceptre in his left.

More indicative of Anatolian religious character is a type which occurs more than once, a coiled serpent with raised head and protruding tongue riding on the back of a horse. The serpent is, without doubt, the representative of Asklepios, but it is probable that the type is not in a further sense religious: it does not indicate any connection in myth or cult between Asklepios and the horse, but merely that a horse-race was a prominent feature in the games celebrated under the name Asklepieia.

Inscriptions give some information, which the Hellenised coins refuse, about the cults practised in the city, and prove that the Anatolian character was strongly marked. In those Graeco-Asiatic cities there is no sign that the Greek spirit in religion took the place of the Anatolian to any great extent. The Greek character in religion was confined to superficial show and festivals: in heart the religion was thoroughly Anatolian. Many of the formulae characteristic of the religion practised in the Katakekaumene (a district described below), confession of sin, punishment of sin by the god, thanks to the god, publication of the circumstances on a stele erected as a testimony, etc., occur in inscriptions found at Philadelphia.

The Pergamenian king selected an excellent situation for the new city. A long vale runs up southeast from the Hermus Valley into the flank of the central plateau: this is the vale down which comes the river Cogamis to join the Hermus. The vale offers the best path to make the ascent from the middle Hermus Valley, 500 feet or less above the sea, to the main plateau: the plateau is over 3,000 feet above sea-level, and its outer rim is even higher. It is not easy for a road to make so high a step, and even by the Cogamis vale there is a very steep and long climb to the top of the hills which form the rim of the plateau. But this is the path by which trade and communication from the harbour of Smyrna and from Lydia and the northwest regions are maintained with Phrygia and the East. It was at that time an important road, rivalling even the great trade-route from Ephesus to the East; and in later Byzantine and medieval times it was the greatest trade-route of the whole country. Its importance is now continued by the railway, which connects Smyrna with the interior.

Moreover, the Imperial Post-Road of the first century, coming from Rome by Troas, Pergamum and Sardis passed through Philadelphia and went on to the East; and thus Philadelphia was a stage on the main line of Imperial communication. This ceased to be the case when the later overland route by Constantinople (Byzantium, as it was then called) and Ancyra was organised in the second century.

The Cogamis Vale is enclosed between Mount Tmolus on the left (south and west) and the plateau proper on the right. A site for the city was found on a broad hill, which slopes gently up from the valley towards Tmolus. In a too close view from the plain the hill seems to merge in the main mass of Tmolus, but when one ascends through the streets of the modern town to the highest point, one finds that the hill is cut off from the mountains behind. Thus the site was susceptible of being made a very strong fortress in ancient warfare, provided it were carefully fortified on the lower slopes and courageously defended in the hour of trial; and its strength was proved in many long and terrible sieges by the Mohammedans in later centuries.

From these general considerations the modern scholar has to reconstruct in imagination the character of the city at the beginning of our era. It was then an important place with a considerable coinage: the great Swiss numismatist, M. Imhoof Blumer, assigns a large body of coins to the reign of Augustus.

Then Philadelphia emerges into world-wide fame through a conspicuous disaster. It was situated on the edge of the Katakekaumene, a district of Lydia where volcanoes, now extinct, have been active in recent geological time, where the traces of their eruptions in rivers of black lava and vast cinder-heaps are very impressive, and where earthquakes have been frequent in historical times. In A.D. 17 an unusually severe earthquake destroyed twelve cities of the great Lydian Valley, including Sardis and Philadelphia. Strabo, who wrote about two or three years after this disaster, says that Sardis suffered most at the moment, but gives a remarkable picture of the long-continued terror at Philadelphia. Apparently frequent shocks were experienced there for a long time afterwards. It has been the present writer's experience in that country that the first great shock of earthquake is not so trying to the mind as the subsequent shocks, even though less severe, when these recur at intervals during the subsequent weeks and months, and that people who have shown conspicuous courage at first may give way to utter panic during some of the later shocks. This state of panic set in at Philadelphia, and continued when Strabo wrote, A.D. 20. Many of the inhabitants remained outside the city living in huts and booths over the vale, and those who were foolhardy enough (as the sober-minded thought) to remain in the city, practised various devices to support and strengthen the walls and houses against the recurring shocks. The memory of this disaster lived long; the very name Katakekaumene was a perpetual warning; people lived amid ever threatening danger, in dread always of a new disaster; and the habit of going out to the open country had probably not disappeared when the Seven Letters were written.

Philadelphia shared in the bounty of the Emperor Tiberius on this occasion, and took part with the other cities in erecting in Rome a monument commemorating their gratitude. It also founded a cult of Germanicus, the adopted son and heir of Tiberius (according to the will of Augustus), who was in Asia at the time, and who was probably the channel through which the bounty was transmitted. In spite of this liberality the city suffered severely; its prosperity was seriously impaired; and no coins were struck by it throughout the reign of Tiberius.

It was probably in commemoration of the kindness shown by the Emperor on this occasion that Philadelphia assumed the name Neokaisareia: the New Caesar was either Tiberius (as compared with Augustus) or Germanicus (as compared with Tiberius). The name Neokaisareia is known both from coins and epigraphy during the ensuing period. At first the old name was disused and the new name employed alone; then the old name recurred alongside of or alternately with the new; and finally about A.D. 42-50 the new name disappeared from us. Philadelphia was the only one of the Seven Cities that had voluntarily substituted a new name for its original name: the other six were too proud of their ancient fame to sacrifice their name, though Sardis took the epithet Caesareia for a short time after A.D. 17.

This explanation of the name Neokaisareia differs from that given by M. Imhoof Blumer, who says that the name was assumed in honour of Caligula. His reason is that the name is found only on some coins of Caligula and of his successor; but it was impossible to put it on coins of Tiberius, for no coins were struck under that Emperor. The new name began to fall into disuse even during the short reign of Caligula, and disappeared entirely soon after the accession of Claudius.

Subsequently, during the reign of Vespasian, A.D. 70-79, Philadelphia assumed another Imperial title and called itself Flavia; and the double name remained in use occasionally on coins through the second and third centuries.

Thus Philadelphia was distinguished from the other cities by several characteristics: first, it was the missionary city: secondly, its people lived always in dread of a disaster, "the day of trial": thirdly, many of its people went out of the city to dwell: fourthly, it took a new name from the Imperial god.

Philadelphia, during the second century and the third, more than recovered its prosperity; and under Caracalla it was honoured with the title Neokoros or Temple-Warden in the State religion. This implies that a Provincial temple of the Imperial cult was built there between A.D. 211 and 217; and henceforward the Commune of Asia met there occasionally to hold some of its State festivals.

The history of the Philadelphian Church was distinguished by a prophetess Ammia, who flourished apparently between A.D. 100 and 160. She was universally recognised as ranking with Agabus and the four daughters of Philip, as one of the few in the later time who were truly gifted with the prophetic power. She remains a mere name to us, preserved in Eusebius' history, v., 17, 2.

In Byzantine and in medieval times its importance increased steadily. Civilisation of a kind became more firmly settled in the heart of Asia Minor in the centuries following the foundation of Constantinople as capital of the Roman Empire. The inner lands of Asia Minor became more important. Their trade now flowed to Constantinople rather than to Rome; and the coast-towns on the Aegean Sea became less important in consequence. The centre of gravity of the world, and the moving forces of civilisation, had shifted towards the East; and the connection of Asia Minor with the West was no longer of such pre-eminent importance as in the Roman time. The Empire of Rome had been strongly orientalised and transformed into a Roman-Asiatic Empire, on whose throne sat successively Phrygians, Isaurians, Cappadocians, and Armenians. In that period the situation of Philadelphia made it a great city, as a centre of wide influence, and the guardian of a doorway in the system of communication.

In the last stages of the struggle between the decaying Empire and the growing power of the Turks, Philadelphia played a noble part, and rose to a lofty pitch of heroism. Long after all the country round had passed finally under Turkish power, Philadelphia held up the banner of Christendom. It displayed all the noble qualities of endurance, truth and steadfastness, which are attributed to it in the letter of St. John, amid the ever threatening danger of Turkish attack; and its story rouses even Gibbon to admiration.

During the fourteenth century it stood practically alone against the entire Turkish power as a free, self-governing Christian city amid a Turkish land. Twice it was besieged by great Turkish armies, and its people reduced to the verge of starvation; but they had learned to defend themselves and to trust to no king or external government; and they resisted successfully to the end. Philadelphia was no longer a city of the Empire; and the Emperors regarded rather with jealousy than with sympathy its gallant struggle to maintain itself against the Turks. At last, about 1379-1390 it succumbed to a combined Turkish and Byzantine army; what the Turks alone had never been able to do they achieved by availing themselves of the divisions and jealousy among the Christians. Since that time Philadelphia has been transformed into the Mohammedan town of Ala-Sheher, the reddish city, a name derived from the speckled, red-brown hills around it.

In the last period of its freedom, it succeeded, as even the stubbornly conservative and unchanging ecclesiastical lists allowed, to the primacy among the bishoprics of Lydia, which had belonged for more than a thousand years to Sardis.

Chapter 28: The Letter to the Church in Philadelphia

These things saith he that is holy, he that is true, he that hath the key of David, he that openeth, and none shall shut, and that shutteth, and none openeth.

I know thy works: behold I have given before thee an opened door, which none can shut, because thou hast little strength, and didst keep my word, and didst not deny my name. Behold, I give of the synagogue of Satan, of them which say they are Jews, and they are not, but do lie; behold I will make them to come and worship before thy feet, and to know that I have loved thee. Because thou didst keep the word of my patience, I also will keep thee from the hour of trial, that hour which is to come upon the whole world, to try them that dwell upon the earth. I come quickly: hold fast that which thou hast, that no one take thy crown.

He that overcometh, I will make him a pillar in the temple of my God, and he shall go out thence no more: and I will write upon him the name of my God, and the name of the city of my God, the new Jerusalem, which cometh down out of heaven from my God, and mine own new name.

He that hath an ear, let him hear what the Spirit saith to the churches.

The address of the Philadelphian letter is conceived with evident reference to the topics mentioned in the body of the letter, and to the character and past history of the Church. The writer is "he that hath the key of David, that openeth and none shall shut"; and the history of Philadelphia and its Church has been determined in the past, and will in the future be determined, mainly by the fact that "I have set before thee a door opened, which none can shut."

The writer of the letter is "he that is true"; and the Philadelphian Church "kept my word and did not deny my name," but confessed the truth, whereas its enemies are they "which say they are Jews, and they are not, but do lie." The writer of the letter is, "he that is holy"; and the picture of Philadelphia that is given in the letter marks it beyond all others of the Seven as the holy city, which "I have loved," which kept my word and my injunction of endurance (a commendation twice repeated).

It may fairly be considered a complimentary form of address when the writer invests himself with the same character that he praises in the Church addressed. That is also the case in the Smyrnaean letter: there he "which was dead and lived" addresses the Church which, as he anticipates, will suffer to death and thereby gain the crown of life. But it is hardly the case in any other letter. In addressing Ephesus and Pergamum and Thyatira the writer speaks as holding that position and authority and power, which they are by their conduct losing. The writer to Sardis occupies the honourable position which Sardis has lost beyond hope of recovery. The writer to Laodicea is faithful and true, addressing a Church which is reproached for its irresolution and want of genuineness.

In this respect, then, the letters to Smyrna and Philadelphia form a class by themselves; and the analogy extends to other characteristics. These two Churches are praised with far more cordiality and less reserve than any of the others. They have both had to contend with serious difficulties. The Smyrnaean Church was poor and oppressed, the Philadelphian Church had but little power. Before both there is held forth a prospect of suffering and trial; but in both cases a triumphant issue is confidently anticipated. Life for Smyrna, honour and dignity for Philadelphia, are promised--not for a residue amid the unfaithful, as at Thyatira or Sardis, but for the Church in both cities. It is an interesting coincidence that those are the two cities which have been the bulwark and the glory of Christian power in the country since it became Mohammedan; they are the two places where the Christian flag floated latest over a free and powerful city, and where even in slavery the Christians preserved cohesion among themselves and real influence among the Turkish conquerors.

Another analogy is that in those two letters alone is the Jewish Nationalist party mentioned. Now in every city where there was a body of Jews settled, either as resident strangers or as citizens of the town, the Nationalist party existed; and there can hardly be any doubt that in every important commercial centre in the Province Asia there was a body of Jews settled. In every one of the Seven Cities, we may be sure, there was a Nationalist Jewish party, opposing, hating, and annoying the Jewish Christians and with them the whole Church in the city. If that difficulty is mentioned only in those two cities, Smyrna and Philadelphia, the natural inference is that it had been more serious in them than in the others; and that can only be because the Jews were, for some reason or other, specially influential there. Doubtless the reason lay in their numbers and their wealth; and hence the weakness and poverty of the Christian party is specially mentioned in those two Churches, and in none of the other five.

The body of the letter begins with the usual statement that the writer is familiar with the history and activity of the Philadelphian Church: "I know thy works." Then follows, as usual, an outline of the past achievements and conduct of that Church; but this outline is couched in an unusual form. "See, I have given before thee a door opened, which no one is able to shut." There can be no doubt what the "opened door" means. It is a Pauline metaphor, which had passed into ordinary usage in the early Church. At Ephesus "a great door and effectual was opened" to him (1 Cor 16:9). At Troas also "a door was opened" for him (2 Cor 2:12). He asked the Colossians to pray "that God may open unto us a door for the word, to speak the mystery of Christ" (Col 4:3). In these three Pauline expressions the meaning is clearly explained by the context: a "door opened" means a good opportunity for missionary work. In the Revelation this usage has become fixed, and the word "door" is almost a technical term, so that no explanation in the context is thought necessary; unless the Pauline use had become familiar and almost stereotyped, the expression in this letter would hardly have been possible.

The history of Philadelphian activity had been determined by its unique opportunity for missionary work; there had been given to it a door opened before it. The expression is strong: it is not merely "I have set before thee a door"; it is "I have given thee (the opportunity of) a door (which I have) opened before thee." This opportunity was a special gift and privilege and favour bestowed upon Philadelphia. Nothing of the kind is mentioned for any other city.

The situation of the city fully explains this saying. Philadelphia lay at the upper extremity of a long valley, which opens back from the sea. After passing Philadelphia the road along this valley ascends to the Phrygian land and the great Central Plateau, the main mass of Asia Minor. This road was one which led from the harbour of Smyrna to the northeastern parts of Asia Minor and the East in general, the one rival to the great route connecting Ephesus with the East, and the greatest Asian trade-route of medieval times.

The Imperial Post Road from Rome to the Provinces farther east and southeast coincided for some considerable distance with this trade-route. Through Troas, Pergamum, Thyatira, it reached Sardis; and from thence it was identical with the trade-route by Philadelphia up to the centre of Phrygia. Along this great route the new influence was steadily moving eastwards from Philadelphia in the strong current of communication that set from Rome across Phrygia towards the distant East. As we have seen in chapter 15, it had not yet penetrated beyond the centre of Phrygia into the northeast, so that there was abundant opportunity open before it.

Philadelphia, therefore, was the keeper of the gateway to the plateau; but the door had now been permanently opened before the Church, and the work of Philadelphia had been to go forth through the door and carry the gospel to the cities of the Phrygian land.

It is not stated explicitly that Philadelphia used the opportunity that had been given it; but that is clearly implied in the context. The door had been opened for the Philadelphia Church by Him who does nothing in vain: He did this because the opportunity would be used.

Here alone in all the Seven Letters is there an allusion to the fact which seems to explain why those special Seven Cities were marked out for "the Seven Churches of Asia." But it would be wrong to infer that Philadelphia alone among the Seven Cities had a door before it. Each of the Seven Cities stood at the door of a district. In truth every Church had its own opportunity; and all the Seven Churches had specially favourable opportunities opened to them by geographical situation and the convenience of communication. But it lies in the style and plan of the Seven Letters to mention only in one case what was a common characteristic of all the Seven Cities; and Philadelphia was selected, because in its history that fact--its relation to the cities on the near side of the Central Plateau--had been the determining factor. Philadelphia must have been pre-eminent among the Seven Cities as the missionary Church. We have no other evidence of this; but the situation marks out this line of activity as natural, and the letter clearly declares that the Philadelphian Church acted accordingly.

The construction of the following words in the Greek is obscure, and it is possible to translate in several ways. But the rendering given in the Authorised Version (abandoned unfortunately in the Revised Version) must be preferred: "I know thy works; see, I have given thee the opportunity of the opened door, because thou hast little power, and didst keep my word and didst not deny my name." The opened door is here explained to have been a peculiar favour granted to Philadelphia, because in spite of its want of strength it had been loyal and true.

If the Philadelphian Church had little power, so also had the city. It had suffered from earthquakes more than any other city of all Asia. In A.D. 17 a great earthquake had caused very serious damage; and the effects lasted for years after. The trembling of the earth continued for a long time, so that the inhabitants were afraid to repair the injured houses, or did so with careful provision against collapse. Two or three years later, when Strabo wrote, shocks of earthquake were an everyday occurrence. The walls of the houses were constantly gaping in cracks; and now one part of the city, now another part, was suffering. Few people ventured to live in the city; most spent their lives outside, and devoted themselves to cultivating the fertile Philadelphian territory. There is an obvious reference to this in a later sentence of the letter, where the promise is given to the faithful Philadelphians that they shall go out thence no more. Those who stayed in the city had to direct their attention to the motions of the earth, and guard against the danger of falling walls by devices of building and propping.

Such a calamity, and the terror it had inspired, naturally hindered the development and prosperity of Philadelphia. The Emperor Tiberius indeed treated Philadelphia and the other eleven Asian cities, which suffered about the same time, with great liberality; and aided them to regain their strength both by grants of money and by remission of taxation. Though at the moment of the great earthquake Sardis had suffered most severely, Philadelphia (as is clear from Strabo's account) was much slower in recovering from the effects, owing to the long-continuance of minor shocks and the reputation of the city as dangerous. The world in general thought, like Strabo, that Philadelphia was unsafe to enter, that only a rash person would live in it, and only fools could have ever founded it. No coins appear to have been struck in the city during the twenty years that followed the earthquake; and this is attributed by numismatists to the impoverishment and weakness caused by that disaster.

Gradually, as time passed, people recovered confidence. Subsequent history has shown that the situation about A.D. 17-20, as described by Strabo, was unusual. Philadelphia has not been more subject to earthquakes in subsequent time than other cities of Asia. So far as our scanty knowledge goes, Smyrna has suffered more. But when the Seven Letters were written the memory of that disastrous period was still fresh. People remembered, and perhaps still practised, camping out in the open country; and they appreciated the comfort implied in the promise, verse 12, "he shall go out thence no more." They appreciated, also, the guarantee that, as a reward for the Church's loyalty and obedience, "I also will keep thee from the hour of trial, that hour which is to come upon the whole world, to try them that dwell upon the earth." The Philadelphians who had long lived in constant dread of "the hour of trial" would appreciate the special form in which this promise of help is expressed.

The concluding promise of the letter resumes this allusion. "He that overcometh, I will make him a pillar in the temple of my God, and he shall go out thence no more." The pillar is the symbol of stability, of the firm support on which the upper part of the temple rests. The victor shall be shaken by no disaster in the great day of trial; and the shall never again require to go out and take refuge in the open country. The city which had suffered so much and so long from instability was to be rewarded with the Divine firmness and steadfastness.

That is not the only gift that has been granted the Philadelphian Church. "See! I am giving of the Synagogue of Satan, who profess themselves to be Jews, and they are not, but do lie: see! I will make them come and do reverence before thy feet and know that I have loved thee." This statement takes us into the midst of the long conflict that had been going on in Philadelphia. The Jews and the Jewish Christians had been at bitter enmity; and it must be confessed that, to judge from the spirit shown in St. John's references to the opposite party, the provocation was not wholly on one side. The Jews boasted themselves to be the national and patriotic party, the true Jews, the chosen people, beloved and favoured of God, who were hereafter to be the victors and masters of the world when the Messiah should come in His kingdom. They upbraided and despised the Jewish Christians as traitors, unworthy of the name of Jews, the enemies of God. But the parts shall soon be reversed. The promise begins in the present tense, "I am giving"; but it breaks off in an incomplete sentence, and commences afresh in the future tense, "I will make them (who scorned you) to bow in reverence before you, and to know that you (and not they) are the true Jews whom I have loved."

A characteristic which distinguished Philadelphia from the rest of the Seven Cities was that it alone abandoned its old name and took in its place a name derived from the Imperial religion. The others were too proud, apparently, of their own ancient and historic names to abandon them even for an Imperial title. Sardis, indeed, which had suffered very severely from the earthquake in A.D. 17, and had been treated with special kindness by Tiberius, had assumed the title Caesareia then; but Caesareia was a mere epithet, which was used along with the old name and not in place of it; and the epithet soon fell into disuse, and is never used on coins later than the reign of Caligula 37-41. Some other less important cities of Asia had in like manner assumed an Imperial name in place of their own. Thus, for example, Hierokome in Lydia had abandoned its name, and in gratitude to Tiberius for his kindness in A.D. 17 had taken the name Hierocaesareia, which lasted through the subsequent history of the city. Similarly, Philadelphia assumed the name Neokaisareia and disused its own.

Now, according to the Roman regulations, it was not permitted to a city to assume an Imperial name when it pleased. Such a name was regarded as highly honourable, and as binding the city closely to the Imperial service. Permission had to be sought from the Senate, which governed Asia through the Proconsul whom it selected and sent for the purpose; but, of course, the Emperor's own will was decisive in the matter, and the Senate would never grant permission without ascertaining what he wished. Tiberius had crowned his kindness to the city by permitting it to style itself Neokaisareia, the city of the Young Caesar, viz., either himself or Germanicus, who was in the East on a special mission in A.D. 17-19, and had perhaps been the agent through whom the Imperial bounty was bestowed. A shrine of Germanicus was erected then.

Philadelphia was thereby specially consecrated to the service, i.e. the worship, of the Young Caesar. There can be no doubt that a shrine of the Neos Kaisar, with a priest and a regular ritual, was established soon after A.D. 17 and not later than 19. Philadelphia wrote on itself the name of the Imperial god, and called itself the city of its Imperial god present on earth to help it.

Erected in the time of Philadelphia's great poverty, immediately after the disaster that had tried its credit and weakened its resources, yet raised without aid from the Commune of the Province, this temple of the Young Caesar could not have been fit to compare with the splendid buildings for the Imperial worship in Smyrna or Pergamum or Ephesus. As the worship of Germanicus disappears completely from notice after A.D. 50, and as the other buildings of the city seem to have been in a perilous condition for years after the shock of A.D. 17, we may conjecture that the humble temple at Philadelphia had not withstood the assaults of earthquake and the slower influence of time: moreover, there was little temptation to maintain the worship of Germanicus (who did not rank among the regular Imperial gods) after the death of his son Caligula and his brother Claudius.

It may therefore be fairly gathered that the new shrine was in a state of dilapidation and decay when the Seven Letters were composed. We know from a letter of Pliny to Trajan, that the same thing had happened to a temple of Claudius, which stood on private ground in the wealthy city of Prusa in Bithynia; yet the soil on which that ruined temple had stood was declared by Trajan to be for ever exempted from profane and common use. Accordingly there would be an opening for a telling contrast, such as St. John so frequently aims at, between the shifting facts of ordinary city life and the more permanent character of the analogous institutions and promises of the Divine Author.

Here, on the one side, were the ruined temple and the obsolete worship of the Imperial god and the disused new name which for a time the city had been proud to bear--a name that commemorated a terrible disaster, a period of trial and weakness, and a dole of money from the Imperial purse: none of all these things had been permanent, and there remained from them nothing of which the city could now feel proud.

On the other hand the letter gives the pledge of safety from the hour of trial, of steadiness like the pillar of a temple, of everlasting guarantee against disaster and eviction, of exaltation above the enemies who now contemn and insult; and in token of this eternal security it promises that the name of God and of the city of God and of the Divine Author shall be written upon the victor. When a Philadelphian read those words, he could not fail to discover in them the reference to his own city's history. Like all the other cities he read the words as an engagement that the Author will do far better for his own everything that the enemy tries to do for the pagan city.

It is often incorrectly said that the victor receives three names--of God, of the Church, and of Christ; but the real meaning is that a name is written on him which has all three characters, and is at once the name of God, the name of the Church, and the new name of Christ. What that name shall be is a mystery, like the secret name written on the white tessera for the Pergamenian victor.

In the times when we can catch a glimpse of its condition, Philadelphia was living amid ceaseless dangers, of old from earthquakes, at last from Turkish attack. It was always in dread of the last hour of trial, and was always kept from it. It stood like a pillar, the symbol of stability and strength. In the middle ages it struggled on, a small and weak city against a nation of warriors, and did not deny the Name, but was patient to the end; and there has been written on its history a name that is imperishable, so long as heroic resistance against overwhelming odds, and persevering self-reliance, when deserted by the world, are held in honour and remembered.

Chapter 29: Laodicea: The City of Compromise

Laodicea was founded by Antiochus II (261-246 B.C.). As a Seleucid foundation, it was probably similar to Thyatira in respect of constitution and law; but no information has been preserved. It was situated at a critical point in the road system of the country. The great road from the west (from Ephesus and from Miletus) ascends the Meander Valley due eastwards, until it enters "the Gate of Phrygia." In the Gate are a remarkable series of hot springs, and warm mud-baths, some in the bed of the Meander, others on its banks. "The scene before the traveller as he traverses the Gate is a suitable introduction to that Phrygian land, which always seemed to the Greeks something strange and unique."

Immediately above this point lies a much broader valley, in which Lydia, Phrygia, and Caria meet. The Meander comes into this valley from the north, breaking through a ridge of mountains by a gorge, which, though singularly beautiful in scenery, is useless as a roadway. The road goes on to the east up the glen of the Lycus, which here joins the Meander, and offers an easy roadway. The Lycus Glen is double, containing a lower and an upper glen. Laodicea is the city of the lower glen, Colossae of the upper. Due north of Laodicea, between the Lycus and the Meander, stands Hierapolis, in a very conspicuous situation, on a shelf below the northern mountains and above the valley, with a cascade of gleaming white cliffs below it, topped by the buildings, still wonderfully well preserved, of the old city.

The glen of the Lycus extends up like a funnel into the flank of the main plateau of Anatolia. Between the lower and the upper glen there is a step about 400 feet high, and again between the upper glen and the plateau there is another step of about 850 feet; but both can be surmounted easily by the road. The lower glen, also, slopes upwards, rising 250 feet; and the upper glen slopes much more rapidly, rising 550 feet. In this way the rise from the Meander Valley, 550 feet above the sea, to the plateau, 2,600 feet (an exceptionally low elevation), is achieved far more easily by this path than at any other point. Hence the Lycus Glen was always the most frequented path of trade from the interior to the west throughout ancient time.

Laodicea was placed as a guard and door-keeper on this road, near the foot of the Lycus Glen, where it opens on the main valley of the Meander. The hills that bound the glen on the south run up northwards to an apex, one side facing northwest, the other northeast; this apex lies between the river Lycus (the Wolf), and its large tributary the Kapros (the Boar), which comes in from the south and passes near the eastern gate: the Lycus is about three miles to the north of the city.

Laodicea was placed on the apex; and the great road from the coast to the inner country passed right through the middle of it, entering by the "Ephesian Gates" on the east. The city was nearly square, with the corners towards the cardinal points. One side, towards the southwest, was washed by the small river Asopus.

The hills rise not more than one hundred feet above the glen; but they spring sharply from the low and level ground in front; and, when crowned by the well-built fortifications of a Seleucid city, they must have presented a striking aspect towards the glen, and constituted an admirably strong line of defence. Laodicea was a very strong fortress, planted right on the line of the great road; but it had one serious weakness. It was entirely dependent for water-supply (except in so far as wells may have existed within the walls, of which there is now no trace) on an aqueduct conducted from springs about six miles to the south. The aqueduct was under the surface of the ground, but could hardly remain unknown to a besieging army or be guarded long against his attack. If the aqueduct was cut, the city was helpless; and this weakness ruined the character of the city as a strong fortress, and must have prevented the people from ever feeling secure when threatened with attack.

Planted on the better of the two entrances from the west to the Phrygian land, Laodicea might have been expected to be (like Philadelphia, which commanded the other) a missionary city charged at first with the task of spreading Greek civilisation and speech in barbarian Phrygia, and afterwards undertaking the duty of spreading Christianity in that country. It had, however, made little progress in Hellenising Phrygia. As has been sated before, Phrygia was the least Hellenised part in all the Province; as a whole, it still spoke the native tongue, and was little affected by Greek manners, in contrast with Eastern Lydia, which was entirely Greek-speaking and Hellenised (at least superficially). Why it was that Laodicea had failed and Philadelphia had succeeded in diffusing the Greek tongue in the districts immediately around, we have no means of judging. But such was the case.

Laodicea was a knot on the road-system. Not merely the great eastern highway and central route of the Roman Empire, as already described, but also the road from Pergamum and the Hermus Valley to Pisidia and Pamphylia passed through its gates; while a road from Eastern Caria, and at least one from Central and West Phrygia, met in the city. In such a situation it only needed peace to become a great commercial and financial centre. It was, as Strabo says, only a small city before the Roman time; but after Rome kept peace in the land, it grew rapidly. Cicero brought with him in 51 B.C. orders to be cashed in Laodicea, as the city of banking and exchange.

It was also a manufacturing centre. There was produced in the valley a valuable sort of wool, soft in texture and glossy black in colour, which was widely esteemed. This wool was woven into garments of several kinds for home use and export trade. Small and cheap upper garments, called himatia, two kinds of birros (another sort of upper garment), one of native style and one in imitation of the manufactures of the Nervii, a tribe in French Flanders, and also tunics of several kinds, were made in Laodicea; and one species of the tunics, called trimita, was so famous that the city is styled Trimitaria in the lists of the Council of Chalcedon, A.D. 451, and in some other late documents.

It is pointed out elsewhere that this kind of glossy black wool, as well as the glossy violet-dark wool produced at Colossae, was probably attained by some system of breeding and crossing. The glossy black fleeces have now entirely disappeared; but they were known in comparatively recent times. Pococke in the eighteenth century saw a great many black sheep; but Chandler in the early part of the nineteenth saw only a few black and glossy fleeces. The present writer has seen some black-fleeced sheep, but the wool was not distinguished by the gloss which the ancients praised and prized so much. Certain systems of breeding animals, and improving them by careful selection and crossing with different stocks, were known to the native Anatolian population in early times: the rules were a matter of religious prescription, and guarded by religious awe, like almost every useful art in that primitive period. But the system has now been lost.

Between Laodicea and the "Gate of Phrygia" lay a famous temple, the home of the Phrygian god Men Karou, the Carian Men. This was the original god of the valley. His temple was the centre of society and administration, intercourse and trade, as well as of religion,--or, rather, that primitive religion was a system of performing those duties and purposes in the orderly way that the god approved and taught--for the valley in which the Lycus and the Meander meet. A market was held under the protection of his sacred name, beside or in his own precinct, at which the people of the valley met and traded with strangers from a distance; and this market continued to meet weekly in the same place until about fifty years ago, when it was moved two or three miles north to the new village called Serai-Keui.

In connection with this temple there grew up a famous school of medicine. The school seems to have had its seat at Laodicea, and not at the temple (which was about thirteen miles west of Laodicea and in the territory of the city Attoudda); and the names of the leading physicians of the school in the time of Augustus are mentioned on Laodicean coins. These coins bear as type either the serpent-encircled staff of Asklepios (chapter 14) or the figure of Zeus. The Zeus who was worshipped at Laodicea was the Hellenised form of the old native god. Men had been the king and father of his people. When the new seat of Hellenic civilisation and speech was founded in the valley, the people continued to worship the god whose power was known to be supreme in the district, but they imparted to him something of their own character and identified him with their own god Zeus. Thus in Sardis and elsewhere the native god became Zeus Lydios, "the Zeus whom the Lydians worship"; and the same impersonation in outward appearance was worshipped at Laodicea, though with a different name in place of Lydios. The Laodicean god was sometimes called Aseis, perhaps a Semitic word meaning "powerful." If that be so, it would imply that a body of settlers from Syria were brought into the new city at its foundation, and that they had imparted an element of their own character to the god who was worshipped in common by the citizens generally.

This Laodicean school of physicians followed the teaching "of Herophilos (330-250 B.C.), who, on the principle that compound diseases require compound medicines, began that strange system of heterogeneous mixtures, some of which have only lately been expelled from our own Pharmacopoeia."

The only medicine which is expressly quoted as Laodicean seems to be an ointment for strengthening the ears made from the spice nard; Galen mentions it as having been originally prepared only in Laodicea, though by the second century after Christ it was made in other cities. But a medicine for the eyes is also described as Phrygian: Galen describes it as having the form of a tabloid made from the Phrygian stone, while Aristotle speaks of it as Phrygian powder; the two are probably identical, Aristotle describes the powder to which the tabloids were reduced when they were to be applied to the eye. There can be no doubt that this Phrygian powder came through Laodicea into general use among the Greeks. Laodicea was the one famous medical centre in Phrygia; and to the Greeks "Phrygian" often stood in place of "Laodicean"; thus, for example, the famous orator of the second century, Polemon of Laodicea was called simply "the Phrygian." The Phrygian stone was exported after a time to all parts of the Greek and Roman world; and as the powder had now become common, and was prepared in all the medical centres, Galen does not mention it as being made in any special place; but Laodicea was probably the oldest home of its use, so far as the Greeks knew.

Jews were an important element in the population of this district in the Graeco-Roman age. In 62 B.C. the Roman governor of Asia refused to permit the contributions, which were regularly sent by the Asian Jews to Jerusalem, to go out of the country; and he seized the money that had been collected, over twenty pound weight of gold at Laodicea and a hundred pounds at Apameia of Phrygia. Such amounts prove that Laodicea was the centre of a district in which a large, and Apameia of one in which a very large, Jewish population dwelt. According to the calculation of M. Th. Reinach, the gold seized at Laodicea would amount to 15,000 silver drachms; and as the annual tax was two drachms, this implies a population of 7,500 adult Jewish freemen in the district (to which must be added women and children).

Of the Jews in Laodicea itself no memorial is preserved in the few inscriptions that have survived; but at Hierapolis they are several times mentioned, and the Hierapolitan Jews may be taken as occupying a similar position to the Laodicean. There were Jews in Laodicean, which was such an important centre for financial transactions (Josephus, Ant., xiv., 10, 20); but there is no evidence whether they were citizens or mere resident strangers (see chapter 12). If they were citizens, they must have been one element in the population planted in the city by Antiochus. Thus we can detect in the original Laodicea the following elements, some Greek or Macedonian colonists, probably some Syrians and also some Jews, in addition to the native Phrygian, Carian and Lydian population of the district.

To these there were added later some new classes of citizens, introduced by Eumenes II or by Attalus II. When Phrygia was given to Eumenes by the Romans, in 189 B.C., it was soon found to be necessary to strengthen the loyalty of the Seleucid colonies by introducing into them bodies of new citizens devoted to the Pergamenian interests. It is known that a Tribe Attalis was instituted in Laodicea; and we must infer that it contained some or all of those new Pergamenian settlers, who were enrolled in one or more Tribes. These later colonists were probably in part Thracian and other mercenaries in the service of the Pergamenian kings. Thus Laodicea and the Lycus Valley generally had a very mixed population. No better example could be found of the mixed Graeco-Asiatic cities described in chapter 11.

The Jews at Hierapolis were organised in trade-guilds, the purple-dyers, the carpet-makers, and perhaps others. These guilds were recognised by the city, so that money could be left to them by will. "The Congregation of the Jews" was empowered to prosecute persons who had violated the sanctity of a Jewish tomb, and to receive fines from them on conviction; and it had its own public office, "the Archives of the Jews," in which copies of legal documents executed by or for Jews were deposited. These rights seem to imply that there was a body of Jewish citizens of Hierapolis.

The Jews of Hierapolis were settled there by one of the Graeco-Asiatic kings, for their congregation is in one inscription called "the Settlement or Katoikia of the Jews," and the term Katoikoi was appropriated specially to the colonists planted by those kings in their new foundations.

Hierapolis seems to have preserved its pre-Hellenic character as a Lydian city, in which there were no Tribes, but only the freer grouping by Trade-guilds. The feasts of Unleavened Bread and of Pentecost are mentioned in inscriptions; and by a quaint and characteristic mixture of Greek and Jewish customs, money is left to the two Jewish guilds (naturally, by Jews), the interest of which is to be distributed annually on those feasts.

Laodicean Jews may be estimated on the analogy of the Hierapolitan Jews (chapter 12).

Laodicea was, of course, a centre of the Imperial religion, and received the Temple-Wardenship under Commodus, A.D. 180-191. Its wide trading connection is attested by many "alliance-coins," in company with Ephesus, Smyrna, Pergamum, most of the neighbouring cities (except Colossae, which was too humble), and some distant cities like Nikomedia and Perinthus. As a specimen it shows an agreement between Smyrna and Laodicea: the latter being represented by its god Zeus, while Smyrna is represented by Zeus Akraios who sits with sceptre in left hand, holding out on his right the goddess Victory.

There is no city whose spirit and nature are more difficult to describe than Laodicea. There are no extremes, and hardly any very strongly marked features. But in this even balance lies its peculiar character. Those were the qualities that contributed to make it essentially the successful trading city, the city of bankers and finance, which could adapt itself to the needs and wishes of others, ever pliable and accommodating, full of the spirit of compromise.

The Lycus Valley, in a larger sense, is a deep cleft between two lofty mountain ridges. On the south are Salbakos and Kadmos, both slightly over 8,000 feet above the sea; on the north is a lower ridge over 5,000 feet in height. The ridges converge towards the east, and in the apex lies the ascent to the plateau already described. Thus the valley is triangular, the base being the opening on the Meander Valley. Low hills occupy the southern half of this greater valley; these hills are drained by the Kapros and the Asopus; and Laodicea stands on their northern apex, about half-way between the two mountain-ridges. It is the only one of the Seven Cities in which no relation is discernible between the natural features that surround it and its part and place in history.

Chapter 30: The Letter to the Church in Laodicea

These things saith the Amen, the faithful and true witness, the beginning of the creation of God: I know thy works, that thou are neither cold nor hot: I would thou wert cold or hot. So because thou art lukewarm, and neither hot nor cold, I will spew thee out of my mouth. Because thou sayest, I am rich, and have gotten riches, and have need of nothing; and knowest not that thou art the wretched one and miserable and poor and blind and naked: I counsel thee to buy of me gold refined by fire, that thou mayest become rich; and white garments, that thou mayest clothe thyself, and that the shame of thy nakedness be not made manifest; and eyesalve to anoint thine eyes, that thou mayest see.

The tone of the exordium is one of thoroughness, consistency from the beginning of the creation of God to the end of all things, a consistency that springs from faithfulness and truth. In the letter itself those are the qualities in which Laodicea is lacking. The Laodicean Church is neither one thing nor another. It is given to compromise. It cannot thoroughly reject the temptations and allurements of the world. And therefore it shall be rejected absolutely and inexorably by Him whose faithfulness and truth reject all half-heartedness and compromise.

The characteristics described in the previous chapter are insufficient to give a clear idea of the special and distinctive character of Laodicea as a city. There is a want of definiteness and individuality about them. They do not set before us the picture of a city recognisable in itself and distinguishable from other cities. But may not this be in itself a distinction? Of the Seven Cities Laodicea is the one which is least determined in character, the one of which the outline is least clearly and sharply defined in history. In the special duties imposed on it as the end and aim of its foundation, to guard a road and gateway, and to be a missionary of Greek language and culture in the Phrygian land, it proved unsuccessful. The one respect in which it stands forth pre-eminent is that it is the adaptable city, able to suit itself to the needs of others, because it has no strongly pronounced character of its own. Such a nature would be suited for the successful commercial city, which it was. But such a nature would least commend the city to St. John. Laodicea must appear to him undecided, devoid of initiative, pliable, irresolute, and unsatisfactory.

The ordinary historian would probably not condemn the spirit of Laodicea so strenuously as St. John did. In the tendency of the Laodiceans towards a policy of compromise he would probably see a tendency towards toleration and allowance, which indicated a certain sound practical sense, and showed that the various constituents of the population of Laodicea were well mixed and evenly balanced. He would regard its somewhat featureless character and its easy regular development as proving that it was a happy and well-ordered city, in whose constitution "the elements were kindlier mixed" than in any other city of Asia. He would consider probably that its success as a commercial city was the just reward of the strong common-sense which characterised its people. St. John, however, was not one of those who regarded a successful career in trade and money-making as the best proof of the higher qualities of citizenship. The very characteristics which made Laodicea a well-ordered, energetic and pushing centre of trade, seemed to him to evince a coldness of nature that was fatal to the highest side of human character, the spirit of self-sacrifice and enthusiasm.

An account which has been given elsewhere of the development of Christianity in Eumeneia, a city in the Laodicean circuit where Christian inscriptions are specially numerous, may be quoted here as an illustration of the probable character of the whole district of Laodicea. The evidence proves that Eumeneia was to a large extent a Christian city in the third century; and there is considerable probability that Eumeneia was the city whose fate is recorded by Eusebius and Lactantius, two excellent authorities, practically contemporaries of the event. In this city people and magistrates alike were Christian in the early years of the fourth century. During the last great persecution, A.D. 303-313, the population, when threatened, collected at the Church (which was in itself a defiance of the Imperial orders). They were surrounded by a ring of soldiers, and the usual alternative was offered, compliance or death. In ordinary circumstances, doubtless, some or even many of them would have lacked the boldness to choose death; but it lies in human nature that the general spirit of a crowd exercises a powerful influence on the individuals who compose it; and even those who, taken singly, might have compromised with their conscience, and shrunk from a terrible death, accepted it when inspired with the courage of the whole body. The entire people was burned with the church; and they died "calling upon the God over all." Eusebius writes as an epitaph over their ashes words that read like a memory of the formula by which the Christian character of the epitaphs on the tombs of their predecessors during the third century has been recognised.

Those inscriptions, by which we trace the character of that Christian city about A.D. 240-300, convey the impression that there was no violent break between Greek and Christian culture in Eumeneia, as it existed in that period. There is no sign of bitterness. The monuments place before us a picture of rich and generous development, of concession, and of liberality, through which people of diverse thought were practically reconciled in a single society; they exemplify the accommodation of two hostile religions in a peaceful and orderly city. This was impossible for the Christians without some sacrifice of strict principle to the exigencies of the situation and the demands of the Imperial government. The spirit of accommodation and even of compromise must have been strong in Eumeneia.

The result has been told: it was, first, the practically universal triumph of Christianity in the city, and thereafter the extermination of the Christian population in a great massacre. In their death no signs can be detected of the spirit of compromise which they had showed in practical matters during their life.

In view of these facts about Eumeneia, and a somewhat similar history in Apameia, another city of the Laodicean circuit, we may fairly regard the spirit of compromise, which is stigmatised in the Laodicean letter, as having been common to the district as a whole and as capable of showing at need a finer side than is recognised in the letter.

The Laodicean letter is the only one in which we have recognised the applicability of the letter to the district or circuit which was connected with the city. There seemed always to the Greek mind to be a certain homogeneity of spirit characterising Phrygia as a whole, which they regarded with some contempt as an indication of lower intelligence, contrasted with the strong development of individual character in the Greek cities. A tendency to compromise in religion was, indeed, never regarded as characteristic of the Phrygian spirit, which was considered prone to excess in religious devotion: the extremest examples of horrible actions under the stimulus of religion, such as self-mutilation, were associated in the ancient mind with Phrygia. But the tendency to excess inevitably results in failure to reach even the mean. The Church blamed the extravagant Phrygian provocation of martyrdom, because frequently overstrained human nature failed in the supreme test, and the would-be martyr, overconfident in his powers, became a renegade in the hour of trial.

It is characteristic of a city devoted to commercial interest and the material side of life, that the Church of Laodicea is entirely self-satisfied. It says, as the city said in A.D. 60, when it recovered its prosperity after the great earthquake without any of that help which the Imperial government was generally ready to bestow, and which the greatest cities of Asia had always been ready to accept, "I have grown rich, and have need of nothing." It has never seen its real condition: it is poor and blind and naked.

There is only one way open to it. It must cease to trust to itself. It must recognise that it is poor, and seek riches where the true riches can be found. Its banks and its wealthy money changers can give it only false money; but the Author can sell it "gold refined by fire." He does not give this gold for nothing: it must be bought with a price, the price of suffering and truth, fidelity and martyrdom.

The Church must recognise that it is naked, and seek to be clad. Its manufacturers cannot help it with their fine glossy black and violet garments, which they sell and export to the whole world. Only white garments, such as the faithful in Sardis wear, will be of any use to cover their shame; and those are sold only by the Author. They too must be bought with a price.

The Laodicean Church must also learn that it is blind, but yet not incurably blind. It is suffering from disease, and needs medical treatment. But the physicians of its famous medical school can do nothing for it. The tabloids which they prescribe, and which are now used all over the civilised world, to reduce to powder and smear on the eyes, will be useless for this kind of ophthalmia. The Laodiceans must buy the tabloid from the Author himself, at the price of suffering and steadfastness.

The description of the medicine here mentioned is obscured by a mistranslation. It was not an ointment, but a kollyrium, which had the form of small cylinders compounded of various ingredients, including some mineral elements, and was used either by simple application or by reduction to a powder to be smeared on the part. The term used by St. John is the same that Galen uses to describe the preparation of the Phrygian stone employed to strengthen weak eyes.

The Laodicean Church is the only one which is absolutely and wholly condemned. Not even a faithful remnant is left, such as even in Sardis, the dead Church, kept itself pure and white. No exception is allowed in Laodicea: advice is given, but there is no appearance that it will be taken. The weakness of the city will become apparent in the testing.

In the rest of the letter there is no recognisable allusion to the character or circumstances of an individual Church. The conclusion is rather an epilogue to the Seven Letters, treated as a literary whole, than an integral part of the Laodicean letter.

Chapter 31: Epilogue

As many as I love, I reprove and chasten: be zealous therefore, and repent. Behold, I stand at the door and knock: if any man hear my voice and open the door, I will come in to him, and will sup with him, and he with me.

He that overcometh, I will give to him to sit down with me in my throne, as I also overcame, and sat down with my Father in his throne.

He that hath an ear, let him hear what the Spirit saith to the churches.

The first sentence in what we take to be an epilogue might quite well be regarded as part of the Laodicean letter. The words seem at first to express naturally the reaction from the sharp censure conveyed in the preceding sentences. But, as we read on, we become conscious that all reference to the Laodiceans has ceased, and that the writer is drifting farther and farther away from them. The final promise has no apparent relation to their situation and character.

Now, when it is remembered that the Seven Letters were not real letters, intended to be sent separately to Seven Churches, but form one literary composition, it becomes evident that an epilogue to the whole is needed, and that this is the epilogue. One might hesitate where the Laodicean letter ends and the epilogue to the Seven Letters begins. The writer passes almost insensibly from the one to the other. But it seems best to suppose that the epilogue begins at the point where clear reference to the circumstances and nature of Laodicea ceases. And when the transition is placed here a difficulty is eliminated. After the extremely sharp condemnation of Laodicea, it seems hardly consistent to give it the honour which is awarded to the true and courageous Church of Philadelphia alone among the Seven, and to rank it among those whom the Author loves. We can understand why Philadelphia, the true city, the missionary Church, in danger even yet ever enduring, should receive that honourable mention; but we cannot understand why Philadelphia and Laodicea should be the only two that receive it.

But, as part of the epilogue, this first sentence unites all the Seven Churches and the entire Church of Christ in one loving waning: the Seven Letters have conveyed much reproof and chastisement, but the Author reproves and chastens those whom he loves. The admirable suitability of the remainder as an epilogue is a matter of expository interpretation rather than of the historical study at which the present book has aimed.

In a few words the historical epilogue to this historical study is summed up.

Among the Seven Churches two only are condemned absolutely and without hope of pardon: Sardis is dead: Laodicea is rejected. And among the Seven Cities two only are at the present day absolutely deserted and uninhabited, Sardis and Laodicea. Two Churches only are praised in an unreserved, hearty, and loving way, Smyrna and Philadelphia. And two cities have enjoyed and earned the glory of being the champions of Christianity in the centuries of war that ended in the Turkish conquest, the last cities to yield long after all others had succumbed Smyrna and Philadelphia. Other two Churches are treated with mingled praise and blame, though on the whole the praise outweighs the blame; for their faith, steadfastness, works, love, service and patience are heartily praised, though they have become tainted with the false Nicolaitan principles. These are Pergamum and Thyatira, both of which still exist as flourishing towns. One church alone shall be moved from its place; and Ephesus was moved to a site about three kilometres distant, where it continued an important city until comparatively recent time, though now it has sunk to an insignificant village.